Relationship Marketing

and

Customer Relationship Management

Third edition

Adele Berndt and Madéle Tait (Editors)

JUTA

Relationship Marketing and Customer Relationship Management

First published 2008
Second edition 2012
Reprinted 2013 (Twice)
Third edition 2014

Juta and Company Ltd
First Floor
Sunclare Building
21 Dreyer Street
Claremont
7708

PO Box 14373, Lansdowne, 7779, Cape Town, South Africa

© 2014 Juta & Company Ltd

ISBN: 978 1 48510 264 9

Project manager: Carlyn Bartlett-Cronje
Editor: Rae Morris
Proofreader: Karoline Hanks
Indexer: Annette Gerstner
Typesetter: PH Setting cc
Cover designer: Adam Rumball
Print administration by DJE Flexible Print Solutions

Contents

PART 1 Building blocks of Customer Relationship Marketing

CHAPTER 1 The nature of Relationship Marketing (RM) and Customer Relationship Management (CRM)

CHAPTER 2 Building relationships

CHAPTER 3 Service issues in RM and CRM

PART 2 The markets of CRM

CHAPTER 4 Internal marketing

CHAPTER 5 One-to-one marketing and mass customisation

CHAPTER 6 Business-to-business (B2B) marketing

CHAPTER 7 Stakeholders in Relationship Marketing

PART 3 The management of CRM

CHAPTER 8 Planning a CRM strategy

CHAPTER 9 Implementing CRM in an organisation

CHAPTER 10 Technologies and metrics in CRM

About the authors

Professor A Berndt is Associate Professor of Marketing, Jönköping International Business School in Jönköping, Sweden.

Professor M Tait is Head of the Department of Marketing Management, Nelson Mandela Metropolitan University, South Africa.

Professor C Rootman is a Lecturer in the Department of Business Management, Nelson Mandela Metropolitan University, South Africa.

Professor M Roberts-Lombard is a full professor of Marketing and Deputy HOD of the Department of Marketing Management, University of Johannesburg, South Africa.

Professor MC Cant is Head of the Department of Marketing and Retail Management, Unisa, South Africa.

CH Bothma is a Senior Lecturer in the Department of Marketing and Retail Management, Unisa, South Africa.

Preface

The Relationship Marketing (RM) and Customer Relationship Management (CRM) concepts represented a new marketing paradigm, a shift in business thinking, and (CRM), became the 'battle cry' of the 1990s.

Relationships are regarded as fundamental assets of an organisation. More than anything else, relationships determine the future of an organisation. Relationships predict whether new value will continue to be created and shared with a variety of stakeholders. The purpose of RM is thus to create meaningful relationships with strategically-significant parties and to indicate how these relationships can be created on a one-to-one basis. If stakeholders are amenable to a deepening bond with a particular organisation, they will do more business with it and support the organisation and its activities. If employees like working for the organisation they will continue along their learning curve and produce more and better. If investors and bankers are happy with their returns, they will continue to keep their funds in the organisation.

One specific focus area of RM is with customers. Marketers are aware of the importance of customers and customer retention for the long-term survival of an organisation. This is reflected in the shift that has taken place within marketing—from transactional marketing to building long-term relationships with customers. By building relationships, organisations are able to obtain a competitive advantage in the marketplace over their competitors, thus increasing the overall profitability and success of an organisation. In terms of CRM, all customers are not equal and so different customers need to be treated differently. It is imperative that marketers view their organisation from a relationship perspective, and not only with customers, but also with all stakeholders.

Implementing a CRM strategy in an organisation may require extensive changes in the way in which the organisation does business. A CRM strategy has the potential to change the processes, training and leadership within an organisation. Thus it requires a total transformation!

CRM is technology-driven. By using technology appropriately, an organisation can serve customers as individuals. However, technology is merely the facilitator of CRM and does not solve any problems a business may have. Before any organisation decides to deploy CRM technology it must first include customer centricity as part of its corporate vision and mission. This management view is reflected in the development of RM-specific metrics that can be used in the evaluation of CRM activities.

In this book we deal with all the basic principles of RM and CRM in building relationships with a variety of stakeholders. One important element required for the implementation of CRM is excellent customer service, thus this is also dealt with. We also focus on the individual customer approach, business-to-business markets, and how to build relationships with all key stakeholders. In the final part we show how a CRM strategy can be planned and implemented, the role of technology in RM and the ways in which RM success can be determined. The book concludes with three case studies that illustrate the place of both RM and CRM within South African organisations.

As authors, we trust that you will enjoy reading the text and find its insights interesting and valuable in your RM journey.

Editors: Adele Berndt and Madéle Tait

Bookplan

This book focuses on the following components of Relationship Marketing (RM) and Customer Relationship Management (CRM):

PART 1 Building blocks of Customer Relationship Marketing		
Chapter 1	The nature of relationship marketing (RM) and customer relationship management (CRM)	In this chapter, the philosophies of RM and CRM are introduced, as well as the organisational requirements of these philosophies.
Chapter 2	Building relationships	This chapter focuses on the nature of relationships, the driving forces of relationships, customer retention through customer bonding and the lifetime value of customers.
Chapter 3	Service issues in RM and CRM	This chapter deals with the various dimensions of service and their effect on relationship building issues.
PART 2 The markets of CRM		
Chapter 4	Internal marketing	Employees interact with the customer on a daily basis, and these are the people who can have the greatest effect on customer behaviour. Employees form a crucial group with whom the organisation needs to develop relationships, as is examined in this chapter.
Chapter 5	One-to-one marketing and mass customisation	For needs to be met, customers are able to have products specifically developed to satisfy their needs, a process known as customisation. How organisations can customise their products and services is discussed in this chapter.
Chapter 6	Business-to-business (B2B) marketing	Relationships that are built with customers differ from those that are developed and maintained with other business organisations, such as suppliers and competitors. These relationships form the focus of this chapter.
Chapter 7	Stakeholders in relationship marketing (RM)	This chapter examines the way in which organisations build relationships with other stakeholders, such as the community and the intermediaries in the distribution channel.

PART 3 The Management of CRM		
Chapter 8	Planning a CRM strategy	This chapter details the suggested stages in the CRM planning process. A business must actually plan how it will create, implement and manage a programme to ensure building relationships with its customers.
Chapter 9	Implementing CRM in an organisation	All plans have to be implemented if they are to be regarded as a success. Implementing CRM faces a number of challenges and these are discussed in this chapter.
Chapter 10	Techologies and metrics in CRM	This chapter shows how technology can be used to not only facilitate CRM, but also to keep track of the organisation's CRM efforts.

PART 1

Building blocks of
Customer Relationship
Marketing

The nature of Relationship Marketing (RM) and Customer Relationship Management (CRM)

Learning outcomes

After studying this chapter, you should be able to:

- explain the concept of customer relationship management (CRM);
- compare and contrast the traditional marketing approach and the relationship marketing approach;
- illustrate the focus areas of RM;
- explain the new capabilities that an organisation requires to implement RM and CRM.

Introduction

The new 'mantra' of marketing is customer relationship management (CRM). With the use of highly accessible technology now available, businesses have a better chance of responding immediately to the requests of their customers than previously (in the offline world). It is now possible to provide a highly competitive and personalised experience and in doing so, develop, nurture and sustain long-term customer relationships.[1] In the past, most businesses produced products and rendered services without the involvement or participation of their customers.[2] As the environment in which businesses are operating has become more competitive, customer co-creation (co-production) has become an increasingly important competitive advantage.[3] Customers are jointly involved with the business to provide value.[4] By co-creating value, more creative ideas are produced and by involving customers, deeper relationships are built with them.[5]

The relationship marketing concept has evolved from the marketing concept.[6] In order to obtain a better understanding of relationship marketing and customer relationship management, it is important to discuss the marketing concept first.

This book is divided into three parts, namely the building blocks of customer relationship marketing (part 1), the markets of customer relationship marketing (part 2) and the management of customer relationship marketing (part 3).

The marketing concept

Marketing is a business function and can be defined as a process which satisfies consumer needs by adding value through the provision of appropriate products or services, at reasonable prices, through acceptable distribution channels using promotional strategies and marketing communication in an ever-changing business environment.[7]

The essence of the marketing concept is an understanding of customer needs and wants. The focus is thus on the customer. If a business offers goods and services that satisfy the needs of and create value for the customer – providing customer satisfaction and the right customer-perceived quality – the business stands the best chance of maximising profitability.[8]

The 'marketing mix' as we know it, was given its name by Professor Neil Borden of Harvard University in 1953. In 1960 McCarthy refined the marketing mix to 4 Ps, namely product, price, place and promotion.[9] It was soon realised that the 4 Ps were not sufficient and in 1967 Philip Kotler was responsible for the first edition of his world-renowned textbook, *Principles of Marketing*. With this book he laid the foundation for the extended marketing mix, namely an additional 3 Ps, which are people, processes and physical surroundings.[10]

In order to have a better understanding of CRM, it is necessary to first consider the traditional marketing approach.

The traditional marketing approach

In the sections that follow the traditional marketing approach is discussed under the headings: the marketing mix, transactional marketing and market segmentation.

The marketing mix

As mentioned earlier, the original marketing mix comprises the product or service, price, distribution (or place) and promotion. In terms of this marketing mix, the business would make all the key decisions regarding the research that would be conducted, the product concept and the value that would be provided, the advertising message and the services that would be delivered to a segment of the market. Customers within each segment, would be served as though they all wanted the same products or services. The main problem confronting the marketer was to find the optimal mix that would obtain a superior response in the market and at the same time, create profits.

Research began to show that this marketing mix model of marketing was too restrictive for business-to-business and services marketing. Moreover, it was also becoming an out-dated concept for consumer goods marketing, as the importance of intangible service characteristics and customer service considerations became prime differentiating factors among products.[11] It was felt that the original marketing mix represented the seller's view of marketing and it was suggested that marketers should view the 4 Ps from a customer-oriented perspective.

Transactional marketing

According to the traditional (transactional) marketing concept, the major focus of marketing programmes has been to make customers buy, regardless of whether they are existing or new customers. Often, only a small part of the marketing budget has been allocated directly towards existing customers. One axiom of transactional marketing is that it is believed that competition and self-interest drive value creation. Buyers can be offered a choice through competition; this choice of suppliers motivates marketers to create the best product offering possible as well as satisfy their self-interest, for example, increased profit margins.[12] It was argued that this approach was no longer broad enough because of the importance of customer retention, the changes in the competitive environment and the limitations of transactional marketing.[13]

In transactional marketing situations, customers, as unidentified members of a segment, are exposed to a number of competing products and they are supposed to make independent choices from among the available options. The two parties (business and customer) have conflicting interests. The starting point is that the customer does not *want* to buy; he or she has to be *persuaded* to do so.

However, businesses are confronted with many competitive challenges. Markets have generally become mature and there is only limited possibility for product differentiation; therefore customer retention is becoming more important than simply attracting new customers.[14]

Market segmentation

Businesses cannot use the same marketing strategy for all of their products and services as customers have unique needs; this implies that each customer is potentially a separate market. Most businesses thus look for broader classes of consumers who differ in their product and service needs.[15] The traditional approach to market segmentation focuses on dividing the heterogeneous market into fairly homogeneous sub-sets of customers. Each segment of the market, it is assumed, will have similar needs and will respond in a similar way to the market offering and strategy. The business then has to decide which of the potential market segments it can best satisfy and develop a product offering and strategy around the needs of that particular segment.[16]

Consumer segmentation can be divided into three main types: behavioural (ie grouping buyers on the basis of their buying behaviour such as benefits sought, loyalty status and attitude toward the product); psychographic (ie segmentation by means of categories such as social class, lifestyle and personality); and profile segmentation (ie segmentation that allows for consumer groups to be classified in such a manner that communication media can target them, for example, geographic, demographic and socio-economic segmentation).[17]

For decades, market segmentation strategies were proving particularly vulnerable, and market segmentation, a central marketing concept, no longer appeared to be operating effectively.[18] While markets were still being presented demographically, geographically and psychographically, marketers were beginning to realise that the only category that was really meaningful was actual – as opposed to speculative – buyer behaviour. It was therefore becoming increasingly difficult to categorise buyers.

Buyers seem to do unusual things, such as saving their money or deferring spending in some areas and then buying heavily in others. Some customers within a historically defined segment are much more sensitive to certain media than others. Some are sensitive to price, others to service. This points to the fact that if the only categorisation that is meaningful is actual buyer behaviour rather than the underlying drivers of that behaviour; then there are no more market segments, but just individual customers.[19] A shift is clearly necessary: from marketing to anonymous masses of customers, to developing and managing relationships with more or less well-known, or at least somehow identifiable, customers.

A 'paradigm shift' was thus needed if marketing was going to survive as a discipline.[20] It was clear that there was a need to transform marketing from a narrow set of functional skills based on the conventional marketing mix to a broader business orientation where delivery of 'superior' customer value was a key objective. In this context, relationship marketing may be a very practical and appropriate approach for marketers to use to regain their edge as the business's strategic driver.

Relationship Marketing

Berry was the first scholar to use the term 'relationship marketing' for the idea of building relationships with customers and managing those relationships.[21] However, relationship marketing was being practised (although to a lesser extent) long before the scholars recognised its presence and gave it a name.

Relationship marketing aims to satisfy existing customers and so spread the word through those customers about how well the product or the service works. Once the customer has decided to use the service of a business, customer relationships are important to retain the customer.[22] Relationship marketing helps to show the customer that the business cares for its existing customers just as much as its new ones and that long-term customer satisfaction is the business's main purpose. Customer retention places the focus of much of the marketing-related activities of the business on its existing customers.[23] Retention of existing customers is based on customer satisfaction.

Thus relationship marketing aims to retain customers through various means (such as customer care and after-sales services) to ensure future transactions with these customers by delivering what they want. In other words, a mass marketer is a hunter, a relationship marketer is a farmer.[24]

The example that best explains relationship marketing is the one of the retail bank and its clients. Consider a client who has a problem with the bank fees which his/her bank is charging. The client wants to sort out the fees and would like to make an appointment with an employee of the bank, who is referred to as a relationship manager, or a relationship consultant. The client would like to see the relationship manager or relationship consultant in person. The client also wants to see the same person in future years in order to avoid discussing confidential banking issues with a stranger. The relationship manager or relationship consultant needs to be knowledgeable about the products and services that the bank offers. The client would also like the relationship manager, or consultant, to be empowered to take important decisions regarding his/her business with the bank. In order for banks to stay in business they need to be up-to-date regarding any new developments in relationship marketing.

> ## Definition of Relationship Marketing
>
> Relationship marketing is the process of building and maintaining profitable customer relationships by delivering superior customer value and satisfaction. Satisfied customers are more likely to be loyal customers and to give the organisation a larger share of their business.[25]
>
> Relationship marketing is particularly relevant when a customer has alternative service providers to choose from, when the customer makes the selection decision and when there is an ongoing desire or need for a product or service, such as in the banking industry.[26]

Focus areas of Relationship Marketing

The main focus areas covered in this section are the individual customer approach as well as how traditional market segmentation and the traditional marketing mix need to be reconsidered in terms of relationship marketing.

Individual customer approach

One of the key aspects of customer relationship management is to focus on individual customers. In the new economy, the business is supported by information which has the ability to differentiate, customise and personalise, and which enables it to gather information about individual customers and business partners such as suppliers. Customisation can be defined as tailoring some feature of a product/service so that the client enjoys more convenience, lower cost or some other benefit.[27] It is thus possible to be more flexible and the business has the ability to individualise the market offerings, messages and media. For example, a bank may customise written or electronic content based on the client's information needs.

Not all customers are the same, so different customers should be treated differently.[28] The key is to know who the best customers are and to treat them as such. For a business that has two million customers, the prospect of cost-effectively communicating, one-to-one, with all of them is an impossible task. Instead, customers should be categorised or segmented, based on what is known about them. The future of a business may depend on the way the market is segmented, and therefore it is regarded as a key task, requiring the correct identification of the market which the business wants to serve and the correct basis on which to segment it. These segments can be described and quantified in terms of their value and potential value to an organisation and appropriate communication strategies can be designed for each segment. Through effective

CLL = Segment

segmentation a retailer, for example, will know that customers from one particular segment are three times more likely to respond to a promotional offer than customers from any other segment.

A business's success increasingly hinges on using customer-level information and interaction to create long-term, profitable, one-to-one customer relationships. The concept of 'a segment of one' can be seen as a further extension of CRM. In terms of CRM, the marketer should focus on the most profitable customers and reject the unprofitable ones.

Customer knowledge[29]

Employees should have the required product/service knowledge and expertise in order to effectively address or respond to the needs of the client.

Already the most successful businesses in a wide variety of industries are those that have succeeded in developing and maintaining long-term relationships with customers and, more importantly, that embrace the principles of one-to-one marketing – notably KidsRKids, (daycare centre in the USA)[30], Amazon.com and American Express. These businesses have built their success on customer knowledge and interaction.

However, one-to-one marketing is not suitable for every business company.[31] Customisation may be very difficult to implement for complex products such as motor cars. It can raise the cost of goods by more than the customer is willing to pay. Some customers do not know what they want until they see actual products. Customers cannot cancel the order after the business has started to work on the product. The product may be hard to repair and have little sales value. In spite of this, customisation has worked well for some products such as laptop computers, clothes, skincare products and vitamins.

CRM has been defined as building relationships with strategically significant customers. In other words, the business has to decide who are regarded as significant customers and how it will build relationships with them.[32] It is felt that customers who are unprofitable today will most probably be unprofitable tomorrow and they do not merit further attention.[33]

One-to-one marketing is basically a simple idea. However, implementing a one-to-one marketing programme is not as simple. In order to build one-to-one relationships, a business must learn continuously from interactions with individual customers and it must respond dynamically to the information those interactions elicit – it must engage its customers, particularly its best customers and ensure that they never want to leave. The concept of one-to-one marketing is discussed further in Chapter 5.

The question that then arises is: How should a market be segmented in terms of CRM?

Reconsidering traditional market segmentation

In the section above, it was mentioned that market segmentation, as practised for decades, was in need of revision. Businesses are experiencing increased pressure from their competitors, as many of them are offering one-to-one or customised marketing strategies. With advances in technology and segmentation methods, segmentation strategies are evolving to reflect this shift in power toward the customer.

Traditionally, objectives of segmentation strategies focused on identifying groups of potential customers, for example, profiling prospects for product development, identifying appropriate prospects for marketing campaigns and classifying groups in accordance with the potential response to specific pricing strategies. The advantages of market segmentation include the designing of responsive products that would meet the needs of the marketplace, the fact that the business is the focus point, the maintenance of effective relationships with customers, retaining existing and attracting new customers, reducing cost on various marketing activities and better allocation of funds.[34] In terms of CRM, a customer lifetime value (CLV)-based segmentation is a segmentation approach that groups customers into meaningful segments based on customer profitability and lifetime value, and other factors. Moreover, the concepts of customer profitability and CLV are fast becoming accepted as new bases for customer segmentation.[35] CLV enables an organisation to focus on improving the effectiveness of marketing expenditures. For example, using CLV as a basis, a segmentation objective may focus on evaluating customer migration expenditures.

How is customer profitability measured? Many organisations measure customer profitability on the level of sales, the increase in order volume and the size of transactions. Indirect costs (mainly the costs of sales, marketing and general administration) are then allocated across the customer base, often in proportion to the total sales of each customer.[36]

Customer lifetime value is seen in customer equity, which is defined as the total number of the discounted lifetime value of all the customers of the business. It is thus the sum of value equity (determined by price, service, quality and convenience), brand equity (determined by brand awareness, ethics and brand perceptions), relationship equity (determined by loyalty programmes, affinity and, community and knowledge building) and perception equity (determined by word of mouth and buying other products from the business).[37]

With advances in technology, organisations also have access to an abundance of data about their customers, including their purchasing history, attitudinal data collected from customer satisfaction surveys, and demographic and socioeconomic data collected from reward/loyalty programmes.[38] Segmentation offers marketers one approach to utilise this data to customise the organisation's marketing efforts, but successful segmentation efforts require sophisticated models in order to use relevant information and to most effectively target specific customers with appropriate offers to maximise response. In addition, cost-benefit analysis suggests that, in some industries, a CLV segmentation strategy, ie clustering customers into meaningful segments based on customer profitability and other variables, may be a more appropriate use of an organisation's resources than individual-level customer profitability models.[39]

CLV looks at what the retained customer is worth to the organisation now, based on the predicted future transactions and costs. Looking forward to the value of future purchases and costs, expressed as the present value of a stream of future profits, fits more comfortably with the development of a relationship marketing approach that is concerned with unlocking value for the organisation and its key customers.[40] Effectively, relationship marketers need to predict the future purchasing behaviour of key customers to arrive at the latter's CLV.

The concept of CLV is based on specific assumptions, for example, it is assumed that the business will be able to ensure customer retention amongst these customers. It is further assumed that the customer will continue to make use of the service of the business and that he or she will continue to buy from this business.[41] CLV analysis suggests that the value of a relationship with a customer can be increased either by increasing the amount of profit or by extending the relationship lifetime. Customers at the beginning of their relationship lifetime will need a different relationship marketing strategy to those approaching the declining stage of their relationship lifetime. Retail banks understand this principle well; they have identified students as potentially high-value customers over a lifetime, even though in the short term they may be unprofitable.

It is important to remember that customer relationship management is designed to provide increased value to the customer, which ultimately yields a lifetime value to the marketer (service provider).[42] The reason is that higher customer value increases customer satisfaction, thereby instilling customer loyalty, which, in turn, creates higher profit due to increased volume resulting from repeat purchases and positive word-of-mouth referrals.

The next section focuses on the traditional marketing mix in terms of CRM.

Reconsidering the traditional marketing mix[43]

The traditional 4 Ps of marketing, namely product, price, promotion and place/distribution, need to be approached differently according to the new focus on customer relationships. Technology can assist in combining the 4 Ps in numerous ways, thereby offering the customers many choices so that they can obtain precisely what they want (product), when and how they want it (distribution), and at a price that represents the value they wish to receive (price). Technology also enables the business to engage individual customers with whom they wish to communicate (promotion). Through digitising the traditional combination of the marketing mix (the 4 Ps) technology can therefore assist in offering the customer many choices. The focus has changed too: it is for the customer to choose, not for the marketer to provide what he/she thinks the customer wants.

By using technology appropriately, an organisation can serve customers as individuals. The introduction of the Carver 3-wheeled 'learning' motorbike is an example of a product that incorporates substantial changes – the Carver remains a motorbike, but it functions quite uniquely. As the driver turns into a corner, the motorbike tilts or leans in the direction of the corner.[44] A data-driven approach enables organisations to assess each customer's needs and potential profitability, and to tailor sales offers and service accordingly. This involves using multiple channels – the Internet, direct mail, telesales and field sales – to improve effectiveness and efficiency. Businesses using technology have the potential to be close to the customer and to gain a competitive advantage.

The traditional 4 Ps of marketing need to change in terms of RM and CRM, as discussed below.

Product

Traditionally, the marketer developed product concepts, researched the customers and then developed the product that would yield the desired profit margin to the business. This never took into account the fact that customers want different things at different times and are often not interested in one standard product or service.

Relationship marketing (as stated earlier) takes into account the needs of different customers. For example, Gary and Diane Heavin, the founders of the Curves brand, opened the first Curves in 1992 in Harlingen, Texas. It was an overnight success, as it was able to provide women with a supportive and comfortable atmosphere in which to work out. What is interesting is that the company's unofficial motto became 'no makeup, no men, and no mirrors'.[45]

For products and services where the lifetime, volume and margin warrant it, individual customers should be considered in every aspect of the business, including the processes that drive new product and service design. This recognises that customers are different – they want different things in different amounts at different times – and the profit derived from each customer may therefore vary.

Since the 1990s, in another industry, Dell Computer has applied the principle of customer involvement in product specification. Dell overtook Compaq as the leading personal computer seller in the United States of America. While Compaq distributed through traditional computer retailer channels, Dell used a direct channel by selling to customers via the Internet.[46] Customers choose from many options, and Dell assembles products as requested by the customer. This, in addition to Dell's innovation in distribution channel directness, has enabled it to become a major contender in a very competitive industry. Making products according to customer order has a side benefit: total costs can go down as the 'less-finished goods' inventory becomes obsolete.

Practically, in the near future, management may decide that the costs of full-blown technology implementation cannot be justified economically. However, technology throws down this challenge: if you ignore opportunities to serve customers uniquely using advanced technologies and your competitors decide to adopt this approach, what will your response be? An example is given below.

Car manufacturers could consider offering customers the following:

- the opportunity to have a GPS in every motor vehicle;
- the flexibility to choose the colour of a particular car, as opposed to being offered a limited range of colours;
- the opportunity to have a steering wheel customised to suit particular needs.

It is interesting to note that some of the American car manufacturers, such as General Motors, are offering customers the opportunity to order customised motorcars, to their exact specifications, on the Internet!

The key challenge for the marketer is to identify the core strategic value that will be delivered to the customer and the elements that the customer can change, allowing the buyer to be firmly in charge, assembling the value he or she wants. For most organisations, mass customisation requires a material shift in current practice – and the marketer can lead the change. Examples of businesses that are addressing this challenge are given on page 14.

Rethinking products/services

- Some excellent banks in the United States are customising their services to meet the particular needs of their clients. For example, the client assists in designing his/her chequebook, credit card and savings account to meet his/her personal needs. Does this ever happen in South Africa?

- General Electric makes jet engines capable of meeting Boeing's specifications. General Electric engines for one type of Boeing plane differ from another, partly because Boeing's knowledge and direction are incorporated in the design and development process.

Price

Traditional marketing sets a price (value given) for a product and offers the price of the product in the market in exchange for something else (money). The price seeks to secure a fair return on the investment the business has made in its more-or-less static product.

With relationship marketing, the product varies according to the preferences and dictates of the customers, with the value varying commensurately. So, when customers specify that a product should have specific features and that certain services should be delivered before, during and after the sale, they naturally want to pay for each component of the value bundle separately. Just as the product and services are set in a process of collaboration, so too will the price need to reflect the choices made and the value created from those choices.

Customers want to participate in decisions regarding the value they receive and the prices they pay. Give them a standard offering and they will expect to pay a single price. But offer them options in the product and they will want some more than others, and will pay more for these. Give them a chance to have an even more tailored solution, and they might pay more again. Give them options they don't want, and they will expect these to be removed and deleted from the price.

Relationship marketing, especially in the case of industrial marketing, therefore invites customers into the pricing process and all other value-related processes, giving customers an opportunity to make any desirable trade-offs and to further develop trust in the relationship.

Marketing communication (or promotion)

Traditional marketing uses one-way mass advertising to communicate with customers. This one-way communication, typically employed by marketers with their customers, such as mass advertising, promotional offers, manuals, price lists and warranty response cards, must be replaced with integrated marketing communication, which means customer-centred communication with the customer and is driven by the need to convey certain messages to the customer.[47] Technology can make promotion become *communication*, because technology can engage individual customers when and how they wish to relate. Relationship marketing gives individual customers an opportunity to decide how they wish to communicate with the business.

Customers can be served as individuals by using technology appropriately. With technology, individual end customers can be interactively and uniquely engaged. Using technologies such as the Internet, computer-telephony integration at all centres, intelligence at point-of-sale, smart cards and interactive voice response, businesses can give customers a host of options to communicate with the business and have information on hand to engage, inform and direct each customer with complete knowledge as to their preferences.

Distribution (place)

Traditional marketing sees distribution as the channel which usually consists of producers, consumers and any intermediaries who are aligned to provide a means of transferring title or possession of a product or service from a producer to a consumer. The participants are selected on their ability to satisfy customers in terms of product availability, price, convenience and after-sales service.[48] For example, in the case of the computer industry, Dell sees distribution as a direct sales approach, primarily using telephone sales and other placement, while IBM uses many approaches to distribution, including its own stores, a direct sales force and retailers that resell the firm's personal computers.

Relationship marketing instead considers distribution from the perspective of the customer who decides where, how and when to buy the combination of products and services that comprise the supplier's total offering. Seen in this way, distribution is not a channel, but a process. The process allows customers to choose where and from whom they will obtain the value they want (see the example that follows on page 16).

> ### Buying a computer the relationship marketing way
>
> The customer can choose whether to buy a computer off the shelf from a reseller and take it home immediately, order one that is built to his/her individual preferences at the factory and shipped within a week or so, or have one that is configured in-store and available within a few days.

It is thus more accurate to think of distribution as a 'placement', using the customers' choice to direct the location at which they will specify, purchase, receive, install, repair and return individual components of the products and services. While traditional marketing considered a product as a bundled package of benefits, relationship marketing unbundles the product and service, and allows the customer to initiate a placement decision for each element.

The traditional 4 Ps of marketing have been extended in recent times to include three additional Ps, namely people, physical surroundings (organisational structure and technical infrastructure) and processes. These will be discussed in chapter 3, as well as their effect on RM and CRM.

Relationship marketing thus offers an opportunity for the business and the marketer to break out of existing frameworks such as the traditional 4 Ps, and to glue the firm into its customers' minds and wallets. It offers marketers a chance to help the business to grow in a competitively challenging environment. Enabled by new technologies, relationship marketing provides the marketer with the tools needed to serve individuals as they wish to be served, throughout their purchasing and consumption lifetimes. Businesses that are first to adopt relationship marketing principles in their industries and to apply the concepts with vigour have the potential to gain a first-mover advantage that is difficult for competitors to emulate. Importantly, this means that companies have the potential to gain a pre-emptive position with the best customers and to ensure that the needs of these customers are well addressed long before competitors try to copy and target these same individuals or businesses.

It has been proven over time that CRM means better profits, if implemented correctly. However, as outlined below, new capabilities need to be in place before a business can implement CRM.

Businesses require new capabilities

Before embarking on CRM, a business must know who its customers are, their value, what they buy, where they are located and through which channels they want to interact with the business. Management needs to formulate a CRM strategy at all levels, including the people, the business processes and physical surroundings.[49] To implement CRM, the support of executive or top management is essential.

Support at the executive level

An organisation wishing to implement CRM must have support at executive level and there needs to be a commitment to CRM, initiated by top management. In fact, the whole culture of the organisation must change.

The CEO must take the lead and ensure that the message is broadcast throughout the organisation, must understand the real meaning of a relationship before committing the business to CRM and must focus on the value that can be created through relationships with key stakeholders – a value that must be shared by the business and the customer. Also, the most profitable customers to focus on must be identified and the CEO needs to be strong enough to terminate relationships with unprofitable customers.[50] In some businesses, executives try to ensure that they maximise the value of each deal with every customer. However, businesses trying to forge relationships with this underlying approach to customers will find that customers have no interest in long-term bonding with such suppliers. The opportunity to create continuously new and mutual value over time will go to competitors who are more amenable to sharing customers.

Management needs to recognise the fact that relationships with customers need to be managed. A relationship manager should work with customers to ensure that they receive the value they seek. Each person within the business communicates and creates value with his/her customer counterpart, with the relationship manager guiding the overall process. In this process it is necessary to integrate all communications with the customer, with the aid of technology.

Without this commitment by top management, CRM cannot succeed. The successful businesses in South Africa are those that receive enthusiastic support from customers and who have recognised the importance of adopting CRM as a philosophy behind the business – CRM should be one of an organisation's core values.[51] What is therefore expected from top management to ensure the successful implementation of customer relationship management? A CEO could consider some of the following actions to create, first of all, a customer-centric approach in the business:[52]

- Convince senior management of the need to become customer focused. Here the CEO personally exemplifies strong customer commitment and rewards those in the business who do likewise. For example, IBM's top 470 executives are personally responsible for more than 1 300 customer accounts;

17

- Obtain outside help and guidance. Consulting firms have the experience to help businesses move toward a customer orientation;

- Develop strong in-house marketing training programmes for corporate management, divisional managers, marketing and sales personnel, manufacturing personnel and others similar to those run by successful businesses such as Motorola and Accenture;

- Establish an annual marketing excellence recognition programme. Reward the winning teams at a special ceremony; and

- Dhift from a department focus to a process-outcome focus. This means appointing process leaders and cross-disciplinary teams to re-engineer the processes around the customer and implement such processes. It also means empowering employees. Progressive CEOs empower their employees to settle customer complaints and other problems in order to retain the customer's business.

A mutually beneficial relationship is imperative for customer retention. However, it is becoming more difficult to connect with customers and even harder to understand customers' needs. Ernst & Young have found in a study amongst 25 000 consumers from around the globe in 34 countries that a number of trends can be identified, namely:

- consumers have different preferences;

- brands and brand names influence consumer decisions now more than ever;

- personalised communication and service are important to customers; and

- consumers want to be active rather than passive spectators.[53]

Some lessons for implementing CRM can be learned from Accenture's experience, as shown in Box 1.1 on page 19. The next important prerequisite for CRM to be successful is a change in the organisation's processes.

1.1 STUDY ON CRM FAILURE BY ACCENTURE[54]

A study by Accenture found the following:

- While business executives overwhelmingly agree that technology has helped them strengthen relationships with their customers the majority say that CRM shortfalls can be attributed in part to inadequate support from top management.

- Many CRM initiatives fail because of the flawed execution of plans. This echoes the view that the full potential of CRM can be achieved through making sure that there is a connection between the organisation's vision and its execution.

- CEOs need to take a closer look at innovative and proven methods of maximising the return on investment of CRM and customer value indicators by going back to basics.

- Too many CRM projects focus on the mechanics, such as technologies, rather than on the ultimate goal, which is to increase the value of the customer relationship.

- Other factors that explain the failure of CRM programmes are: the lack of a long-term vision for the business; the need for investment in CRM is not justified; investments are not prioritised; and the return on investment is not calculated.

Processes

A process refers to the procedures, mechanisms and flow of activities and operations by which the service is delivered.[55] Service quality management, service recovery and complaint management are three processes that can help to create customer-perceived value. Two perspectives have influenced service quality management, namely conformance to specification and fitness for purpose. Conformance to specification might mean to produce error-free invoices, or to deliver on time, or to produce an initial response to customer complaints within 24 hours. Fitness for purpose might mean to allow the customer to select a preferred communication channel, or to recruit customer contact staff members who are responsive and empathic, or to customise products for customers.

Service recovery includes the actions taken by a business when there has been a service failure. Customers are not concerned with who is to blame – they just want the situation resolved. They want the business to fix the imbalance. There are different ways to do this, namely the business can compensate the customer for service failure or offer apologies. In this case we call it distributive justice. Procedural justice takes place when the customer has a perception of the process to obtain recovery; some procedures offer prompt recovery, whilst others offer delayed recovery. Interactional justice takes place when the customer has a perception about the performance of service recovery people, for example their empathy, courtesy and effort.

A complaints management process should enable businesses to capture customer complaints before customers start spreading negative word-of-mouth or take their business elsewhere. People are the key differentiators from competitors and a major source of customer value. In the next section we will take a closer look at this very important CRM capability.[56]

People

People refer to all aspects of employee involvement, including interaction with customers, employee recruitment, training, motivation, rewards and teamwork.[57] There are many important roles that people need to fulfil for CRM strategies to work well. One of the more important jobs in CRM is the customer contact role. These staff members have two fundamental roles, namely information management and relationship management. They are accountable for collecting information about customers. This information enables them to manage the customer relationship. This might involve winning, growing and maintaining the customer's business, handling customer queries and complaints, representing the customer's interests to the business and ensuring customer satisfaction.

The interaction between employees and customers is referred to as the *service encounter* – this is the actual service the customer receives either face to face, or by telephone, email or through the mail. The service encounter is extremely important for all types of business. Even the interaction between the customer and the provider's service system should be customer friendly, for example a bank's interaction between customer and ATM or Internet bank. Unfriendly systems scare customers away.

For example, a customer calling to enquire about the operation of a new product should be met by someone who has the appropriate information. The information will come either directly from that person or indirectly from data warehouses or people with the knowledge, in which case it requires a person with the ability to engage new processes to access, assess and communicate the relevant information.[58]

The value of CRM capabilities[59]

An important question to ask at this point is: How much are these CRM capabilities worth to a business? Research indicates that the most profitable businesses develop a very specific set of CRM capabilities. Conversely, those that do not invest in building such capabilities leave millions of rand in profit on the table (see Box 1.2). Each business must reinvent itself to produce CRM benefits. The world's leading business software suppliers have also reinvented themselves to focus on CRM.

The end result of establishing a relationship with profitable customers is customer loyalty and, ultimately, greater profitability.

1.2 CRM CAPABILITIES INCREASE PROFIT[60]

In one study, it was found that a typical one billion rand business could add R40–50 million in profit by enhancing specific CRM capabilities by just 10 per cent, whereas businesses that achieve the highest level of CRM performance could improve their pre-tax profit by as much as R120–140 million.

Anderson Consulting survey[61]

In a study by Anderson Consulting, it was found that businesses that enjoy the highest profitability are those that have invested in developing CRM capabilities. Twenty-one such CRM capabilities were identified. Topping the list was motivating and rewarding employees, followed by excellence in delivering customer service, turning customer information into insight, attracting and retaining the right personnel, and building selling and service skills. The influence of technology accounted for about 40 per cent of CRM's impact and will become important with the rapid growth of e-commerce.

The survey further indicated that the highest-performing businesses gave frontline employees quick and easy access to critical customer information. And top performers even shared this information with channel partners outside their organisation.

Summary

Successful companies never lose sight of their customers' demands and are careful to keep track of their customers' needs as they evolve and change.

A company can attract and retain customers by knowing and delivering what they want, when they want it, how they want it, and making it an easy and problem-free process for customers to interact with the organisation. Thus CRM solutions have become strategic requirements in a customer-focused economy.

These solutions can help organisations attract and retain customers in highly competitive markets.

DISCUSSION QUESTIONS

1. Discuss what is meant by relationship marketing.
2. Contrast the traditional marketing approach and the relationship marketing approach.
3. How do relationship marketing and customer relationship management solve the problems that are encountered with the traditional approach to marketing?
4. An organisation wishing to implement CRM needs to change many of the old traditional approaches of marketing, and it also requires new capabilities that can be considered as prerequisites for the implementation of CRM. In light of this statement, explain these prerequisites or new capabilities for CRM.
5. Discuss the value of CRM capabilities.
6. Discuss the focus areas of relationship marketing.

Mini case study

Mass customisation at Amazon.com[62]

Amazon.com has become the world's largest and also most successful online retailer. It has diversified from books and CDs into other areas, for example electronics and clothing.

Its success has been related to its CRM strategy of retaining and gaining increased sales from its customers. Based on available information such as previous purchases and products that have recently been browsed, its CRM software can predict a range of other products in which the customer is likely to be interested.

A customer who selects to purchase for example, an Ernest Hemingway novel, may receive a recommendation to purchase another novel by Hemingway or a DVD documentary of his life.

MINI CASE STUDY QUESTIONS

1. Compare the individual customer approach and the approach that Amazon.com is following.
2. Advise Amazon.com on market segmentation.

Building relationships

Introduction

Due to increasing rivalry in most industries, management has come to realise that they can no longer afford to take their customers for granted. The nature of business today makes it easy for customers who are unhappy with a particular product or service to switch to a competing brand or service without much difficulty.

Customer relationship management (CRM) focuses on building a learning customer relationship, developing a base of loyal customers and at the same time increasing profitability. Nurturing and building a meaningful relationship with customers will ensure customer loyalty and decrease the chance of the customer switching to the organisation's competitors. Implementing strategies such as customisation, following up and providing excellent customer service will lead to long, successful customer relationships.

Focus on customer relationships

More and more organisations are beginning to understand the importance of customer relationships.[1] Managing relationships with customers has become the core of marketing. Goods and services are no longer sufficient to differentiate organisations from their competitors and are therefore adopting a customer relationship marketing approach to differentiate themselves.[2]

This chapter deals with customer relationships and how to build them. We will explore the nature of a learning relationship and how to improve it. We will also look at which relationships are not realistic, and the stages in relationship development. We will explore customer retention, which is a prerequisite for relationship loyalty; the lifetime value of a customer; and its implications for profitability.

The learning relationship

In order for a company to establish and improve a relationship, the marketer needs to acquire knowledge about the customer; be able to develop insight into this knowledge as well as interact regularly with the customer to acquire new information.

Learning relationships are built on knowledge

As the interaction between the customer and the organisation increases, the learning relationship between the two parties should continue to improve, defining in ever more detail the customer's own individual needs and tastes.[3] The more customers interact and influence a company, the better it becomes at providing exactly what the customer wants, and the more difficult it will be for a competitor to lure them away. Even if a competitor were to provide exactly the same offerings, for a customer already involved in a learning relationship with another company the competitor would have to spend an inordinate amount of time and energy learning about the customer and teaching the customer about their offerings. Thus, a powerful competitive advantage has been created by the first company. An example of such a learning relationship is shown in Box 2.1 on the following page.

2.1 BUILDING RELATIONSHIPS WITH GARY ROM HAIRDRESSING CLIENTS[4]

The Gary Rom Hairdressing (GRH) team works long and hard at building good foundations with their clients and each employee understands the importance of this process.

Below are some of the innovative ways in which GRH builds relationships:

- The GRH loyalty programme helps maintain a relationship with customers, thus communicating that GRH cares about the money spent at its salons. The programme awards clients points on each visit that can be redeemed to provide a discount on a later consultation.

- GRH employees communicate with their clients and ensure that they are satisfied and happy with the GRH experience, or ascertain of there is anything that can be improved on.

- Courtesy calls are made to clients to enquire whether or not the service they received was up to standard, if they are happy with their stylist or if there is something that needs to be improved.

In order to gain knowledge of customers, as well as insight into this knowledge, it is, necessary to obtain information. This information is then used to create a database for the customer, which becomes the foundation for subsequent CRM activities. Technology enables companies to gather and store information about every individual customer in a sophisticated customer database. After you have bought a new car, for example, the dealer could compile a database with information about your purchase, as well as your personal needs and preferences. After a year or two, he or she could contact you to enquire if you are thinking of buying a new car. Thus, companies that focus on gaining customer knowledge and developing insight into this knowledge can deepen and extend customer relationships. The database of a clothing retailer, for example, should ideally contain the following information:[5]

- **transactions:** a complete history of the purchases made by the customer, including the purchase date, the price paid and whether or not the merchandise was purchased in response to a special promotion or marketing activity;

- **customer contacts:** a record of the interactions that the customer has had with the store, including visits to the website and enquiries made by telephone, plus information initiated by the retailer, such as direct mail sent to the customer;

- **customer preferences:** what the customer likes, such as favourite colours, brands, fabrics and flavours, as well as clothes sizes;

- **descriptive information:** demographic data (such as age, race or gender) and psychographic data (for example lifestyle and social class) describing the customer that can be used to develop market segments; and

- **responses to marketing activities:** the analysis of the transaction and contact data provides information about the customer's responsiveness to marketing activities.

The customer database can provide important information for planning, for example, merchandise assortment in a store, provided that the necessary insight into this knowledge can be developed.

Whereas traditional marketing tended to regard information as a source of power, learning relationships imply that information is a valuable resource in building relationships. Because of the competitive advantage based on knowledge about customers, a company that can cultivate learning relationships with its customers should be able to retain their custom virtually forever, provided that it continues to supply high-quality customised products or services at reasonably competitive prices and does not miss the next technology wave. Learning relationships would not have saved an ox wagon manufacturer from the motorcar!

Most relevant knowledge comes not only from customers, but through and with them. Increasingly, companies are recognising that they should work with their customers in joint knowledge-creating processes to develop deep bonding and a more informed capability to respond to customers.

Customer interaction enhances relationships

Interacting with a customer to learn how satisfied the customer is, or whether the customer has an unspoken complaint, is really just another way of obtaining information about that customer's needs.[6] What the organisation really wants to know is how to make the service experience better for that customer at the next opportunity. If a company can find out how to treat a specific customer better the next time it has dealings with him/her, it can begin to lock that customer into a learning relationship. If, every time a customer deals with you, it is more satisfying for that customer than it was the previous time, you are creating a learning relationship with the customer, and, after just a few interactions, the customer will become very loyal. However, this type of interaction should not be used in excess, otherwise the customer will begin to resist interacting at all. One good principle to apply is to check on a customer's satisfaction whenever anything out of the ordinary has occurred in the relationship, for example, a particularly large purchase such as a car, or a problem in financing.

It is important to keep in mind the following rules of engagement when interacting with customers:[7]

- Have a clear objective before interacting with the customer.
- Only ask the customer something once.
- Find out which communication medium would suit the customer best.
- When engaging in an interaction, start with the customer, not the product.
- Put effort into personalised interaction with the customer.
- Ensure that your interactions with customers are always welcomed.
- Always put the customer's privacy first.
- Invite dialogue by printing toll-free numbers and website URLs on everything.
- Be clear in demonstrating the value of the interaction to the customer.
- Be sensitive to the customer's time; do not try to learn everything about a customer all at once.

As technology has made interactions increasingly less costly, businesses are finding that they can afford to interact economically with a wider range of customers. Technology also allows an organisation to streamline and automate many of the manual interactions required in serving customers, thus reducing costs and saving time, often quite dramatically (see the example in Box 2.2). It is, however, important to note that if customers are bombarded with electronic media that can lead to resistance as well.

2.2 GARY ROM HAIRDRESSING[8]

A customer-care line is also provided on all GRH products to ensure that clients have a direct contact line for both compliments and complaints. GRH is also active on social media sites such as Facebook and Twitter which facilitate two-way communication and encourage feedback.

As most companies attempt to establish relationships with their customers, they should bear in mind that in some cases there are reasons why attempting to develop a relationship may be a fruitless pursuit, because some relationships are simply unrealistic.

Unrealistic relationships[9]

It is not possible for all types of businesses to develop learning relationships, because there are no powerful benefits to be gained from some relationships. Some customers may not be suitable for the investment needed in developing a relationship, as it may prove to be too costly. Frequently, there may be a need to change an organisation's marketing activities and increase the marketing expenditure on the relationship-building elements of the marketing mix. Marketers therefore need to consider the potential lifetime value of a customer and determine whether it is appropriate to make this commitment. When is a learning relationship therefore appropriate?

There are many situations where relationship development is unrealistic, from either the customer's or the supplier's point of view. For example, it may not be a viable proposition for a supplier to embark on costly relationship-building strategies, or there may be no reason why the seller would ever see the buyer again. See the examples in Box 2.3.

2.3 APPROPRIATE RELATIONSHIPS[10]

Companies such as home builders, real estate brokers and appliance manufacturers – which do not interact frequently with end users of their products – cannot learn enough to make a learning relationship with those customers work. But they might find it beneficial to develop such relationships with general contractors.

Manufacturers of products such as paper clips, whose revenue or profit margin per customer is too low to justify building individual learning relationships with customers, might find it advantageous to cultivate learning relationships with businesses in office-supply chains, that interact directly with end users of their products.

A number of scenarios exist in which it would be unrealistic to develop customer relationships, for example:[11]

- where there is no reason why, or little likelihood that, a buyer will purchase again from a supplier. A buyer who is unlikely ever to patronise a supplier will see no benefit from establishing a relationship and may indeed be annoyed by the tactics associated with it, such as data capture;

- where buyers want to avoid a relationship, as it may lead to a dependency on a seller. This situation may exist when any benefits associated with the relationship are outweighed by lost opportunities elsewhere;

- where buying processes are formalised in a way that prevents either party developing relationships based on social bonds. Formalised buying situations may be compromised and jeopardised by too close an association between buyer and seller (for example, those involving government agencies); and

- where the costs associated with a relationship put the buyer at a cost disadvantage in a price-sensitive market. It may be more profitable for buyers in certain markets to keep their eyes open for the best deal available, rather than narrow the field and commit themselves to one supplier. Indeed, they may well prefer to play suppliers off against one another using an organisation's potential insecurity to gain added value.

Certain requirements for a relationship will also indicate whether CRM strategies should be considered. These requirements are essential ingredients for a relationship to be successful.

Essential ingredients of a relationship

The success of a business relationship lies in the development and growth of trust and commitment among partners. The two parties also need to have shared goals and mutual benefits to build a successful relationship.

Trust and commitment

In order to build successful customer relationships, relationship commitment and trust is essential. Interactions between customers and business which lack these elements do not develop into relationships.[12] According to the Commitment-Trust Theory of Relationship Marketing[13], relationships exist through the retention of trust and commitment; thus, when both commitment and trust are present – not just one or the other – they produce outcomes that promote efficiency, productivity and effectiveness.

Trust

Trust is seen as an expression of confidence between parties in the exchange that they will not be harmed or put at risk by either party's actions. Thus, trust is the willingness to rely on an exchange partner in whom one has confidence; it is a generalised expectancy held by an individual that the word of another can be relied upon. These descriptions of trust highlight the importance of confidence, ie the firm belief that the trustworthy party is reliable and has high integrity, and are associated with such qualities as consistency, competence, honesty, fairness, responsibility, helpfulness and benevolence.

There would appear to be a considerable overlap between trust and satisfaction, as they both represent an overall evaluation, feeling or attitude about the other party in a relationship. Satisfaction may be developed through personal experience or, less directly, through opinion and the experience of peers. It is associated with the perceived standard of delivery and may well be dependent on the duration of the relationship. We can therefore say that high levels of service need to be present throughout the product service delivery process. This would enable customers to receive what they want, when they want it – a perfect delivery each and every time with the desired levels of service that appeal to the consumer. This, in turn, may motivate customer retention. Further, satisfaction over a long period of time reinforces the perceived reliability of the firm and contributes to trust; and anticipated levels of satisfaction may also have an important effect on the duration of the trust.[14]

To build trust is to ensure that customers know that the business will stand behind its promise of service and honour its commitments. In the service sector, for example, trust is particularly relevant, because customers often do not buy services as such. What they buy are implicit and explicit promises of service, for example:

- promises that insurance companies will honour future claims;
- promises that banks will correctly process cheques; and
- promises that home security systems will promptly contact the armed response when burglars break in.

Trust is therefore an important element of a relationship-building programme, because it builds confidence, fosters co-operation and gives the service provider a second chance when inevitable mishaps occur. It may not be possible to rebuild customer relationships when trust is broken.

Trust is a major determinant of relationship commitment.

Commitment

Commitment is undoubtedly connected with the notion of trust. Commitment is the belief that the importance of a relationship with another is so significant that it warrants maximum effort to maintain it.[15] Commitment implies that both parties will be loyal, reliable and show stability in their relationship with one another. It is, therefore, a desire to maintain a relationship and it is often indicated by ongoing investment in activities that are expected to maintain that relationship. As it may take time to reach a point where a commitment may be made, it may also imply a certain 'maturity' in a relationship.

Trust facilitates commitment to a relationship, because commitment creates a sense of vulnerability, but this risk is reduced with trust. One exchange partner accepts a lower immediate return with the expectation that their exchange partner will allow them a larger future benefit. Buyers and sellers who accept the premise of an unequal exchange benefit with parity being achieved over time will seek trust-based relationships and will partner only with trustworthy partners. Trust reduces the perception of vulnerability, because it reduces the expectation that a partner would engage in opportunistic behaviour while increasing confidence that short-term inequalities will be equalised over time.[16]

Therefore, when both commitment and trust are present, they produce outcomes that promote efficiency, productivity and effectiveness. In short, commitment and trust lead directly to cooperative behaviours that are conducive to relationship marketing success.

Is a must! But not enough - today!

In a business relationship, <u>excellent customer service is,</u> of course, a major prerequisite. Some customers are known to have said, 'Stop sending the birthday cards, just answer the phone the first time!'

A relationship is further sustained through the same shared values, together with relationship benefits.

Shared goals and mutual benefits

Shared goals and mutual benefits are also key factors in building effective business relationships. The extent to which the partners have beliefs in common about behaviours, goals and policies that are important, appropriate and right for a particular situation is likely to affect commitment to a relationship.[17]

The existence of shared goals has been found to have significant effects on relationships that could be profoundly useful to the sellers of products and services. People with shared goals expect to receive help from each other; they share relevant information, and trust the information that they receive, because it is in the interests of both sides to maximise their joint effectiveness and their joint goal attainment. In contrast to what has been said about factors such as trust and commitment being essential ingredients of a relationship, absence of commitment to a relationship is, however, possible in workable relationships, as illustrated in Box 2.4 on the following page.

As mentioned earlier, the purpose of building relationships with customers is to retain customers. And by retaining customers, loyalty is created; loyalty, in turn, results in superior long-term financial performance. So let us explore relationship loyalty in more detail.

objective

2.4 RELATIONSHIPS WITH NO TRUST AND COMMITMENT

In the retailing sector, consumers have no reason to commit themselves to one or a few retailers, because of the availability of a large supply of retailers in a largely undifferentiated market. What at first might appear to be 'commitment' on the part of consumers may hide the fact that they have few other exchange possibilities and are 'trapped' rather than committed to the relational exchange.

The irony is that the retailing sector, where commitment is low, is the industry most heavily involved in 'loyalty schemes'. If commitment is a rarity in these businesses, then loyalty is also in short supply. Indeed, most loyalty schemes, while rewarding repeat behaviour, are little more than technically advanced promotions that have little to do with retention and may actively work against the development of long-term commitment.

Uncommitted customers will be attracted by the best deal with little regard to who supplies it. Once a better brand appears, the consumer will easily switch to another supplier, as there is no trust and commitment.

Relationship loyalty

Loyalty is a concept close to the heart of customer relationship management. To fully understand relationship loyalty, it is necessary to look at loyalty in perspective – to explore customer retention as well as customer migration, customer bonding strategies and the lifetime value of customers.

Customer loyalty in perspective

Customer loyalty, the objective of CRM, is more than having customers make repeat purchases as well as being satisfied with their experiences and the products or services which they purchased. Customers who are committed and loyal towards an organisation will not be open to advances made by competing organisations. Loyal customers have a deeper level of trust, and even a bond with the organisation.

Loyalty towards a retailer[18]

Loyal customers have an emotional connection with the retailer. Their reasons for continuing to patronise the retailer go beyond the convenience of the retailer's store or the low prices and specific brands offered. They feel such goodwill toward the retailer that they will encourage their friends and family to buy from it.

Loyalty can be defined as the

> ... *biased behavioural response, expressed over time by customers with respect to one supplier out of a set of suppliers, which is a function of decision making and evaluative processes resulting in brand or store commitment.*[19]

Simple patronage, therefore, is not enough. Loyalty, if it is to be genuine, must be seen as biased repeat-purchase behaviour, or repeat patronage accompanied by a favourable attitude.

Many companies, having secured a customer's order, turn their attention to seeking new customers without understanding the importance of maintaining and improving the relationships with their existing customers. Too little emphasis is therefore placed on generating repeat business. The objective of relationship marketing is to turn new customers into regularly purchasing customers, and then progressively to move them towards being strong supporters of the company and its product, and finally to being active and vocal advocates for the company, thus playing an important role as a referral source. And in this process, customer service has a pivotal role to play in achieving this progression up the ladder of customer loyalty.[20]

Developing customer loyalty is not a question of making 'unloyal' customers loyal. Some customers will never be loyal to a company or its competitors and companies must accept this. However, companies can make sure that they keep existing customers loyal by giving them more reasons to stay so. They can also encourage uncommitted customers to become more loyal and, by profiling the types of customers who are loyal, they can actively seek other customers who have similar profiles. The retention of loyal customers is of great importance to any organisation.

One of the key elements of customer retention is customer satisfaction. As a rule, the more satisfied the customer, the more durable the relationship. And the longer this lasts, the more money the company stands to make.

There are a number of techniques for measuring customer satisfaction and linking them directly to corporate profitability. The simplest, yet one of the most effective, is 'customer retention', where satisfaction is measured by the rate at which customers are kept – the 'customer retention rate'. This is expressed as the percentage of customers at the beginning of the year that still remain at the end of the year. The more satisfied the customers are, the longer they stay and thus the higher the retention rate. A retention rate of 80 per cent means that, on average, customers remain loyal for five years, whereas one of 90 per cent pushes the average loyalty period up to ten years. And as the average 'life' of a customer increases, so does the profitability of that customer to the company.[21]

Ways of retaining customers will be dealt with under loyalty strategies in Chapter 8.

Customer retention

Many companies spend a great deal of effort, time and money wooing new customers, yet surprisingly few take equal trouble to retain existing customers, as illustrated in Box 2.5.

2.5 CUSTOMER SERVICE – 1ST FOR WOMEN[22]

Selling a policy is one thing, but it is quite another thing to retain a customer, especially in an industry notorious for its churn and price sensitivity. With this in mind, 1st for Women has an on-going challenge to maintain relationships with its customers and to meet and exceed their expectations.

In order to understand what these expectations are, 1st for Women conducts both qualitative and quantitative research on a regular basis. The purpose of this research is to find out what its customers' expectations are in key areas of interaction.

One such key interaction with customers is 1st for Women's Lifestyle Networking events, which are run every year. These events have become somewhat of an institution and were launched so that like-minded women could meet, network, talk and ultimately learn and grow.

Very few companies actually go to the trouble of regularly measuring customer satisfaction in any systematic way, partly because they are obsessed by a perceived need to win new business and partly because they fail to understand the very real and demonstrable relationship between customer retention and profitability.

Know your customer 80/20 Principle

> ## The effect of customer retention on profits
>
> Acquiring a new customer costs more than retaining an existing one.
>
> Normally 80 per cent of the profits are derived from 20 per cent of the customers (according to the Pareto Principle). It thus makes sense to concentrate on those clients that produce profits, in other words, the existing customers.
>
> Regular customers tend to place frequent and consistent orders, thereby decreasing the costs of servicing those customers.
>
> Efforts to retain customers make it difficult for competitors to enter the market or to increase their share of the market.
>
> Improved customer retention can lead to an increased level of employee satisfaction, which leads to increased employee retention and which feeds back into an even greater customer longevity.
>
> Long-time customers tend to be less price sensitive, permitting the charging of higher prices, for example, they will not move for the extra 5 per cent difference in banking charges.
>
> Long-time customers are likely to provide free word-of-mouth advertising and referrals.

Customer retention can be improved upon if the organisation focuses on customer migration.

Customer migration

Customer retention is crucial to all businesses but it should not be their sole focus. They also need to investigate customer migration before it leads to defection.[23] Upward migration means that customers spend more, while downward migration refers to customers spending less and less. Managing migration – from the satisfied customers who spend more to the downward migrators who spend less – is crucial in customer-retention strategies.

Many more customers change their spending behaviour than defect. So the spending behaviour typically accounts for larger changes in value. Managing migration not only gives companies an early chance to stem the downward course before their customers defect entirely, but also helps them to influence upward migration earlier. One should also keep in mind that a broad measure of satisfaction can tell a company how likely customers are to defect, but satisfaction alone does not tell an organisation what makes customers loyal. The product or the difficulty of finding a replacement can also be factors, for example. Nor does gauging satisfaction levels tell an organisation how susceptible its customers are to changing their spending patterns. Understanding the other drivers of loyalty is crucial to having an influence on migration.

Normally, customers are loyal because they are emotionally attached to the supplier, and have rationally chosen it as the best option. Downward migrators have several reasons for spending less: their lifestyle has changed, so they have developed new needs that the organisation is not meeting; they continually reassess their options and have found a better one; or they are actively dissatisfied, often because of a single bad experience (for example, with a rude salesperson).

Organisations often make little effort to meet their customers' changing needs, which might include new financial or insurance products for ageing customers and new travel arrangements made necessary by updated corporate travel policies. Changing needs are not uncontrollable; they can be addressed and the new needs form a relevant part of the overall loyalty opportunity.

The case for increasing customer retention is captured in the concept of customer lifetime value (CLV).[24] Organisations can use their customer database to determine how profitable existing customers are before expensive efforts are made to retain them.

Customer lifetime value

The old concept of customer lifetime value (CLV), introduced in chapter 1, has been revived by CRM and has become one of the key tenets of CRM in that it recognises the value of customers over their purchasing lifetimes.[25] In recognising lifetime value, CRM seeks to bond progressively more firmly with customers.

Customer lifetime value can be defined as the present value of the stream of future profits expected over the customer's lifetime purchases. CLV is estimated by using past behaviours to forecast the future purchases, the gross margin from these purchases and the costs associated with servicing the customer.[26] Costs associated with a customer include the cost of advertising and promotions used to acquire the customer and the cost of goods returned. Other costs could include such factors as the profit earned on referrals made by a customer, the monetary value of collaborative assistance from the customer in designing new products or services, the benefit of the customer's own reputation among other current and potential customers and so on. The figure you could come up with if you were able to factor in all these variables is the customer's lifetime value.

The assessment of CLV is based on the assumption that the customer's future purchase behaviours will be the same as they have been in the past. Sophisticated statistical methods are typically used to estimate the future contributions from past purchases. For example, think of a customer who has shopped at Pick n Pay for the last three years and has generated a profit every month for the company. We can assume that this customer will continue to generate that profit level for some period of time in the future, although any number of forces may arise that will change this simplistic trend at any moment.[27]

One has to also consider that certain goods, such as children's cereals and toys, are only of interest during a limited period in a family's lifetime.

Customers have different values to a business and they need different things from the business. What do the customers want and what is the customer worth? The value of a customer relative to other customers allows the business to prioritise its efforts, allocating more resources to ensuring that the more valuable customers remain loyal and grow in value.[28] And catering to what a specific customer needs is the basis for creating a relationship and winning customers' loyalty. It is therefore necessary to rank customers by their value and to differentiate them by their needs.

There is one other critical element of the customer's lifetime value: the customer's growth potential or strategic value. Strategic value is the additional value a customer could yield if you had a strategy to get it.[29]

A customer's growth potential or strategic value

A banking customer could have both a cheque and a savings account. Every month the customer provides a certain profit to the bank and the net present value of this continuing profit stream represents the customer's actual value to the bank. But the home mortgage, which that same customer has at a competitive bank, represents strategic value: potential value that the first bank could realise if it had a proactive strategy to obtain it.

Knowing both actual and strategic value allows an organisation to calculate its 'share of wallet' (ie the percentage of the customers' purchases made from the organisation) with these customers. Remember, you cannot calculate this precisely. Instead, you create a financial model for it, try to get a better and better handle on it, and in the end, settle for a good-enough substitute variable. A simple way of calculating the lifetime value of an average supermarket customer can be done as shown on page 38.

CLV of a supermarket customer

The customer's expenditure per week	R1 200
Thus he spends per month	R4 800
He spends per year	R57 600
Assume he remains loyal for 30 years	× 30
Then his lifetime value is	R1 728 000

However, as you can see, no costs have yet been calculated, such as advertising, so the actual lifetime value would be less.

Box 2.6 shows a more sophisticated way of estimating CLV.

2.6 CALCULATING CLV [30]

A company could analyse its new-customer acquisition cost as follows:

- Cost of an average sales call (including salary, commission, benefits and expenses) R1 200
- Average number of sales calls to convert an average prospect into a customer × 5
- Cost of attracting a new customer R6 000

This is an underestimate, because the cost of advertising and promotion has been omitted, plus the fact that only a fraction of all potential customers end up being converted into actual customers.

Now suppose the company estimates average CLV as follows:

- Annual customer revenue R6 000
- Average number of loyal years × 3
- Company profit margin 0.2

CLV R3 600

This company is spending more to attract new customers than they are worth. Unless the company can sign up customers with fewer sales calls, spend less per sales call, stimulate higher new-customer annual spending, retain customers longer or sell them higher-profit products, it is headed for bankruptcy.

When an organisation has determined the CLV of its customers, it should have a well-informed financial view of its customer base. In particular, it will know that a relatively small number of customers account for the majority of the profits. A retailer, for example, could group its customers into a commonly used segmentation scheme that divides customers into four segments, as illustrated in Figure 2.1.[31]

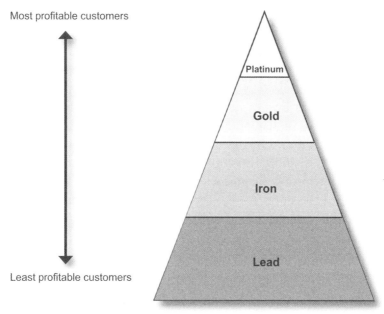

Figure 2.1 The customer pyramid

The four segments of the customer pyramid are outlined below.

- **Platinum segment:** This segment is composed of the customers with the top 25 per cent CLVs. Typically, these are the most loyal customers who are not overly concerned about price, and place more value on customer service.

- **Gold segment:** The next 25 per cent of customers have a lower CLV than platinum customers because they are more price sensitive. Even though they buy a significant number of products, they are not as loyal as platinum customers and probably patronise competitors as well.

- **Iron segment:** These customers do not deserve much special attention due to their modest CLV.

- **Lead segment:** These customers are in the lowest segment and often demand a great deal of attention but do not buy much. They, in fact, cost the organisation money.

In the same way as the customer pyramid, segmentation schemes can be drawn up for other types of companies, such as airlines. However, the pyramid will be quite different. Some schemes break customers into ten deciles according to their CLV, rather than the quartiles illustrated above. In this case, the 10 per cent of the customers with the highest CLV would be in the top segment. (In chapter 8 targeting customers based on their profitability will be discussed.)

When segments or segmentation schemes are designed, a good starting point is to investigate the stages of relationship development.

Stages of relationship development

Once a customer has been acquired, the relationship with the company can develop in one of two fundamentally different directions, depending on the level of customer satisfaction. On the one hand, if the company is able to keep a customer lastingly satisfied, ideally the customer may turn into an 'enthusiast' for the company. This means the customer becomes more and more loyal, making significant use of the entire range of company services, while not considering competitive offers. On the other hand, in the case of a customer who becomes dissatisfied, it is possible that the customer may even turn into a 'terrorist' with regard to the company, not only by causing the organisation extra costs, but also by dissuading other current or potential customers from dealing with the organisation.[32]

The well-known relationship marketing ladder of loyalty identifies six stages of relationship development; these also represent the different stages of relationship development, or customer bonding, in order to achieve loyalty. This ladder of loyalty is illustrated in Figure 2.2.[33]

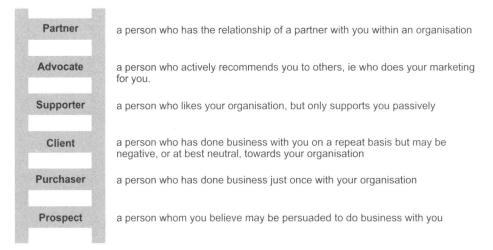

Figure 2.2 The relationship marketing ladder of loyalty

The six stages of relationships development are described below.

1. **Prospect:** The first task is to identify prospects who offer interesting potential and may want to do business with you. Prospects usually have limited awareness of an organisation and its relevance, but are unlikely to become purchasers until awareness increases. Thus, elevating levels of company or product/service awareness may be an important issue for shifting customers from prospects to purchasers. These prospects then need to be moved up to the first rung to become a purchaser.

2. **Purchaser:** During the purchaser phase, potential consumers have begun to explore the extent to which your company is relevant to them, perhaps with initial trial purchases. Based on their satisfaction with this experience, they will wish to assess the potential to establish a more significant flow of business to your company. Needless to say, excellent service and follow-up interaction are important in moving these customers to the next rung on the ladder.

3. **Client:** The company should now try to turn the new purchaser into a client who purchases regularly. If clients are satisfied with all their contact with the company, they may become more significant. Even small mistakes or problems can create the dissatisfaction that can erode the trust relationship that is beginning to be forged in this stage.

4. **Supporter:** The next stage of advancement up the loyalty ladder is the supporter of the organisation and its products, the longer-term buyers whose trust you now have. These consumers, who are satisfied with their initial experience, have begun to do business with your company, but not as a matter of course. They are likely to continue to do business with their current supplier, but are interested enough in your offer that they consider your company an appropriate second source in the event that their main supplier fails to satisfy them in some way.

5. **Advocate:** The advocate on the next rung provides powerful word-of-mouth endorsement of an organisation. With advocates, your company has customers who are so committed to your organisation that only a major violation of trust would erode this goodwill. You have virtually their entire attention in this product or service category. An advocate will make business referrals; they will also be good complainers, inviting you to improve without being negative in their guidance.

6. **Partner:** In an organisation-to-organisation context, advocates may ultimately develop into partners who are closely linked in trusting and mutually sharing relationships with their suppliers. Trust is gained once a company has successfully fulfilled these customers' needs over a period of

time. Partners consider the company to be a vital role player in fulfilling their needs.

Summary

CRM focuses on improving learning relationships with customers. These learning relationships are based on obtaining information by interacting with customers. An organisation cannot, however, focus on all relationships, since some are simply not appropriate and thus do not justify the time and money that need to be invested to maintain them. In order to build and improve relationships, marketers need to take into account the essential requirements for a relationship, namely trust, commitment, shared goals and mutual benefits, as, without these, the relationship would not be successful. The main reason why a marketer wants to build these relationships is to create customer loyalty, which means that customer retention, customer migration and the lifetime value of customers are important factors to be considered. Once the profitability of customers has been established, different strategies of loyalty can be put in place, depending on the nature of the customers' profitability and loyalty. (These strategies will be dealt with in Chapter 8.)

DISCUSSION QUESTIONS

1. How can a learning relationship be built between a customer and his/her bank where almost all his/her accounts are kept?

2. Why are some relationships unrealistic? Illustrate your answer with practical examples.

3. Explain, with the aid of practical examples, the essential ingredients of a relationship, highlighting how these ingredients should be applied by a bank.

4. Explain and illustrate why a marketer should take into account customer retention and customer migration in order to develop customer loyalty.

5. An organisation wishing to determine the profitability of its customers has requested that you explain the lifetime value of customers to it, and to illustrate how this value can be determined and applied by the organisation. Explain how you would approach this request.

6. What are the segments of the customer pyramid?

7. How should a firm of attorneys use the stages of relationship development to attract and keep more clients?

Mini case study

Gary Rom Hairdressing (GRH) gets to know its clientele personally[34]

As part of the GRH experience, appointments are scheduled hourly. This enables stylists to have a 30–40 minute consultation with their clients prior to working on their hair. This process separates GRH from the rest of the salons in the industry. GRH firmly believes in consultation, as it allows stylists to get to know their clients on a personal level. Understanding one's customers and gaining insight and valuable information from them assists in building that long-term relationship that is so vitally important in a service industry.

Each client is taken through a seven-step consultation process in which elements such as skin tone, facial shape, height, career, family, and more are identified to ensure that the best possible haircut/design is given to each client.

GRH's clients are seen as the company's most valuable asset. Clients appreciate the fact that they can walk into any GRH salons and know that their stylist has their best interests at heart and is not interested in how high their docket value could be. At GRH the stylists and management team take time to understand each client's needs, and to continuously ensure that these needs are met with ever-increasing consistency.

MINI CASE STUDY QUESTION

1. Can you identify the important factors in building relationships with customers that Gary Rom Hairdressing has implemented in terms of the following:
   a) Learning relationship?
   b) Customer database?
   c) Customer retention?
   d) Lifetime value?
   e) Managing customer loyalty?

Service issues in RM and CRM

Learning outcomes

After studying this chapter, you should be able to:

- explain the nature of customer service by highlighting its meaning and its role in building customer relationships;
- discuss customer expectations;
- explain and illustrate the factors involved in service quality;
- demonstrate the links between relationships, quality service and customer loyalty;
- explain ways of measuring customer satisfaction;
- discuss the factors involved in moments of truth or service encounters;
- identify and explain the various factors that shape servicescapes;
- explain the impact of service failure and how service recovery can lead to customer satisfaction;
- explain the key success factors of service management;
- explain the relevance, for keeping customers, of the cash value or lifetime value of each customer;
- identify some of the elements of great service;
- discuss the management of the service culture within an organisation.

Introduction

Understanding the importance of and valuing customer insights is crucial not only in improving customer service, but also in the design of the service delivery system. As in many other countries, South Africa is no exception when it comes to poor customer service. This is particularly true in the case of the government sector and the services industry. According to the findings in a national customer satisfaction study by research company, React Surveys[1], it was found that many consumers had more disposable income and were spending money 'without being too fussy' about the service. It is therefore easier to be rude to a customer because there are 100 more behind him/her! The survey also found that most customers returned to the stores and restaurants that provided bad service because of value for money and convenience. Many people also believe that it does not help to complain as nothing can and will be done.

Customer service forms an integral part of CRM and can be used to differentiate a company from its competitors. In spite of this however, many companies still do not give good service. Think of South African companies that could be considered 'excellent' in terms of service. Woolworths is one company that often comes to mind in this regard. It has certainly managed to differentiate itself in terms of product and service quality and is reaping the rewards of this through premier pricing. Yet even Woolworths went through a difficult period when it had to refocus its efforts in terms of the strategic direction of its services and quality to maintain its performance in the marketplace. Therefore, even though an organisation knows what it wants to achieve in terms of service and quality, achieving those objectives is clearly more difficult than it seems, as evidenced by the few companies that can really be considered as giving excellent service.

In the recent worldwide recession many companies went back to basics. They improved their service to customers. High-quality customer service is the key to improving relationships with customers, and an enhanced relationship with one's customers can ultimately lead to greater customer retention, customer loyalty and, more importantly, profitability.[2]

Keeping customers happy is not easy and it must be remembered that if customers are not satisfied they will not come back but try another company.

In today's highly competitive environment, companies must pay attention to fulfilling the needs of each customer quickly and accurately. If an organisation can position itself favourably within a particular marketplace, relative to competitors, it has created a competitive advantage; indeed, stronger relationships with customers result in a number of competitive advantages.

In this chapter, the nature of customer service is described first, followed by service quality and customer expectations of service quality. Other factors discussed are the links between relationships; quality service and loyalty; the moments of truth (or service encounters); and servicescapes. Various other important factors in creating a service culture within an organisation will also be dealt with.

The nature of customer service

What is customer service?

Customer service can be seen as the provision of service to customers before, during and after a purchase. Essentially, customer service is any back-up service that the company provides to customers in order to maintain their loyalty and to secure a sale. In relationship marketing, customer service must be seen in the context of the supply/marketing channel. This view of the supply/marketing channel suggests that customer service should be seen not only in the context of the company and its relationship with its customers, but also in its downstream relationship with its ultimate customers, as well as its upstream relationship with suppliers.

The actual distribution of goods may represent much of the customer service element for a manufacturer supplying branded goods to distribution companies. Similarly, the ability of suppliers to meet promised delivery schedules is the most frequently mentioned aspect of service referred to by buyers.

While to a distributor, delivery schedules may be the most important, other service elements may be relevant to the final consumer. It is for this reason that warranties, unconditional service guarantees, intelligible (ie clear and simple) instruction books and free phone-in advice centres become critical to customer service.

It must be kept in mind that it is not the actual service that is of importance, but rather the *perceptions* that a customer has of the service. Therefore one should always try to see the overall service from the customer's point of view.

Customers have expectations of how they think a service will be provided. These expectations are based on their past experiences, what they have heard from their friends and family and what they have seen in the media, either in advertisements or news reports.

Service and customer service are becoming more important to consumers and organisations, as they impact on the way in which relationships are built. Let us consider the following arguments in this regard:

- **Changing customer expectations:** In almost every market, the customer is now more demanding, knowledgeable and sophisticated than he/she was, say, 30 years ago. Customers have higher expectations and more choices than ever before. This means that marketers have to listen more closely to customers than ever before. They also have to anticipate needs, to solve problems before they start, to provide a service that impresses customers and to offer responses to mistakes that more than make up for the original error. Competitors have not only been meeting these rising customer expectations, but shaping them with yet higher standards of performance and value. And so the cycle repeats itself, with customers asking for more and getting it. So there is no reason why customers should buy one organisation's offerings unless it is in some way better at serving the customers' needs than those offered by competing organisations.

- **The increased importance of customer service:** With changing customer expectations, competitors are seeing customer service as an important competitive weapon by which to distinguish their product(s) from competitors' offerings, thereby successfully differentiating their sales efforts.

- **The need for a relationship strategy:** To ensure a customer service strategy that is formulated, implemented and controlled, and that will create attractive value for customers, it is necessary to establish this strategy as having a central role and not one that is only a sub-component of the elements of the marketing mix.

In the next section, key issues in building relationships through customer service will be detailed.

Customer service in building relationships[3]

Organisations that embrace the marketing concept seek ways to build a profitable long-term relationship with each customer. Even the most innovative organisation faces competition sooner or later. And trying to get new customers by taking them away from a competitor is usually more costly than retaining current customers by really satisfying their needs; satisfied customers buy from the same company again and again. This makes the customer's buying job easier and it also increases the selling organisation's profits. Thus, in an organisation that has adopted the marketing concept with its focus on customer orientation, everyone focuses on customer satisfaction in order to offer superior customer value. That helps to attract customers in the first place and keeps them satisfied after they buy. Because customers are satisfied, they want to purchase from the organisation again. The relationship with customers is profitable, so the organisation is encouraged to find better ways to offer superior customer value. In other words, when a firm adopts the marketing concept, it wins and so do its customers.

Most successful marketers understand that key issues in developing competitive advantage include building long-term relationships and central to these relationships is maintaining customer satisfaction and creating customer value.

Customer satisfaction

A marketer who adopts the marketing concept sees customer satisfaction as the path to profits. To ensure survival and success, organisations therefore have to satisfy their customers.

Customer satisfaction is the customer's feeling that a product has met or exceeded his/her expectations. Organisations that have a reputation for delivering high levels of customer satisfaction do things differently from their competitors. Top management is obsessed with customer satisfaction and employees throughout the organisation understand the link between their job and satisfied customers. The culture of the organisation is to focus on satisfying customers rather than on selling products. Such companies do not pursue one-time transactions; they cultivate relationships.

For an organisation to be focused on customer satisfaction in order to build relationships with customers, employees' attitudes and actions must be customer oriented. An employee may be the only contact a particular customer has with the business. In that customer's eyes, the employee is the business. Any person, department or division that is not customer oriented weakens the positive image of the entire business. For example, a potential customer who is greeted discourteously may well assume that the employee's attitude represents the whole organisation. Leading marketers recognise the role of employee training in customer service to build customer relationships. Consider, for example, how all new employees at Disneyland and Walt Disney World must attend Disney University, a special training programme for Disney employees. Similarly, McDonald's has its own Hamburger University.

Customer value

Building relationships with customers requires that all the employees in an organisation work together to provide customer value before and after each purchase. The long-term relationship with the customer is threatened unless everyone works together to make things right for the customer when he/she has a complaint about service or quality. Any time the customer value is reduced – because the benefits to the customer decrease or the costs increase – the relationship is weakened.

Customer value is the ratio of benefits to the sacrifice (by the customer) necessary to obtain those benefits. Read the extract in Box 3.1 on page 50 about On the Dot.

3.1 CUSTOMER SERVICE – ON THE DOT[4]

On the Dot is the most significant multichannel media logistics company in South Africa driving the sales of products by operating a national network of sales and distribution platforms.

Their three main client groups are: retailers who stock the products that On the Dot distributes; publishers who produce the products; and subscribers whom On the Dot manages on behalf of publishers.

All publishers and retailers are assigned key account managers to assist with queries, provide updates and feedback. They key account managers ensure that clients sign service-level agreements to manage the expectations of clients and to provide clear and measurable service levels. Effective control of all queries is achieved by assigning a key account manager ensuring that client's expectations are managed.

Various call centres are available to log queries and for subscribers to report non-deliveries, late deliveries or query their accounts.

Customer value is not simply a matter of high quality; thus a high-quality product that is available only at a high price will not be perceived as good value, nor will bare-bones services or low-quality goods selling at a low price. Instead, customers value goods and services of the quality they expect that are sold at prices they are willing to pay. Value can be used to sell a top-of-the-range Range Rover Evoque and a buy-one-get-one-free burger meal!

To offer customer value, marketers need to consider the following broad guidelines:

- The bare minimum requirement is to offer products that do what they are meant to do; consumers lose patience with shoddy merchandise that does not work properly.

- Give customers more than they expect by delivering the best customer experience in the market you serve. The customer experience is the sum total of the interactions that a customer has with a company's product, people and processes; in other words, give customers more than they expect.

- Give customers adequate information. Today's sophisticated customer wants informative advertising and knowledgeable salespeople.

- Offer organisation-wide commitment in service and after-sales support.

Box 3.2 on the following page shows how Tracker added value for its customers.

3.2 TRACKER – ADDING VALUE[5]

Tracker has been South Africa's leading vehicle-tracking company since the 1990s. And while vehicle tracking and stolen vehicle recovery (SVR) remains the company's core business, the Tracker of today has evolved into a highly sophisticated technological company offering leading-edge fleeting monitoring and telematics solutions to both individuals and organisations throughout Southern Africa.

Tracker strives to create value for a broad range of people and industries. It is about filtering and processing different strings of vehicle data and providing meaningful information that can be utilised and connected with other layers of intelligence to improve the lives of motorists, the general South African public as well as the wide spectrum of organisations in the insurance, vehicle manufacturer, fleet, dealer and other intermediary markets.

It is about taking vehicle recovery, route and driver information and creating true value propositions for a host of different audiences. Whether it is powering a live traffic product or enabling tailored insurance offerings, Tracker wants to add value wherever it can, to whomever it touches.

Underpinning everything that Tracker does is the belief that the company is making a real difference in South Africa. Whether it is helping to track and recover assets, combating crime or delivering services that enable people and organisations to be more efficient in how they operate, the creation of value is critical to everything that Tracker strives to achieve.

The higher the perceived benefit of a product or service, the higher the customer value and the greater the chance that the customer will choose and keep choosing the product or service in future.

In the next section, customer expectations of service quality will be discussed.

Customer expectations

Central to the effective management of customer service within any organisation has to be the issue of service quality performance. Service quality is the ability of the organisation to meet or exceed customer expectations. In this context, customer expectations may be seen as the desires or wants of customers; in other words, what customers feel a service provider should offer rather than what it does offer. Thus, service quality is measured in terms of the extent to which an organisation's performance is perceived by customers as meeting or exceeding expectations. It is, therefore, the customers' perceptions of performance that count, rather than the reality of performance. Indeed, it can be argued that as far as service quality is concerned, 'perceptions are reality'.[6]

The organisation should know how the customers compare its service in terms of service expected and actual service received (or experienced).

Service expected vs. service received

Customers' expectations are based on their knowledge of and experiences with a particular organisation and its competitors. For example, customers expect a supermarket to have parking facilities. Marketers can also provide unexpected services to increase their competitive advantage and to outsmart competitors. See the examples that follow.

> **Unexpected service**
>
> - The taxi driver hands the customer a bottle of water after picking him/ her up from a long flight.
> - A pizza take away stores the customer's name and phone number to ease the ordering process.
> - An airline allows frequent flyers to upgrade to another class of seat.

Delivering quality service means conforming to customer expectations on a consistent basis. Service quality is thus a measure of how well the level of service delivered matches customer expectations. In line with this thinking, Grönroos[7] developed a model in which he contends that, in evaluating service quality, consumers compare the service they expect with perceptions of the service they receive.

Customer + Staff + Environment

Customers, by their very nature, will evaluate service during and after the service. How this service is evaluated will depend on the quality that he/she expects before the delivery of the service, and the quality of the actual service that is delivered. For example, if the customer expects the food and service from a particular restaurant to be like royal treatment and this does not materialise, the perceived quality will be negatively confirmed. On the other hand if the service expectation is very low and the service is average, the quality will be positively confirmed.

Types of customer expectations[8]

Expectations serve as benchmarks against which present and future service encounters are compared. It is useful to distinguish the following three different types of expectation.

- **Predicted service:** This reflects the level of service customers believe is likely to occur. For example, bank customers tend to conduct their banking business at the same bank over time. They become accustomed to dealing with the personnel at the bank and begin to anticipate certain performance levels. It is generally agreed that customer satisfaction evaluations are developed by comparing predicted service to perceived service received.

- **Desired service:** This is an ideal expectation that reflects what customers actually want compared with the predicted service that they are likely to get. Hence, in most instances, desired service reflects a higher expectation than predicted service. For example, a bank customer's desired service is that he/she not only receives his/her predicted service, but that the tellers call him/her by his/her first name and enthusiastically greet him/her as he/she enters the bank. Comparing desired service expectations to the perceived service received results in a measure of perceived service superiority.

- **Adequate service:** This reflects a minimum tolerable expectation and reflects the level of service that the customer is willing to accept. Adequate service is based on experiences or norms that develop over time. For example, most adult consumers have dined at hundreds of restaurants. Through these experiences, norms develop that consumers expect to occur. Hence, one factor that influences adequate service is predicted service. Encounters that fall below expected norms fall below adequate service expectations. Comparing adequate service with perceived service produces a measure of perceived service adequacy.

Zone of tolerance

The difference between the desired service level and the adequate service level can be called the zone of tolerance, ie the extent to which customers recognise and are willing to accept variation in service delivery from one location to the next and even with the same provider from one day to the next. Consumers who accept this variation develop a zone of tolerance. The zone of tolerance expands and contracts across customers and within the same customer depending on the service and the conditions under which the service is provided. Other factors, such as price, may influence the zone of tolerance. For example, as the price increases, the customer's zone of tolerance decreases as desired service needs begin to dominate and the customer becomes less forgiving of sloppy service.

Factors influencing service expectations

Desired service expectations are influenced by the factors outlined on pages 54–55.

- **Enduring service intensifiers:** These intensifiers are personal factors that are stable over time and that increase a customer's sensitivity to how the service should best be provided. For example, the customer's personal service philosophies or personal view of the meaning of service and the way in which service providers should conduct themselves will heighten his/her sensitivities. These customers hold their own views regarding exactly how service should be provided; they want to be treated in the way they believe they should be treated.

- **Personal needs:** The customer's own personal needs influence desired service expectations. Some customers are more needy than others. Some customers are very particular about where they are seated in a restaurant, while others are happy to sit nearly anywhere. In a hotel, some customers are very interested in the hotel's amenities, such as the pool, sauna, dining room and other forms of available entertainment, while others are simply looking for a clean room. Customers have a variety of needs and no two are alike in every way, thus the organisation is particularly challenged in providing a service.

- **Explicit service promises:** These encompass the organisation's advertising, personal selling, contracts and other forms of communication. The more ambiguous the service, the more customers rely on the organisation's advertising when forming expectations. For example, if a night club projects a fun and youthful atmosphere with music and lights, customers would expect a lot of young people to be dancing and socialising exactly as shown in the advertisement.

- **Implicit service promises:** These promises also influence desired service and predicted service. As the price increases, customers expect the organisation to deliver higher-quality services. For example, customers would probably have higher expectations of service at a boutique fashion store than they would of a cheaper mass producing clothing retailer. The nicer the furnishings and layout of the organisation, the higher customer expectations become.

- **Word-of-mouth communications:** Customers tend to rely more on personal sources of information than on non-personal ones when choosing a service provider. Customers view word-of-mouth information as unbiased information from someone who has been through the service experience. Sources of word-of-mouth information range from friends, family or consultants to product review publications such as Top Car magazine.

- **Past experience:** Service evaluations are often based on a comparison of the current service encounter to other encounters with the same provider, other providers in the industry and other providers in another industry.

In a health spa, for example, clients' desired and predicted service expectations of beauty therapists are likely to be based on past experience in other spa treatments with the same beauty therapist and on other spa treatments with other therapists.

In the next section, service quality will be looked at in greater detail.

Service quality

In the section on Customer expectations, the concept of quality in a service context will be introduced. Service quality comes about through a focused evaluation reflecting the customer's perception of specific dimensions of service.

> **Definition of service quality**[9]
>
> Service quality can be defined as the ability of an organisation to determine customer expectations correctly and to deliver the service at a quality level that will at least equal these customer expectations.

Service quality, as perceived by the customer, is one of the components that would influence the satisfaction of the customer. Although promises of quality may attract customers, marketers (especially service providers), believe that the delivery of quality is essential in building and maintaining customer relationships.[10] Delivering on promises is the essence of mutually satisfying relationships. Service quality refers to the consistency with which customers' expectations are met and the general superiority of the service relative to that of the competition. Accordingly, this initiative includes any practices focused on identifying which services and service attributes customers want, providing them to the customers' satisfaction and at a level superior to the competition. This includes efforts to raise standards and improve service performance, listening to customers' preferences and ensuring that customers' requirements are met. Providing friendly, professional, courteous service that is consistent, fair and reliable is one of the best ways to establish and maintain customer relationships. This is exemplified by making on-time deliveries, supplying a wide range of goods and services, having a knowledgeable staff and providing technical competence. Service quality includes listening to customers, knowing the market and understanding customers' needs. Naturally, consistently meeting customers' expectations includes responses focusing on providing high quality goods and services.

Let us consider the different views as to what constitutes service quality from the customer's point of view.

Evaluating service quality

One way of evaluating service quality is by considering two factors:[11]

- the technical quality of the outcome of service delivery; and
- the functional quality of the service delivery process.

If a service has a specific outcome, such as winning a court case, then a customer can make a judgement on the efficacy of the service on the basis of the particular outcome (ie winning or losing the case). If the service is complex, however, and an outcome is not clear, it may be hard to judge a service on the outcome. The customer could then rely on how the service was done in order to determine quality. In other words, the service is judged by looking at the process (the way it was done). An example follows.

Judging service quality: Architects[12]

The services provided by architects are very complex and the outcome is not always easy to judge. Understanding the process and outcome quality can be important for the success of an architect. If two architects both have good technical skills and certificates, but one has very good interpersonal skills, then the process dimensions such as the ability to solve problems, to empathise, to meet deadlines and to be courteous, could lead to an advantage for one over the other.

Dimensions used for evaluating service quality

As a result of exploratory and quantitative studies, researchers have identified five dimensions that consumers use in order to assess service quality. These dimensions apply across a wide range of industries, but it would be important for a marketer to establish how critical each of the dimensions is to a specific target group. This would help guide the marketer as to which dimension to focus on in that specific segment. The five dimensions are discussed here.

- **Reliability:** This refers to the ability to perform the promised service dependably and accurately and focuses on delivering on promises made by the organisation. Customers expect companies to keep their promises, because, if the organisation does not deliver the core service that customers think they are buying, it will be seen as failing them. Think of other companies that you tend to use: more likely than not, they are the ones that are consistent and reliable. Loyalty, as noted in the previous sections, cannot be earned without consistent and reliable service.

- **Responsiveness:** The willingness to help customers and provide prompt service. Responsiveness implies that the needs of the customer are met in a timely manner and that the organisation is flexible enough to customise a service to the specific customer's needs. It is critical to understand the customer's expectations in terms of time (speed) in order to understand what must be done to be seen as responsive.

- **Assurance:** Assurance refers to the knowledge and courtesy of employees and their ability to convey trust and confidence. This is important in those services that are perceived as high risk or where the customer is not sure about how to evaluate outcomes. Examples of these would be banking, insurance and medical services.

- **Empathy:** The caring and individualised attention a firm gives its customers is known as empathy. This involves confirming for the customer that his/her unique needs and requirements will be met. Many smaller companies can compete with big companies through convincing the customer that they understand him/her better, unlike the cold, formal, by-the-numbers approach of many larger companies. Being perceived as a specialist in a certain field could also help a company be seen as having the ability to meet the specialised needs of customers better than others.

- **Tangibles:** Tangibles include the appearance of physical facilities (offices, showrooms, consulting rooms), equipment, staff and communication materials. It includes anything physical that indicates the quality of the service that customers will receive. This is especially important for a new customer, who looks for cues as to the level of service he/she should expect.

Table 3.1 shows how these five dimensions of service quality can be used to judge the quality of a variety of services.

Table 3.1 Service quality dimensions for selected industries

Industry	Reliability	Responsive-ness	Assurance	Empathy	Tangibles
Doctor's office	Appointments are kept and on schedule; professional service	Appointment starts on time	A thorough consultation and examination is conducted and the relevant information and medical history is checked	Doctor and nurse introduced	Practice layout, hygiene and cleanliness, facilities, waiting room, reception

Industry	Reliability	Responsive-ness	Assurance	Empathy	Tangibles
Car tyre dealer	Appointments are kept and on schedule	Simple and easy paperwork and financing options provided	Trusted brand name; add-on features explained and competent sales staff	Needs and preferences acknowledged	The dealership floor, pamphlets and office environment
Hair salon	Appointments are kept on schedule; reminder email/sms sent to client 24 hours prior to appointment	Appointment starts on time	A thorough consultation is conducted with the client and the relevant information provided	Hairdresser/ stylist introduced	Salon and facilities, layout, music, products on display, wall art

Quality service and customer loyalty[13]

In Chapters 1 and 2, we introduced you to the principles and concepts of customer relationship management. Although this concept was widespread in the past, it is only fairly recently that it has resurfaced as one of the main themes in business. Value exchange is an important part of marketing. These exchanges are in the form of transactions between the customer and the company. If a company is successful in consistently satisfying the customer in terms of this value exchange then it can create a relationship with that customer particularly when these transactions take place regularly.

Reasons for placing emphasis on relationships and not transactions

Many factors have led to this shift in emphasis to a relationship approach. Until a few years ago, many companies faced a situation where many markets were growing, where demand outstripped supply and where competition was not as intense as it is today. In contrast, today many markets are in the mature phase and face overcapacity and oversupply. Since this means that finding new customers becomes increasingly difficult, companies have to take action to keep their good customers. Also, many businesses face the reality of having to keep a customer for a lengthy period before that customer becomes profitable. Through better access to media and information, customers are more knowledgeable about alternative suppliers and products. The international focus on customer and value-added aspects has also led to customers being more demanding. These factors have reinforced the trend for companies to form stronger relationships with their customers.

The payoff of relationships and good service: loyalty[14]

In order to reap the rewards of establishing a relationship, the company has to generate loyalty – and the benefits of loyalty to an organisation can be startling. In order to recoup the costs of acquiring a customer, many companies have to keep that customer for a number of years. In fact, only after a few years do many customers become profitable. If a company is busy 'churning' customers, then it may not be keeping them long enough for them to become profitable and the company's performance suffers as a result. Loyal customers are more profitable, because spending by customers in most businesses tends to accelerate over time. Customer spending should be managed in such a way that it is actually encouraged.

Another reason why loyal customers are more profitable is that customers learn to be more efficient as they learn about a business over time. They no longer waste time asking for the services that the company does not provide. By learning about the company, both the customers and the employees with whom they interact are more productive.

Referrals also are important long-term benefits of loyalty. For example, think of referrals that an automobile dealership can gain through a long-term relationship with a loyal customer. Many customers who are referred are often of higher quality in terms of profitability relationship longevity, than customers who respond to marketing communication efforts.

Lastly, loyal customers often provide the company with more profitability through price premiums than new customers do. By establishing a long-term relationship with a company, a loyal customer gets better value and tends to be less price sensitive on individual product items, than a new customer is.

Loyalty, built up through establishing a relationship, is attained only through customers perceiving a consistent delivery of service quality. Yet, customer service often fails to deliver this quality. Some reasons why customer service fails are discussed next.

Reasons why customer service fails

Many organisations do not understand how to practically implement customer service. Some of the main reasons why customer service fails are listed below and on pae 60:[15]

- **The market is not properly segmented:** The organisation wants to get its product or service to everyone in the world, but does not properly understand the market's needs.

- **The customer database is incomplete or non-existent:** Because of this, improvement in customer service is based on what the managers think is best, instead of what the customers want, ie customers' perceptions are disregarded.

- **The organisation is managed from the inside out:** The organisation uses a push strategy where it tells customers to use the product. This is as opposed to a pull strategy, where research is done to work out what customers need and want. The product or service is then developed; and, due to the need, customers will actively seek out the product or service.

- **All blame is shifted downward:** Front-line employees are blamed for any service failure, regardless of a lack of training and/or the failure of organisational systems, processes or structures.

- **Misunderstanding below the line of visibility:** Employees who are below the line of visibility (ie never in contact with customers) struggle to understand the need for customer service. These employees still, however, have an important role to play in the delivery of exceptional customer service.

- **The focus is on attracting new customers as opposed to the retention of customers:** Little effort is made to keep the company's most profitable segment – its existing customers.

- **Dehumanised customers:** To many employees and managers, a customer does not have a face, which can lead to the customer becoming less human in their minds and therefore less deserving of respect.

- **As mentioned earlier, there is a strong link between customer satisfaction, customer retention and customer loyalty.** The extent of the customer's satisfaction with a product or service will determine its success in the market. It is therefore necessary to look at ways of measuring customer satisfaction.

Measuring customer satisfaction[16]

Since customer satisfaction is the objective of most successful companies, the service quality needs to be measured by how well they in fact satisfy their customers. There have been various efforts to measure overall customer satisfaction.

Benefits of customer satisfaction surveys

Customer satisfaction surveys provide several worthwhile benefits, such as the following:

- **Customer feedback:** Such surveys provide a formal means of customer feedback to the organisation, which may identify existing and potential problems.

- **Show that the company cares:** Satisfaction surveys also convey the message to customers that the organisation cares about their well-being and values customer input concerning its operations.

- **Evaluating employee performance:** Satisfaction results are often utilised in evaluating employee performance for merit and compensation reviews and for sales management purposes, such as the development of sales training programmes.

- **Comparison purposes:** Survey results help a company to identify its own strengths and weaknesses and where it stands in comparison to its competitors. When ratings are favourable, many organisations utilise the results in their corporate advertising.

- **Focus on customer needs:** Ultimately, the major advantage of customer satisfaction measurement is that it helps to secure an increased focus on customer needs and to stimulate improvement in the work practices and processes used within the company.

The placement of customer feedback forms by some companies can make customers wonder if the company really wants their feedback. Customer feedback forms 'hidden' in the desk drawers of a hotel room are an example of this.

Problems in measuring customer satisfaction

There are limits to interpreting any measure of customer satisfaction because of the following reasons:

- **Level of aspiration:** Satisfaction depends on and is relative to customers' level of aspiration or expectation. Less prosperous customers begin to expect more as they see the higher living standards of others.

- **Changes in levels of aspiration:** Aspiration levels tend to rise with repeated successes and fall with failures. Products considered satisfactory one day may not be satisfactory the next day, or vice versa. Years ago, most people were satisfied with a cell phone that could make phone calls. But once they became accustomed to cell phones that could send text messages, have access to the Internet, take photos and store information, the old cell phone is no longer good enough.

- **Personal concept:** Customer satisfaction is a highly personal concept – and looking at the average satisfaction of a whole society does not provide a complete picture for evaluating effectiveness. Some consumers are more satisfied than others. So, although efforts to measure satisfaction are useful, any evaluation of effectiveness has to be largely subjective.

Let us look at a few ways of measuring customer satisfaction.

Ways of measuring customer satisfaction

The use of formal surveys has emerged as by far the best method of periodically assessing customer satisfaction. The surveys are not marketing tools, but information-gaining tools. Enough homework thus needs to be done before carrying out the actual survey.

After-sales surveys

After-sales surveys assess customer satisfaction while the service encounter is still fresh in the customer's mind. Consequently, the information reflects the organisation's recent performance, but may be biased by the customer's inadvertent attempt to minimise cognitive dissonance. After-sales surveys can also identify areas for improvement and are seen as a proactive approach to assessing customer satisfaction. After-sales surveys attempt to contact every customer and allow the company to take corrective action if a customer is less than satisfied with his/her purchase decision. In South Africa, several household appliance retailers use this method after the purchase of an appliance.

Mystery shopping

Mystery shopping is a form of non-customer research that measures individual employee service behaviour. As the name indicates, mystery shoppers are generally trained personnel who pose as customers and who shop unannounced at the business. The idea is to evaluate an individual employee during an actual service encounter. Mystery shoppers evaluate employees on a number of characteristics, such as the time it takes for the employee to acknowledge the customer, eye contact, appearance and other specific customer service factors. Results obtained from mystery shoppers are used as constructive employee feedback. Consequently, mystery shopping aids the business in coaching, training, evaluating and formally recognising its employees.

Customer satisfaction index

One method that can be used is the customer satisfaction index (CSI), which is based on regular interviews with many customers. This index makes it possible to track changes in customer satisfaction measures over time and even allows comparison among companies. The questionnaire must not be complicated or difficult to complete, in order to try to ensure a higher response rate. It must, however, still provide the correct data that is useful to the company and should be accurate and reliable. Questions asked of respondents vary and data can be collected by personal interviews or self-administered questionnaires. Many companies prefer to use short telephone or cell phone interviews.

The questionnaire should contain 'objective'-type questions where the customer has to 'rate' specific aspects about the organisation and its service or its products on a scale of, say, 1 to 5 or 1 to 10. The reason for providing a rating is that it gives respondents a way to express the importance they attach to various survey parameters. Respondents should be asked to give a weighting factor (for example on a scale of 1 to 5 or 1 to 10) for each requirement. This gives a better indication of the relative importance of each parameter towards overall customer satisfaction and makes it easier for organisations to prioritise their action plans by comparing the performance rating (scores) with importance rating (weighting).

SERVQUAL

Various methods have been suggested to measure service quality, the most well-known being that of the SERVQUAL instrument. The importance of SERVQUAL is that it offers managers a systematic approach to measuring and managing service quality. It emphasises the importance of understanding customer expectations and of developing internal procedures that align company processes to customer expectations. The model identifies five core components of service quality: reliability, assurance, tangibles, empathy and responsiveness.[17] Statements are formulated and, based on those statements, the respondent is able to indicate both the expectation and the perception that they have of the specific dimension. The difference between the perceptions and expectations indicates the existence of a gap. In total there are a minimum of 21 statements that cover these five service quality dimensions.[18] This may vary depending on the industry in which the service quality is evaluated.

An example of a statement that can be used in a typical SERVQUAL used to evaluate waiters in a restaurant is shown below:[19]

The waiter at the restaurant is professional							
My expected level of service	Low						High
	1	2	3	4	5	6	7	8
My perception of my waiter's level of service	Low						High
	1	2	3	4	5	6	7	8

Figure 3.1 Example of a typical SERVQUAL

Despite its extensive use in measuring service quality, the SERVQUAL instrument is not without its critics. Cronin and Taylor[20] have specifically commented on the measurement of both the expectations and perceptions in the SERVQUAL instrument. However, despite the criticisms that have been levelled against SERVQUAL, it remains an instrument that is used in all areas of business and industry, including the non-profit sector. Its use has largely been 'institutionalised'.[21]

But how does measuring service quality affect relationship building? Measuring service quality indicates whether a gap exists between the customer's expectations and his/her perceptions. If the customer does not perceive that she/he is receiving a quality service from the organisation, she/he will not want to build a relationship with the organisation. SERVQUAL will indicate what type of actions management needs to take to improve the quality of service and thus the overall relationship with the customer.

Moments of truth or service encounters

The term 'moment of truth' was coined by Jan Carlzon[22], the president of Scandinavian Airline Systems (SAS), following a study commissioned by him to establish what SAS needed to do to improve its service. Carlzon used the phrase to rally the employees of SAS at a time when the airline industry was in dire economic straits. He convinced them that every contact between a customer and any employee of the airline constituted a moment of truth. In these brief encounters, he argued, the customer made up his/her mind about the quality of service and the quality of the product offered by SAS. Carlzon estimated there were 50 000 moments of truth in a given day in the SAS system – 50 000 moments of truth daily that had to be managed. He succeeded in taking SAS from near bankruptcy to profitability in less than two years.

The 'moment of truth' concept literally means that now is the time and the place – when and where – the organisation has the opportunity to demonstrate the quality of its services to the customer. It is a true moment of opportunity. In the next moment, the opportunity will be lost, the customer will have gone and there are no easy ways of adding value to the perceived service quality. If a quality problem has occurred, it is too late to take corrective action. In order to do so, a new moment of truth has to be created. The marketer can, for example, actively contact the customer to correct a mistake or to at least explain why things have gone wrong. This is, of course, much more troublesome and probably less effective than a well-managed moment of truth.

It is important to emphasise the issue of remoteness. We must remember how customer perceptions are formed and can be influenced. These perceptions are directly tied in with the customer's opinion of the service offered by a company. We must also remember that customers view service as they perceive it, not according to reality. Hence, the moment of truth is not only the actual service that the customer receives face-to-face, but could also include contact by telephone or by post. The point to remember is that the moment of truth is any contact customers have where they are able to form an impression about an organisation (see Box 3.3 for some examples).

3.3 SOME MOMENTS OF TRUTH FOR A GUEST STAYING AT A LUXURY RESORT[23]

- Guests drive up to the entrance of the resort. The concierge opens the car door for both the driver and the passenger.

- The front-office staff are alerted by security personnel upon arrival of the guests. Staff members walk up and greet the guests, addressing them by name.

- The barman offers the guests a welcoming drink.

- The guests check into the hotel.

- Basic information is filled in by the staff. The guests complete only what is absolutely necessary. In some instances, registration is done not at the reception, but at the executive floor for the convenience of the guests.

- A member of staff asks if the guests would like to freshen up and accompanies the guests to their room. The guests' bags are attended to by the bell boy.

- The guests take the elevator up to their room.

- Staff have placed a bouquet of flowers and a basket of fruit in the room for the guests with their name written on a personalised welcome card. Also, a copy of the spa treatments and other activities is left on the work station in the room.

- The guests telephone front office. The name of each guest calling is displayed on the telephone's display unit and the front-office staff respond, 'Yes Mr/s X, how can I help you?' The relevant member of staff then attends to their query.

- A cocktail party is organised to formally welcome the guests who have checked in during the previous 48 hours. The Guest Relations Officer (GRO) plays an active role in establishing contact and rapport.

- The guests then move into the main ball room where dinner will be served.

- The Guest Relations Officer (GRO) and other key staff members meet with guests informally and ascertain satisfaction levels. Particular preferences are noted, such as choice of newspaper, and the guests are pleasantly surprised, even delighted, when they receive it.
- The guests check out. A thank you card is sent thanking them for their support with an invitation for them to come again.

An organisation may not have 50 000 moments of truth a day, but it is probably safe to say that there are several hundred that occur every day, and every one of them must be managed to achieve a positive outcome if the organisation hopes to renew customer loyalty on a sustained basis. It is important to remember that a moment of truth is not, in itself, positive or negative. It is how the service encounter is managed that will turn the moment of truth into a positive or negative experience for the customer.

Also, keep in mind that a moment of truth does not necessarily have to involve human contact. The customer experiences a moment of truth when he/she drives into your parking lot. Are there sufficient parking spaces? Are the grounds clean and attractive? Is the entrance to your business easy to find? Are signs placed logically, and are they easy to read? All of these are potential moments of truth and they happen even before you have a chance to perform for your customer.

The major contributing factor to the moment of truth and the impression formed is the customer's interaction with front-line employees; in other words, those who deal with or have personal contact with the customers on a day-to-day basis. These include, for example, the receptionist, the petrol attendant, the switchboard operator and the parts salesperson.

Moments of truth are therefore crucial to perceived quality of service and, as such, can be regarded as a major contributor to the service performance of a company.

Often 'unexpected' services will cause the customer to positively evaluate the organisation's product or service. Customers evaluate a store, for example, on their perceptions of that store's service. In this case, the service of the store depends on the employees working in the store. Employees play an important part in the customer's perception of the service. Customer evaluations of service are often based on the way in which employees provide the service, not just the outcome. Consider the example on page 67.

The way in which employees provide service

A customer goes to a large store to return a product that is not working properly. In one case, the company policy requires the employee to ask the customer for a receipt, test whether the product is not working, ask a manager whether a refund can be provided, complete the paperwork and finally refund the customer the amount paid for the product in cash.

In a second case, the store employee simply asks the customers how much he/she paid for the product and refunds the cash.

The outcome is the same in both cases – but the customer is more satisfied in the second case than in the first.

Types of service encounters

Customers experience three main types of service encounters.

- **Remote encounter:** A remote encounter occurs when there is no human contact. Examples of this include the use of automated teller machines (ATMs) or direct mail methods. Since more and more services are being delivered through technology, this type of encounter is becoming increasingly important. In these encounters, the tangible evidence of service and the quality of the process itself (the process dimension of service quality) become the basis for judging the quality of the service.

- **Telephone or cell phone encounter:** The telephone (or cell phone) encounter is, for many businesses, the most frequent type of encounter with end customers. Important criteria for judging this encounter include tone of voice, an employee's knowledge and his/her effectiveness in handling customer issues. The popularity of call centres has emphasised the importance of this type of encounter for many companies.

- **Direct contact:** An important encounter is direct contact (face-to-face). This is a complex way of trying to establish service quality, because both verbal and non-verbal behaviour need to be considered.

Ingredients of a moment of truth

The ingredients of the moment of truth are the service context, frame of reference and congruence.

Service context

All encounters between the organisation and the customer occur in a specific setting or service context. The service context can be described as the collective impact of all the social, physical and psychological elements that happen during the moment of truth. The service context that is created is the overall effect of the environment created by the attitude and approach of all employees as they assist customers.

A good way to illustrate the service context is by using an example of 1ˢᵗ for Women Insurance, see Box 3.4.

3.4 1ST FOR WOMEN[24]

1ˢᵗ for Women Insurance understands that women have unique insurance needs. It also understands that for women, insurance should be more than a mere product offering, but rather a holistic lifestyle support solution that caters for a woman's distinctive requirements.

1ˢᵗ for Women's value-added products provide peace of mind and ensure that women are covered for every eventuality. They include:

- **Trip Monitor:** This service ensures that the driver and her passengers reach their destination safety.

- **Directions Assist:** This 24-hour helpline offers direction guidance when travelling within the borders of South Africa.

- **Nurse @ First:** This is a personal health advice line that will offer 1ˢᵗ for Women policyholders a better understanding of various chronic ailments such as cancer, HIV/Aids, diabetes, asthma and other conditions.

- **Concierge Assist:** This lifestyle management service provides assistance including booking car services, dentist visits, flights, accommodation, providing tourist information, restaurant bookings, handymen and so much more.

- **Road Assist:** This benefit offers comprehensive solutions for virtually any roadside emergency.

- **Medical assist:** This 24-hour facility provides policyholders with telephonic advice and emergency by doctors, ICU-trained nursing sisters and paramedics.

Frame of reference

Both the customer and the service employee approach the moment of truth encounter from the individual's frame of reference, which then totally dominates his/her thinking processes, attitudes, feelings and behaviour. The frame of reference has a powerful effect upon the meaning that individuals assign to the moment of truth.

Some of the inputs that create the frame of reference may be automatic, for example, both people may speak English and both represent social norms and customs with which they are mutually familiar. Some inputs to the customer's frame of reference may, however, differ from inputs that create the service employee's frame of reference. When that happens, the two individuals view the moment of truth encounter from very different perspectives. It is important to note that frames of reference can change in an instant. As the customer perceives that a need is being met or not being met, the frame of reference filters changes. Along with it, the customer's perception of the moment of truth changes. The same is true for the person who is providing the service or product for the customer.

Among the many possible inputs that help to create the customer's frame of reference are:

- past experience with the business or similar business;
- beliefs about the business;
- expectations formed by previous experiences;
- attitudes, beliefs, ethnic norms and values that have formed during the customer's lifetime; and
- recommendations or warnings from other customers.

Inputs that help to create the service employee's frame of reference include:

- what the company has told the employee to do;
- rules and regulations set for service employees and customers;
- the employee's level of emotional maturity;
- expectations of customer behaviour based on past experience;
- attitudes, beliefs and values formed during the employee's lifetime; and
- the tools and resources, or the lack thereof, used to deliver the service or product.

Congruence

One of the key concepts of the moment of truth is the need for congruence, ie a working compatibility among the three factors of context, the customer's frame of reference and the employee's frame of reference. This means that there must be agreement at the moment of truth. If the inputs to the customer's frame of reference and that of the service employee differ greatly from each other, then the moment of truth could be adversely affected. There must be some alignment of the customer's frame of reference with that of the service employee in order for the moment of truth to be positive for the company on a consistent basis, and both must be congruent with the service context.

When there is a lack of congruence, the probability of a satisfactory result is reduced. This is often the case when a service problem occurs. Customers will describe their own actions as completely reasonable, rational and polite. Service employees will describe their own behaviour in the same way. However, when the customer describes the behaviour of the service employee, the employee's behaviour is described in terms of impatience, exasperation and disrespect for the customer. The service employee, on the other hand, describes the customer's behaviour as arrogant, demanding and rude. Often the truth lies somewhere between the two extremes, but we can see that the underlying cause is that the frames of reference are mismatched, owing to the different inputs of the employee and customer.

Cycle of service

Moments of truth do not happen in a haphazard way. They usually occur in a logical, measurable sequence. By placing the moments of truth in their logical sequence, the organisation can identify the exact encounters for which front-line and other employees are responsible. Once the logical sequence of the moments of truth has been determined, then the cycle of service has been created. The cycle of service, depicted in Figure 3.2 shows the service as the customer experiences it.

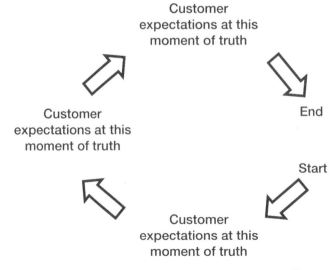

Figure 3.2 Representation of the cycle of service[25]

A cycle of service is a map of the moments of truth as they are experienced by customers. The cycle of service is activated every time a customer comes into contact with the business. Just as there are hundreds of moments of truth in a given business day, so are there many cycles of service. The value of mapping cycles of service for the various departments in the organisation is that one is able to look through the customer's eyes and evaluate the business from the customer's perspective.

Mapping out cycles of service is best done by the manager or supervisor and the employees who are directly involved in delivering service for that particular cycle. It is worth repeating, however, that it must be identified from the customer's point of view. Often, it is only the customer who perceives the full picture of the service experience, while managers and employees are only aware of their part of the cycle. The result is that managers or employees in a section may think they have provided good service, while the customer perceives the whole service experience and may decide that the service has been bad.

A second reason for illustrating service encounters in a cyclical way is to separate the important moments of truth from the critical moments of truth. While all of the moments of truth in a service encounter are important, there is usually a smaller number that are of such importance to the success of the business that they are called the critical moments of truth.

When the cycles of service for the major operations of the organisation have been created, it will be possible to spot those moments of truth that, if not managed positively, will almost certainly lead to customer dissatisfaction, loss of loyalty to your service or product and possible loss of the customer's business. These are the critical moments of truth. It is imperative that people in the organisation whose work centres around these key encounters with customers be equipped with the skills required for positive outcomes. For example, a critical moment of truth for most businesses happens when one of the organisation's systems fails, as one of them certainly will from time to time. At that precise moment, the company's service reputation is at stake. When this happens, it will take a quick-thinking person to make the situation right again with the customer. The 'recovery' record for responding to system failures is one of the hallmarks of credibility for the service-managed business. The critical moments of truth, if left unmanaged, invariably lead to a loss of customer confidence. Once customer confidence is lost, the loss of loyalty and repeat business soon follows.

The cycle of service is therefore the chain of events made up of particular moments of truth or encounters that customers go through as they experience a service. Customers, in their exposure to the cycle, are usually concerned about their needs and expectations. The company, on the other hand, is often more concerned with the systems that are in place to handle any customer interaction.

It is only the customer, however, who actually experiences the full cycle of service. This means that the overall result may still be customer dissatisfaction, even though each service provider feels it treated the customer correctly at its particular moment of truth.

The organisation must ensure that it is managing the moments of truth through the cycle of service so as to deliver excellent service. If the encounters or moments of truth are not managed, the customer's needs will be met only some of the time. This means that the organisation can hope to achieve only mediocrity in terms of service quality, since it will win some encounters and lose others.

Managing the moments of truth implies establishing the customer's expectations at each critical moment of truth and then deciding on how to ensure that service is delivered to meet expectations. Aspects that need to be considered at each encounter include skills, competencies, attitudes, time, knowledge, equipment, decision-making capability and authority.

Sources of satisfaction/dissatisfaction in the moment of truth

Research has identified four factors that can lead to satisfaction or dissatisfaction in terms of the moments of truth. These four are:[26]

- **Recovery:** This includes all incidents where the service delivery system has failed somehow and an employee has to respond to customer complaints. The way the employee responds, in terms of content and form, leads to a favourable or unfavourable memory of the incident for the customer.

- **Adaptability:** The second factor is how adaptable the service delivery system is when the customer has special needs or requests. Customers often perceive that something special is being done for them based on their needs, or they are frustrated by the unwillingness of the company to adapt to or accommodate their needs.

- **Spontaneity:** The third factor encompasses pleasant surprises for the customer, such as special attention to something being done that was not requested. Unsatisfactory incidents often include negative or rude behaviour towards the customer.

- **Coping:** The fourth factor revolves around the customer being uncooperative, where the service provided could do nothing that would satisfy the customer or lead to him/her being pleased about the encounter. Coping is the behaviour of the employees in handling these 'problem' customers.

These four factors and the specific behaviours for each that lead to either positive or negative encounters are summarised in Table 3.2 on the following page.

Table 3.2 General service behaviours for the four factors[27]

Factor	Do	Don't
Recovery	• Acknowledge the problem • Explain its causes • Apologise • Compensate/upgrade • Lay out options • Take responsibility	• Ignore the customer • Blame the customer • Leave the customer to 'fend for him/herself' • Downgrade • Act as if nothing is wrong • 'Pass the buck'
Adaptability	• Recognise the seriousness of the need • Acknowledge • Anticipate • Attempt to accommodate • Adjust the system • Explain rules/policies • Take responsibility	• Ignore • Promise, but fail to follow through • Embarrass the customer • Laugh at the customer • 'Pass the buck'
Spontaneity	• Take time • Be attentive • Anticipate needs • Listen • Provide information • Show empathy	• Exhibit impatience • Ignore • Yell/laugh/swear • Discriminate
Coping	• Listen • Try to accommodate • Explain • Let go of the customer (ie stop dealing with the customer)	• Let the customer's dissatisfaction affect others

Servicescapes[28]

After analysing the moments of truth, we need to understand what a company can do to ensure that the service experience is pleasant for the customer. The actual physical facility where the service is performed, delivered and consumed is referred to as the *servicescape*. A good example of a high-contact encounter would be a visit to uShaka Marine World in Durban where you meet mascots, ticket salespeople, restaurant staff, hotel staff, enquiries staff and sales staff in the stores and entertainment areas. There are many interactions with the employees of uShaka Marine World. In the example of Woolworths, the actual store facility would be the servicescape where the company's service is experienced.

The servicescape forms part of the physical evidence with which companies need to provide the customer as cues for its service quality.

Elements of the servicescape that affect service include both exterior and interior attributes. Exterior attributes are visible on the outside of the facility, while interior ones are visible inside the facility. Figure 3.3 gives a brief view of the elements contained in both the exterior and interior of the facility.

To elaborate on the factors presented in this diagram, regarding, for example, the exterior facility factors, one must keep in mind that not all these factors can be controlled by the company, for example the owner of a shop in a mall does not have the power to change the design of the parking lot; however, if a customer struggles to find parking outside the shop, this will still fall within the overall service cycle.

Figure 3.3 Elements of servicescapes[29]

The interior facility factors can be managed much more extensively by the company, which can improve the interior facility and by so doing still improve the overall impression a customer has. For example, a store with soft lighting, gentle music and air-conditioning may be a very welcome place to be for a customer who has struggled to find parking.

Let us consider the example of Rihanna's live concert in October 2013 at the FNB Stadium in Soweto. What were some of the elements of the servicescape that were considered? Clearly, there are many, but some of the more important ones include parking areas, shuttle services from the parking, the stadium exteriors, the ticket sales areas, the entrances to the facilities, the seating, the restrooms within the stadium, the concession areas and the performance areas themselves. Each of these, working in conjunction with the others, such as the availability of hotels and transport facilities, can give the customers the evidence needed as to the type of service they may expect.

Roles played by the servicescape

We mentioned above that the servicescape is important in providing physical evidence of service. It can play many roles in this regard, as outlined below.

Package the offer

The first role of servicescape is to package the offer. This can give an indication, through the external image, of what the consumer can expect inside. This is often the initial impression and is a moment of truth for the customer, especially for a newly established organisation trying to build a specific image. This appearance can be extended to the actual dress of the staff and other aspects related to their outward appearance.

Facilitator

The second role that the servicescape can fill is that of facilitator in terms of helping the performance of people in that environment. Through good design, the flow of activities can be improved, facilitating goal achievement. Where good design can make the experience a pleasure for the customer, bad design can lead to frustration and even actual discomfort – one only has to think of some of the airline seats that passengers are forced to endure in the name of efficiency and profits!

Aid in socialisation

The servicescape design can also aid in socialisation, in that both customers and employees can better understand their expected roles, behaviours and relationships. By absorbing the position, appearance and placement of the surroundings, employees can deduce what expectations the company has of them. The design can also help to establish, for customers and staff, exactly what types of interactions are encouraged. For example, consider the changes that have occurred in the servicescape related to booksellers. Until recently, browsing through books and magazines was actively discouraged and customers were forced to make their choices standing up, as there was nowhere for them to sit. Staff members were placed behind a desk and the whole feel was unfriendly and spartan. The servicescape in many successful booksellers has changed dramatically. The customer is encouraged to browse and the product is available for easy handling. Comfortable chairs and sofas are provided so that the customer can relax and go through the product at leisure. Many stores now even provide coffee shops within the store to encourage social interaction and further improve the experience. Staff members are encouraged to roam the aisles and socialise with the customers and provide information as needed.

Differentiation

The last role that the servicescape can fulfil is differentiation of the company from its competitors. As alluded to above, changes in the servicescape can be used to reposition a company or even attract new market segments. For example, by adding a gourmet section with detailed information and a wider range of product choices, a food retailer could expand its target market and attract new customers. Consider the launch of LTE (Long Term Evolution) that provides customers with fast, reliable communication at an affordable price. By providing a product with a faster speed at a price that is affordable, Vodacom has attracted new customers who were originally using other service providers.

The servicescape can perform either one or all of these roles simultaneously, but in order to ensure complete management of the service experience, the marketer needs not only to consider physical facilities through the servicescape, but also to look at the culture of the organisation.

A few common examples of poor service (also known as the sins of service) that often lead to upset customers are provided in the next section.

Poor service (sins of service)

It has often been said that 'little things' – the details – affect the customer's perception of quality of service. Most customers are appreciative when they know a company is making a real effort to make things right. The slipping of standards with respect to little aspects can be a death blow to customers' perceptions of service quality. We can identify the following 'sins' of service:

- **Apathy:** The worst form of apathy is when service employees convince customers that they really do not care about the customers' problems. Apathy is an indication of an employee who has lost interest in customers, and when service employees stop caring, they should be replaced.

- **Brushing customers off:** This is when service employees try to dispose of the customers, usually because they have something else to do, especially close to lunch time and closing time.

- **Coolness towards customers:** Here the service employee is overly formal, unsmiling and officious. The service context in this situation is perceived by the customer as cold and uncaring.

- **Treating customers with condescension:** This is shown when service employees talk down to customers, use words that the customer cannot understand or shout at customers who cannot speak a certain language well.

- **Root syndrome:** This occurs when service employees become so used to the routine that they do everything in the same way, day after day. Many times, service employees do not even realise that the customers are there, do not acknowledge their presence and often speak to the social class of the customer rather than directly to the customer. How many times have you tried to pay a bill and the person behind the counter has not acknowledged you as a customer? Employees like this ignore the face-to-face customer contact that is so critical to positive service perceptions.

- **Following the rules:** This occurs when the rules and procedures of a company are created more for the organisation's convenience than for the convenience of customers. Often, systems and procedures are established by employees in an organisation who are far removed from the face-to-face customer's point of view. In terms of CRM, the rules must be designed from the customer's point of view. This will ensure that the company is perceived as service oriented.

- **The customer turnaround:** This is a way of disposing of customers by directing them to another department in the organisation. How many times have you been transferred from one department to another, while nothing is done to deal with your complaint?

By ensuring that a service system that is customer-focused exists in your organisation, the common examples of bad service can be minimised.

Key success factors of service management

Service management should be a total organisational approach so as to ensure that superior service is one of the driving forces of your business. The problem that businesses think they face is that a choice must be made among the three elements, namely, product quality, service quality and cost containment. In order to develop a truly service-oriented organisation, four key success factors of service management, shown in Figure 3.4 on the following page, must be understood.

Employees have a big effect on the process of providing service. Marketers, therefore, need to be reminded that it is not the problem itself, but the way in which the problem is handled that distinguishes good service from bad service. If the customer has been handled in the correct way, the customer will come back to the store and the marketer has succeeded in establishing a long-term relationship. Surprisingly, those customers who have a problem with a supplier, and whose complaint is resolved, stay even more loyal than those who never complained in the first place!

Customers are eager to evaluate service quality when an unexpected event occurs. For example, if customers have a problem locating certain merchandise in a store, they would like some guidance in finding merchandise. Employees must be equipped and trained to help such customers.

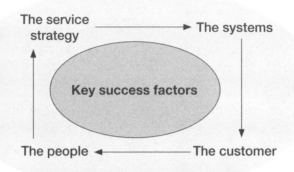

Figure 3.4 Key success factors[30]

In the next section we consider each of the factors in Figure 3.4.

Key success factors

The customer

All of the processes in an organisation revolve around the customer. Customers must be identified and understood. Service management is based on a customer-centred organisation that makes the customer's needs and expectations the central focus of the business. The underlying principle to keep mind is that the customer always comes first.

The service strategy

The service strategy directs the attention of the people in the organisation toward the real priorities of the customer. It has two key parts, the official corporate commitment to service and the service promise to customers. The service strategy becomes the basis for future decisions about the company, its service and its operations.

The people

The managers of service-oriented organisations must help to ensure that service employees focus on meeting the needs of the customer. Effective front-line employees are able to maintain this focus of attention by being aware of the need to provide the service in such a way that customers perceive it as being superior. This makes customers want to tell others about the service and come back for more.

The systems

All employees in an organisation must work within the systems that organise the running of a business. Customers must work their way through these systems in order to do business with the organisation. These systems must be designed for the convenience of the customer rather than the convenience of the organisation. The physical facilities, policies, procedures, methods of communication and processes must all be geared to meet the customer's needs.

It was mentioned earlier that employees must be equipped and trained in customer service. They should understand the value of each customer to the organisation, and be trained to provide excellent service at all times.

Encouraging employees to recognise the cash value of each customer

One way of underlining to employees the importance of keeping customers, is for management to stress the cash value of each customer. Consider the following example.

The cash value of each customer

A fish and chips takeaway restaurant in Cape Town has calculated that a single customer who comes back regularly over a period of 15 years is worth R20 000 to the chain. Employees of the restaurant now recognise that what they do or say can have far-reaching financial consequences beyond the profit on one fish and chips meal. Everybody at the store, from the telephone operator to the delivery person, now knows how important it is to ensure that each and every customer is satisfied.

In Chapters 1 and 2, the lifetime value of each customer (CLV) was highlighted. The lifetime value is the same as the cash value mentioned above.

The CLV is a formula that expresses a customer's present value in monetary terms. CLV consists of three factors, as shown in Table 3.3 on the following page.

Table 3.3 Factors of CLV[31]

	Recency	Frequency	Volume
Definition	Date of last purchase	Average number of purchases a year	Average spend per purchase
To increase CLV	Purchase should be recent	Purchases should be frequent	Spend per purchase should be high

The CLV is based on a combination of the above factors, for example, if the customer purchased a large amount (volume), once (frequency) two years ago (recency), CLV will be low, since both frequency and recency are low. From the above, the importance of building and maintaining a long-term relationship with the customer becomes more important.

Other factors that should be taken into account when measuring the lifetime value of a customer include:

- the period of time over which CLV should be measured;
- the interest rate to be used to determine the present value of the customer; and
- all the costs related to the customer that should be taken into account, for example, costs of merchandise sold, services provided and maintenance.[32]

Elements of great service

To be truly exceptional, customer service should lead to positive word of mouth (WOM) communications.[33] This is more important than ever. It is no longer just a case of a customer complaining about bad service, because most customers are technologically savvy nowadays, and if a customer does or does not like a service provided, he/she can discuss it in his/her blog or start a group on Facebook. He/she may even start a webpage where anyone searching the Internet for the company's name might find a page describing his/her pleasant/unpleasant service experience, which might be easier to find than the company's own website. Positive WOM is therefore more important than ever.

Steps to remarkable customer service

Adapted from the practical experience of Joel Spolsky[34], of the software company Fog Creek, practical steps to exceptional customer service are given below.

Fix everything two ways

When a customer has a complaint, it cannot be ignored. Efforts should be given to finding a solution to the customer's immediate problem. Once the complaint is resolved, the second way to fix the problem is to try to ensure that the same mistake does not happen twice, therefore the root of the problem must be identified and solved throughout the business.

Think laterally to avoid customer offence

Sometimes the problem can be quite easily solved by the customer him-/ herself, especially in the case where a customer has phoned into a help desk. If the problem is solved without the customer having to return the product, it will save the customer time and effort, which he/she will greatly appreciate. However, if the problem is simple to solve, the customer might take offence at your suggestions, for example, suggesting that an electrical appliance is not plugged in. Try to think laterally to solve the problem without offending the customer, for example, suggest that the customer blows the dust off the plug, thereby ensuring that the customer checks that the appliance is plugged in, without insulting his/her intelligence.

Make customers into fans

People make mistakes and it is almost impossible to provide perfect service every time, first time round; however, complete recovery from service failure can sometimes leave a much bigger impact on customer satisfaction and positive WOM than good service the first time round. This is because customers expect the service to go well and will not necessarily think anything of it when it does; however, customers often do not expect their complaints to be resolved and will be pleasantly surprised if they are. This is not to say a company should strive to fail the first time round since customers still prefer a certain amount of consistency. However, when things do go wrong, service recovery processes should be set in place. The following steps are examples of these processes and should be practised by everyone in the company from the top down.

Step 1: Service employees must seem eager to solve problems

Customers should not have to search for a salesperson; salespeople need to be available to the client and must be seen to be keen to solve the problem.

Step 2: Take the blame

In many instances, a service employee may actually blame the customer, which is particularly bad if the fault truly does not lie with the customer. Most customers just want someone to take responsibility for the inconvenience caused by the service failure. Irate customers are often a result of service failure followed by blame shifting or further service failure. When a service employee takes the blame (even when it is not directly his/her fault) it has an emotionally calming effect on customers.

Step 3: Memorise useful phrases

Many service employees do not know what to say to calm a customer after service failure and a few simple phrases can be memorised to help the process. The following are good examples: 'I'm sorry', 'It's my fault', 'Can I offer you the following to make up for your loss?' or 'Please tell me everything that happened so that I can ensure it never happens again.' These phrases may not be easy to say, but perhaps when faced with the prospect of a happy customer in comparison to an angry customer, the happy customer does seem a better choice.

Often the problem here is with managers. Managers need to have the same attitude towards their customers that they expect their employees to have. However, many managers may understand that having a customer focus is beneficial, but also have the attitude that they are in some way above the customer and want to control the customer. This can create a problem of attitude, since the manager, just as much as the service employee, needs to 'serve' the customer.

Step 4: Practise puppetry

Service employees need to understand that the customer's anger is not necessarily directed at them personally. Often the customer does not come into contact with the person responsible for the service failure, but the customer sees the company as a whole and for this reason will take out his/her frustration on the nearest representative of the company. One approach is to have the service employee visualise him/herself as a puppet and a puppet master in a puppet show. As the puppet master, he/she needs to try to discover what would be the best thing for the puppet to say in order to appease or please the customer. In this way, the employee is not party to the argument and can learn not to take the customer's behaviour personally.

Step 5: Go the extra mile

Exceptional service employees do that little something extra. It may just be a small gesture, but it can mean the difference between good and exceptional service, and lead to very positive WOM. For example, if a store is out of stock (because of a delivery failure), the shop assistant could phone other stores in the vicinity and have a product immediately delivered. A good service employee will value a customer's time, realising that time is not only money, but is also keeping a customer away from places he/she would rather be, for example, at home with his/her family.

Step 6: Honour ceremonial expectations

Certain companies offer loyalty cards to offer the customer special services. The services promised should be delivered, because even if the other service offered by the company is exceptional, if the service provider fails to offer what is promised, the customer may still be disappointed.

Step 7: Greed will get you nowhere

The responsibility should not all fall on the shoulders of the service employees; the company needs to put certain processes into place to help the service employee, even if they cost the company money. For example, having a 'no questions asked' return policy helps the service employee provide something of value to the customer and with such a policy, the customer loses the feeling of helplessness, making the likelihood of an irate customer very slim, finally leading to more positive WOM. What the company loses from returns, it will gain from referrals.

Step 8: Provide a performance guarantee

A guarantee removes much of the risk from purchasing a new product or a product that a customer has purchased before, but which has failed. There are a number of situations in which providing a guarantee can differentiate a company from its competitors: when you have a new product; when you have received negative publicity; when the product is complex or technical; when the product is not sold face-to-face; after a service failure; and when the risk of loss is high.

Step 9: Give customer service people a career path

Much of the above cannot be achieved without the co-operation of service employees. By providing customer service people with a career path, the benefits to a company will be two-fold. Firstly, the company will be able to attract the best candidate for the job; and secondly, the company will benefit from a lower staff turnover. The career path needs to have value to service employees. For example, management could set incentives for achieving targets and provide employees with internships at international companies or bursaries at prestigious universities in the world. These must also be realistic; it will not help if a company makes empty promises.

Step 10: Make sure something is in it for the employees

Good-service employees understand that building a long-term relationship with a client will benefit them, because they know that if the client comes back into the store, they will likely be there again and will have to deal with that client.

So if the client was dealt with fairly or received exceptionally good service, it will be much easier to deal with that client in the future. If the client was treated badly however, there is the possibility that they will not return and even if they does return, in all likelihood they will be much more difficult to deal with.

Customer service process model

The rules of the service game are different from the rules of the manufacturing game. Service organisations deliver an experience rather than a tangible product to customers. It is therefore the delivery that counts, since that is what creates the experience. If service organisations need to think differently about how they operate, then managers need to think differently about what their organisation is and how it behaves.[35]

Implementing a process model is another way that service employees can be given a very clear understanding of how to provide excellent service. Figure 3.5 is an example of a service process model for a restaurant.

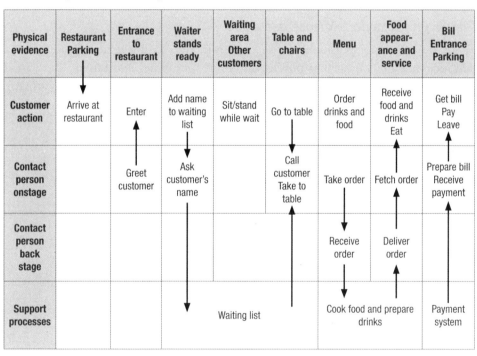

Physical evidence	Restaurant Parking	Entrance to restaurant	Waiter stands ready	Waiting area Other customers	Table and chairs	Menu	Food appearance and service	Bill Entrance Parking
Customer action	Arrive at restaurant	Enter	Add name to waiting list	Sit/stand while wait	Go to table	Order drinks and food	Receive food and drinks Eat	Get bill Pay Leave
Contact person onstage		Greet customer	Ask customer's name		Call customer Take to table	Take order	Fetch order	Prepare bill Receive payment
Contact person back stage						Receive order	Deliver order	
Support processes				Waiting list		Cook food and prepare drinks		Payment system

Figure 3.5 Restaurant visit service blueprint[36]

Managing the service culture: internal service

A service culture exists in an organisation when service orientation and an interest in customers are the most important norms within the organisation.

Many companies have set the objective of being customer-centric, but few seem to have really instilled the culture in the organisation so that it becomes the lifeblood of the organisation. A corporate culture is the set of common norms and values shared by people in the organisation.[37] In common language, it can be described as the internal climate in the organisation. It is important to manage it, because a service culture could be a basis for a sustainable competitive advantage. Southwest Airlines in the USA has been one of the few airlines that has been consistently profitable over the last 40 years and one of its advantages over the competition is the strong service culture that it has. Top management takes care to nurture it and all the activities of the firm are affected by the service imperative. Great care is taken in the selection of potential employees to make sure that they will fit into the service culture of the organisation, so that they will be effective from an early point in their employment.

Requirements for a service culture

In order to implement a service strategy effectively, the organisation will need a service culture. There are four requirements for achieving a service culture and the organisation must manage these.[38]

- **Requirement 1:** A service strategy must be developed. It is important that top management wants and actively aims for a service culture. This means that it must develop a service strategy. This strategy must be clearly stated and must address the strategic aspects of service. The mission statement must include a service vision, establishing the scope and direction of the company in terms of service delivery. The service concepts, therefore, will have to be clearly spelled out: what will be done, for whom and how, as well as the benefits that are to be offered. Resource management – human and other – must be guided by the service strategy, as it is an important part of the service culture. The ways of measuring performance also have to reflect the objectives in terms of the service strategy, and should measure not only efficiency, but also effectiveness.

- **Requirement 2:** All aspects of the organisational structure must reflect the service strategy and processes. This is important, because the more complex the organisational structure, the more difficult it is to consistently deliver good service. The organisational structure of most retail banks in South Africa makes it problematic for them to deliver on their customer service excellence objectives. What is needed is quick and flexible decision-making, and co-operation among the different departments in a company in order to consistently deliver good service. The implications of this for authority and decision-making for front-line employees must be carefully considered. The identification of all customers, both external and internal, must be the basis of the structure decisions. This also means that managers have to understand their roles as facilitators of performance and in providing support for the front-line staff. The design of operational systems, work flows and routines has to be done with the customers' needs and expectations in mind and the use of information technology is an opportunity to make the sharing of the customer service culture a reality.

- **Requirement 3:** A service-oriented leadership must be established. Members of management must support the service initiative in word and deed in order to maintain a service culture. This includes the roles they take as leaders in their teams and how they act and speak. It is important that there should be no ambiguity about the service emphasis and the kind of behaviour expected of employees. It is especially important for the top manager of the company to speak continuously about service excellence and give strong support to it. OUTsurance's 'The Staff Helping SA OUT' campaign is a staff initiative led by top management and is supported by all staff members. The idea was that management must guide the staff as to the correct set of values and attitudes to have, through visible leadership and coaching.

- **Requirement 4:** The knowledge and attitudes needed for good service must be created through service training. This is an important part of internal marketing, which will be discussed in detail in a later chapter. The more knowledgeable employees are about the operations, the customer relationships and the expectations that exist, both in terms of the customers and themselves, the more likely they are to understand what is needed and why it is needed. This assumes that all the necessary information is understood by all concerned, as explained in Requirement 1.

Behavioural code ~Managers & Staff~

Service employees need to understand what is expected of them. Training should therefore be provided so that employees have a clear understanding of what constitutes great service. Providing a code of conduct for employees facilitates this. The following are good examples of how service employees should strive to behave on a daily basis:[39]

- **Only speak well of customers:** Service employees can get into the habit of competing for who has the worst customer, leading to a culture in which the customer is seen as the enemy. This is not beneficial to providing exceptional customer service; rather, employees need to see customers in a positive light, so that they *want* to help them, instead of *having* to.

- **Only speak well of competitors:** Feuding should be discouraged and from the service employees' point of view, the focus should be on improving the company, not on one-upping the competition.

- **No temper tantrums:** Employees should be discouraged from phone slamming, swearing and general poor behaviour. They need to realise that their negative behaviour has a chain reaction on all around them.

- **Speak to managers about issues:** When employees have a problem, they need to be able to speak openly and freely with their supervisors. A culture of open communication should be established.

- **Teamwork:** Offering assistance when other associates are in need should be encouraged; this also applies to supervisors.

Corporate commitment[40]

Exceptional service needs a commitment from the entire organisation in order to be successful. The following are necessary elements of corporate commitment:

- **Commitment is worth more than the paper it is written on:** Raymond Ackerman often uses the expression 'The customer is king'. This is an excellent slogan; however, to have any true value, it needs to be practised constantly.

- **Commitment needs to flow from the top down:** Managers and owners of businesses need to practise what they preach; they also need to invest time and money in exceptional service.

- **Commitment to service needs to become entrenched:** Exceptional service quality needs to be sustained; and service employees need to be continually reminded of the benefits of exceptional service, not only to the enterprise, but to each service employee as an individual.

- **Commitment to service needs to be properly compensated:** To ensure the above, the benefits promised to service employees should not only be stated, but actually delivered.

Summary

In this chapter, the various factors in customer service that influence the building of customer relationships were discussed. Service quality was highlighted, with specific reference to the link between relationships, quality service and customer loyalty. A few methods for measuring customer satisfaction were discussed. The moments of truth concept, or service encounters, formed a large part of the discussion of quality, as well as the cycle of service as experienced by customers when they interact with an organisation. The impacts of servicescapes were highlighted. Numerous practical applications of service quality were highlighted throughout the chapter. Lastly, we discussed the importance of a service culture to an organisation in being able to achieve its service goals.

DISCUSSION QUESTIONS

1. Explain and illustrate the nature of customer service.
2. Explain, with the aid of practical examples, the quality outcomes when consumers compare the service they expect with the actual service they receive.
3. Discuss the different types of customer expectations and highlight the factors influencing service expectations.
4. Explain the dimensions used by consumers when evaluating service quality.
5. Illustrate the link between relationships, quality service and customer loyalty.
6. What are the benefits of customer satisfaction surveys and the problems in measuring customer satisfaction?
7. Explain, with the aid of practical examples, four methods of measuring customer satisfaction.
8. Discuss the moments of truth or service encounters for a bank under the following headings:
   - the meaning of moments of truth or service encounters;
   - types of service encounters in a bank;
   - ingredients of a moment of truth;
   - sources of satisfaction/dissatisfaction in the moment of truth.
9. Discuss which aspects of the servicescape you would consider, in terms of managing the physical evidence of service, if you were the owner of a private educational institution teaching degree programmes under a licence agreement with a major university.
10. Briefly explain the key success factors in service management that should be implemented to ensure that superior service is provided in the whole organisation.
11. Assume that you have been appointed as CEO of a business unit in a major corporation that has been steadily losing customers and whose customers have rated it as 'shocking' in terms of service delivery. Identify the aspects that you should consider in terms of trying to instil a service culture in the unit.

Mini case study

Europcar: delivering world-class products and services to customers[41]

Europcar is essentially the merger of a home-grown brand with an international one, each complementing the other's strengths. Imperial Car Rental's primary focus was the local business traveller, while Europcar's focus was the inbound leisure visitor. Bringing the two together made good business sense.

Realistically, the nature of the car rental market and its key drivers leave very little opportunity for a differentiated product and service offering. The majority of its competitors are positioned around price and service, and none seems to have a unique offering. It was thus important for Europcar to craft a differentiating, strong and attractive positioning away from the plethora of competitors. A necessary prerequisite for this to happen was the ability to deliver the brand promise through tangible 'reasons to believe' (eg service standards, and an efficient and fast car rental process).

To this end, Europcar identified three value proposition anchors that together must communicate the central idea of 'effortless interaction':

- **Simplicity**: the car rental experience must be as user-friendly as possible.
- **High performance**: the service must be efficient, reliable and consistent.
- **Personalised service**: the service must meet individual needs and requirements.

MINI CASE STUDY QUESTIONS

1. In your opinion, how do you think customer expectations of car rental services have changed over the past few years? What do you think would have prompted these changes?
2. Explain how a customer might assess 'responsiveness' as a dimension used for evaluating service quality at Europcar.
3. Identify and explain the top three key success factors of Europcar.

PART 2

The markets of CRM

Internal marketing

Learning outcomes

After studying this chapter, you should be able to:

- define the term 'internal marketing';
- discuss the dimensions inherent to internal marketing;
- identify the different outcomes of an internal marketing strategy;
- discuss the purpose of internal marketing;
- identify and discuss the different components of internal marketing;
- explain the objectives of internal marketing;
- discuss internal marketing as a management strategy;
- discuss the internal environment as a key factor when developing an internal marketing strategy;
- explain the four types of internal customer groups;
- discuss the guidelines for the successful implementation of an internal marketing strategy.

Introduction

One of the key aspects for any organisation implementing Customer Relationship Marketing (CRM) is the area of internal marketing. In the chain of relationships, one of the key relationships is found within the organisation itself and is known as internal marketing. Through internal marketing, the organisation reveals that it consists of individuals and departments who are considered to be each other's customers. However, both educating customers and communicating the benefits of a service present continuing challenges for service marketers. Employees do not only provide a service to the external customers but also to each other within the organisation.

Internal marketing hinges on the assumption that employee satisfaction and customer satisfaction are interlinked, therefore internal marketing must precede external marketing. Organisations must recognise that achieving objectives and creating change can only be achieved through motivated boundary-spanning employees. Organisations therefore need to recruit, train and provide tools to employees to perform superior service. The success of services relies on the internal marketing activities being carried out successfully and being aligned with one another in order to ultimately convey a positive awareness of the brand to customers. Internal marketing can thus be described as the enabler of the promise made to customers.

This chapter explains what the term 'internal marketing' means and why internal marketing is so important for the successful implementation of CRM within an organisation.

A perspective on internal marketing

Internal marketing refers to a structured and planned approach towards the employees (as internal customers) of an organisation. The aim is to deliver employee satisfaction which results in employees feeling valued by the organisation for which they work. The predicted outcome is that employees become more positive towards their work, resulting in greater commitments towards their employer, stronger involvement in their job and the experience of greater job satisfaction. The latter ensures greater external customer satisfaction in the medium to long-term.[1] The focus of internal marketing is to treat employees as internal customers of the organisation.[2]

For internal marketing to succeed, the following internal market orientation objectives need to be in place. Firstly, the organisation needs to derive an understanding of employees' needs and wants, and establish an understanding between the employees and managers. Secondly, the organisation's vision and strategic objectives need to be communicated to all employees mainly through internal mass media communications.[3] If internal marketing is implemented successfully and the objectives are met, it can lead to different benefits such as effective overall communications, stronger individual performance and productivity, better teamwork and improved employee retention producing increased profits.[4] A strong internal marketing strategy can therefore be critical to achieve and sustain a competitive advantage for an organisation, as well as drive organisational change and enhanced organisational performance.[5]

Definitions of internal marketing identify two dimensions to the concept. The first is the 'marketing job' that the organisation has to do in order to attract employees, while the second dimension refers to the nature and execution of the task of internal marketing itself.

Dimension 1

The first perspective of internal marketing relates to the job that is offered to employees. A job can be seen as a 'product' that is offered to an employee.[6] The job and its activities need to be sold (or marketed) in order to attract quality staff, making the job a product offered by the organisation. If the product does not satisfy an employee's needs, they will find an alternate 'product'.[7] This means that the employee will evaluate the job in terms of its ability to satisfy their needs, which refers not only to the financial aspects of the job, but also to their need for personal growth, as seen in the development and training received from the organisation, as well as the personal development of the employee.

The importance of this perspective is found in the assumption that a satisfied employee will assist in creating satisfied customers for the organisation. The job that a person does within an organisation is hence one that will affect not only the employee him/herself, but also the success of the organisation.

> When an organisation employs staff, the job description will indicate the nature of the job to be carried out as well as the remuneration package, while growth prospects will also be discussed with the employee.

Dimension 2

A number of definitions of internal marketing have been offered to identify the nature of the second dimension of internal marketing, namely the nature and execution of the marketing task. Each of these definitions attempts to put the focus on a different aspect of this perspective.

The first aspect refers to the activities of the tasks that are needed to ensure that the external marketing is carried out successfully. This can be seen in the following definition:

> *Internal marketing is any form of marketing within an organisation that focuses staff attention on the internal activities that need to be changed in order to enhance external marketplace performance.*[8]

The focus here is on the purpose of internal marketing, namely that of channelling staff commitment into the activities of the organisation. This staff commitment is channelled specifically into the issues of problem solving and opportunity seeking within the marketing efforts in order to improve customer service. This would imply that without employees who are focused on solving the problems experienced by external markets, the success of the marketing effort will be compromised. An example of this may be the situation where

Corporate Entrepreneurship

employees are encouraged to show initiative and develop new methods of improving customer care, where they see the opportunity. This might involve new processing techniques or the introduction of new production methods, as in the example that follows.

> A home loan consultant working for a Bank should be empowered with decision-making power without needing to obtain the approval of a line manager. Such decision-making can be allowed within a certain framework. For example, when the home loan consultant is evaluating the bond application of an individual, the consultant should have the decision-making power to increase the loan amount by a certain percentage, without prior approval from a line manager. Such decision-making empowerment will enhance the employee's feeling of belonging, strengthen their commitment to the employer, increase their level of motivation towards the task performed and be able to provide a more speedy response to the customer.

Linked to the above is the second aspect, namely that of the human resource issues within the organisation, specifically that of motivation:

> *Internal marketing is a planned effort using a marketing-like approach directed at motivating employees, for implementing and integrating organisational strategies towards customer orientation.*[9]

In this definition, the question of the motivation of staff to attain the goals set for the CRM programme can be seen. Here the focus of marketing activities is the employees, where the purpose of internal marketing is to get the staff motivated so that they are willing and able to implement all the strategies of the organisation, including CRM and other strategies of the marketing department. In attempting to motivate staff, attention is drawn to issues such as performance-based reward systems, training and other techniques that can be used to affect the motivation of the workforce. This can be done by linking staff bonuses to their success in retaining profitable customers for the organisation.

> The CRM programme contains a number of objectives that are to be attained. Goals need to be set that are regarded as challenging for the employees, and for which they will be adequately rewarded.

The third aspect highlighted by internal marketing is the relationships that are created as a result of internal marketing:

> *The objective of internal marketing is to create relationships between management, employees and the various functions within the organisation.*[10]

No function can exist in isolation, hence the aim of internal marketing efforts is to create an efficient unit, where functions are all focused on achieving a common goal. This is done through the creation of relationships among the various functions of the organisation. These relationships are not only created through formal contacts and communication within the organisation, but also through informal contacts such as social events and get-togethers.

Considering the information above, a successful internal marketing strategy can result in the following:

- enhancing the morale levels of employees;
- enhancing the motivational level of employees;
- strengthening the willingness of employees to work as a team;
- providing rewards for employees for their performance in the organisation;
- improving the attitude of employees towards colleagues and external customers; and
- acknowledging departments or business units for their performance.[11]

What is internal marketing?

Internal marketing focuses on people inside business boundaries, and places emphasis on the satisfaction of employee needs. Internal marketing theories state that the business emphasises the importance in employee need satisfaction, and approaches jobs as internal products, aimed towards the development and motivation of best-qualified personnel.[12]

> For the purpose of this chapter and the ensuing discussion, internal marketing refers to:
>
> *Viewing employees as internal customers, and jobs as internal products that satisfy the needs and wants of these internal customers while addressing the objectives of the organisation.*[13]

The purpose of internal marketing

The purpose of internal marketing is to engage employees in order to overcome organisational resistance to environmental and business change.[14] Engagement refers to a positive, fulfilling, work-related state of mind that is characterised by vigour, dedication and absorption. It is composed of two vital components, namely attention and absorption. Attention relates to the level of the employees' cognitive accessibility and the amount of time spent thinking about their function, whilst absorption refers to the intensity of the employees' focus on their function.[15] Employees who feel safe in their environment are far more accessible and highly absorbed in their work as they feel part of something bigger. As a result, employees who are fully engaged are involved and passionate about their work and the services they provide to customers.[16] Internal marketing should be considered as a method for enhancing employee engagement.[17] It must be noted that the role of internal marketing involves far more than the attraction and motivation of employees, it highlights the need for cross-functional co-ordination across employees and business units in order to achieve customer satisfaction.[18] The fundamental nature of internal marketing is to improve internal communications and customer consciousness among employees in an effort to improve external market performance and customer satisfaction. Broadly speaking, the purpose of internal marketing is to involve employees in the organisation's mission and strategy direction as well as to help them understand the organisation's objectives and their role in achieving these objectives in order to create value for customers.[19]

The purpose of internal marketing is to concentrate on the internal relationship between employees and the organisation in order to ensure that employees are motivated, engaged and effectively managed to ensure a customer and service orientation.[20] This will therefore ensure that customers receive higher levels of service quality resulting in increased customer satisfaction and retention.[21]

The components of internal marketing

Taking the perspectives of internal marketing into account, five main components can be identified.[22] These components are regarded as essential for the implementation of a successful internal marketing strategy. They are as follows:

- **Employee motivation and satisfaction:** Here the focus is on the employees of the organisation and their skills, as well as their motivation to provide the expected level of service. If the motivation of employees is not adequate, it will affect the level of service offered, which in turn will impact on the satisfaction experienced by customers.

- **Customer orientation and customer service:** Here the focus of the organisation is on the customer rather than sales. This results in employees being customer aware in the activities that they carry out. Customer satisfaction is the key to maintaining customers and their support of the organisation.

- **Inter-functional co-ordination and integration:** The importance of co-operation among all the functions is identified. No function can operate in isolation, and the success of the entire programme requires that every function needs the other to operate efficiently.

- **Marketing-like approach to the components above:** This approach suggests the use of marketing-like techniques within the organisation. These marketing-like techniques can be used to inform employees about the actions and decisions of the organisation regarding marketing activities. Examples include the use of marketing communication and other promotional activities within the organisation.

- **Implementation of specific corporate or functional strategies:** Employees are the keys to the implementation of any strategy within the organisation. Any CRM strategy needs communication and co-operation within the organisation to aid in its implementation. Internal marketing can thus be used to assist in strategy implementation, while also improving inter-functional co-operation within the organisation.

The objectives of internal marketing

The underlying objective of internal marketing is the development of a marketing programme that is aimed at the internal market of an organisation and that is parallel to the marketing programme aimed at external customers. Internal marketing is part of the quality and service initiatives of the organisation and encompasses the following objectives:

- to enable all the employees of an organisation to focus on similar broad organisational objectives;

- to create an awareness of both internal and external customers; and

- to establish a team spirit amongst the employees of the organisation.

The following objectives of internal marketing were developed from a relationship marketing perspective:

- to create, develop and retain internal relationships between employees of the organisation irrespective of their position. Employees must be motivated by it to deliver a quality service to both internal and external customers;

- to provide employees with the required skills, knowledge, support, internal service providers, systems and technology from a management and supervisor level that will empower them to deliver a customer-orientated service to internal customers;

- to ensure that employees are motivated to deliver customer and service driven performance of a high quality and so be responsible as 'part time internal customers' within the interactive marketing process;

- to recruit and retain qualified and skilled individuals;

- to ensure that internal service delivery is done on a customer service basis within the organisation or between partners within a network context;

- to provide sound internal and external service delivery through the provision of management and technology support that will empower employees to function as 'part time marketers' of the organisation;

- to manage employees in a more service-orientated way; and

- to manage a culture of continuous change in the organisation. This must be done from the perspective of 'how activities *are* performed' to 'how activities *should* be performed'. The outcome of this should be to achieve success and to manage and implement the marketing plan successfully.

Internal marketing as a management strategy

Internal marketing examines what is <u>required</u> and by <u>whom</u> it is required. In most instances, the organisation predetermines much of the employee's role as described in a formalised job <u>description</u>, which is more or less well specified, depending on the service delivery process. Internal marketing can be used to identify the type of role that is required by employees to execute <u>strategies</u>. The identified role is contingent to organisational circumstance and situation and is linked to the specific skills and capabilities of the specific employee. Internal marketing makes the assessment of employees for specified roles more visible, since it looks at deployment of individual competence from an opportunity-cost point of view, taking into consideration both the organisation's and employee's perspective.

Once the roles of employees have been clarified, the relationships between them and the rest of the organisation have to be managed. This requires understanding and managing internal relationships, functions and interactions in an effective and profitable manner. Successful reciprocal exchange relationships within the organisation can be established through understanding and intimacy; trust and commitment. These concepts are discussed in more detail in the section that follows which focuses on the internal environment as a key factor when developing an internal marketing strategy.

> To be able to achieve its goals, an organisation needs to build trust and commitment, which can only be done if the organisation knows and understands its employees and itself intimately.

Internal marketing assists in developing and growing trust and commitment within the organisation if interactions are aligned through explicit consideration of stakeholders' needs, if the needs of employees are taken care of and the organisation clearly indicates that it values its employees. The human resources department plays a critical role in internal marketing management, since it offers tools that can be used in internal marketing, such as training, hiring and career planning. Internal marketing offers guidance on how these and other tools should be used, i.e. to improve interactive marketing performance through customer focused and skilful employees.

The effective management of an organisation requires a variety of inter-functional and well established activities that form part of an overall process aimed at a common objective. Internal marketing allows management to approach all of these activities in a more systematic and strategic manner and to gear them towards the external performance of the organisation. Although internal marketing emerged from services marketing, it has widened to be applicable to any type of organisation, not merely those in the service sector. This has led to internal marketing being a general technique for the implementation of internal and external organisational strategy.[22]

The internal environment as a key factor when developing an internal marketing strategy

The internal marketing environment of organisations consists of two characteristics, namely tangible and intangible characteristics. Tangible characteristics include organisational resources, functional departments, systems and processes, while intangible characteristics would be human capital, culture, mission and objectives, leadership, alignment and teamwork.[23] When both the tangible and intangible aspects are aligned with the external marketing objectives, the organisation has a higher chance of actioning its strategy.[24]

Employees are at the heart of organisations. They pull everything together, so it is essential that their needs are taken into consideration when designing and developing the organisational strategy.[25] It is also essential that employees are included in the development of the organisational strategy and are informed about the organisation's customer needs, expectations, products, services, concepts and business initiatives. Through this approach, shared goals can be created which results in a common understanding of tasks and outcomes. This results in employees working together as a unit to achieve the organisational objectives.[26] For this reason, internal marketing aims at creating an appropriate internal environment where strong internal relationships are created in which employees are engaged and encouraged to work together in a co-ordinated fashion in order to transfer knowledge and generate ideas and innovations that create value for customers.[27]

In this way organisations can ensure that a continuous flow of knowledge takes place between employees, as well as between the various business units. It is widely recognised that the successful management of tacit knowledge transfer can make a significant contribution to an organisation's success. Tacit knowledge is defined as knowledge which is derived from personal experience, it is subjective and difficult to formalise, and is generally transferred from one person to another through an apprenticeship. It is tacit knowledge that the organisation needs to nurture and manage in order to develop individual skills and expertise.[28]

It is argued that if two people exchange knowledge with each other, both gain information and experience resulting in a linear growth. However, if both of them share their new knowledge with others, the benefits are exponential. Furthermore, if organisational knowledge is shared, it becomes entrenched in the organisation's processes, products and services which makes these unique to the organisation and therefore difficult to copy, giving the organisation a unique competitive advantage. The development of an appropriate internal environment characterised by strong internal relationships provides the motivation and ability for employees to transfer tacit knowledge within the organisation.[29]

Trust and commitment

Trust and commitment have been identified as key virtues which underpin relationships.

> Trust refers to 'a willingness to rely on an exchange partner in whom one has confidence' and commitment as 'an enduring desire to maintain a valued relationship'.[30]

Trust, commitment and understanding are fundamental to internal marketing and the creation of the internal environment. These factors create psychological safety for the employee. Psychological safety is the state in which people feel safe enough to be honest about what they think and feel. Relationships can thus be successfully developed as employees are more likely to act transparently and with integrity when they feel psychologically safe in their environment.[31]

In addition, this psychological safety ensures that employees are fully engaged which allows them to perform their roles more competently and deliver service excellence to customers.[32] It is important therefore that all internal marketing processes are conditioned in trust, referring to trust in leadership, processes and systems. To build trust and commitment an organisation needs to know and understand its employees and itself thoroughly. Internal marketing helps in the development and growth of trust and commitment among parties. By looking after the needs of the employees, internal marketing provides a clear message to the internal market that the organisation values its employees. If employees feel valued and psychologically safe they will be more willing to share knowledge and generate ideas.[33]

The role of cross-functional co-ordination in creating relationships in the internal environment

Throughout the value chain, each employee is responsible for generating customer value, either directly or through internal cross-functional relationships and teamwork with the aim of creating value in all steps of the value chain.[34] Cross-functional co-ordination brings employees from all parts of the organisation together in order to achieve the organisational objectives. Through the internal customer-supply chain (value chain) a network of relationships is created and through internal marketing practices, all employees understand their role and their impact on the next customer in the value chain.[35]

Cross-functional co-ordination is therefore essential in creating and aligning relationships within the internal environment and assisting in the transfer of knowledge. Personal relationship theory suggests that mutual interdependence is also created between parties in the value chain which reduces the risk of one party acting in their own interests as this adversely affects the partnerships. Relationships between internal customers and suppliers are crucial as the outcome of these alliances depends not only on what each party does individually, but also on the joint decisions and actions.[36] It is therefore important for organisations to build relationships with their employees on all levels from top management level right down to shop-floor level.[37] This helps to establish an internal environment which is based on trust, where employees feel psychologically safe, are fully engaged, motivated and committed to the transfer of knowledge and improved collaboration.[38] The management of internal relationships and the creation of an appropriate internal environment are essential for the satisfaction of employees and their loyalty and retention in the long run.[39]

Four types of internal customer groups

There are typically four different types of internal customer groups. They consist of contractors, modifiers, influencers and isolateds and will be discussed briefly below.[40]

Contractors

Contractors often have numerous and regular interactions with an organisation's clients and are closely involved with everyday marketing actions. Such contractors include, for example, all the Account Executives and Client Relationship Managers of a staffing agency.

Due to the frequent interactions that contractors have with clients, they are required to be well trained, equipped and motivated to deliver a quality service in a responsive way on a daily basis. Contactors also need to be aware of their central role in achieving client satisfaction and gaining a competitive advantage. They should be recruited, assessed and rewarded based on their actual and prospective responsiveness to client needs. It is the organisation's responsibility to ensure that contractors are well trained and motivated to provide services to clients in a responsive way in order to reinforce a favourable image of the organisation.

Modifiers

Modifiers are employees that have frequent contact with an organisation's clients but are not traditionally involved in marketing the organisation's offering. They do not play an active role in the conventional marketing mix and their contact with clients is frequently not in person. These employees could include all secretaries and client contact administrative personnel such as collections clerks.

Since modifiers do have some level of contact with clients; they have a chance to influence an external client's ideas, feelings, intentions and actions towards the organisation and its marketing initiatives. They are required to understand the marketing exchange process and overall marketing goals of the organisation from the clients' and organisation's viewpoint. Modifiers need to be aware that their responsiveness to the needs of clients, or lack of it, will affect the clients' perceptions of the organisation. The organisation should screen modifiers for their existing communication skills and responsive attitude and train them in further communication skills.

Modifiers should be measured not only on the quality of their work but also on how effectively they represent the organisation when interfacing with clients. They should be rewarded on the basis of their performance in such interactions.

This is important, as such interactions ultimately affect the clients' overall perception of the organisation.

Influencers

Influencers usually have no direct contact with the external client. They do however, have a large amount of knowledge concerning the capabilities and resources of the organisation. They are involved in indirectly implementing the organisation's marketing strategy. These employees include marketing, information technology and human resource professionals as well as management. Perceptions of the organisation and its marketing are affected quite significantly by how effectively influencers execute their responsibilities.

Influencers need to be aware of their pivotal role in creating and supporting a client orientation for the organisation. When hiring influencers, management should seek client-responsive individuals as they ultimately have an influence on the behaviour of contractors and modifiers. Client-orientated influencers will ultimately lead to higher levels of internal service delivery since satisfying the client is the primary responsibility of employees. Influencers who provide high levels of internal service delivery to other employee segments will facilitate the achievement of higher levels of external service delivery. Influencers should be assessed and remunerated based on client-focused performance standards, as these standards impact on the work of contractors who ultimately satisfy the client, through final service delivery.

Isolateds

Isolateds are support personnel who do not have direct contact with clients and are not involved in the creation or implementation of marketing strategies. They include data processors and administrative employees. The efficiency and effectiveness of their support activities affect the performance of other organisational functions which directly deliver on clients' needs. They need to be aware that their services are required to help the organisation to deliver its clients' needs.

In order for isolateds to be client focused and to deliver exceptional internal services, they require an understanding of the organisation's marketing strategy and how the organisation serves its clients. Isolateds, in particular, should be made aware of clients' needs on a daily basis. As they do not have direct contact with external clients and so may lose sight of clients' needs unless they are frequently reminded of them. This could be done on an ongoing basis through occasional intentional exposure to the client or through written, visual or audio materials that relate to the needs of the client and the function of the organisation in meeting those needs. See the example that follows on the following page.

The staff recruiting brand, Kelly Group, use a corporate DVD that indicates the personality of the organisation and the goals it desires to achieve, both internally and externally. This corporate video indicates each staffing brand within the Kelly Group and how each brand serves its relevant client base. The DVD assists in providing a vision of the client and the client's needs to isolateds.

The successful implementation of an internal marketing strategy

The modern organisation faces the challenge of having to focus on two customer segments, namely the internal and external segment of the organisation. This has far-reaching implications for an organisation with regard to the satisfaction of customer needs and the implementation of the organisation's strategies. The following aspects can serve as guidelines for an organisation that wants to initiate an internal marketing strategy.[41]

- **The personal training and development of employees** is especially relevant to those employees that are responsible for addressing the internal and external needs of customers.

- **Continuous communication to employees** must also provide feedback to employees to ensure that the internal culture and climate can be determined.

- **The empowerment and participation of employees** must be done according to clearly formulated guidelines and predetermined frameworks. This will ensure that an improved service is delivered to the organisation's customers and that employees will experience improved work satisfaction.

- **Internal consumer segmentation** can be done according to the manner in which employees have contact with customers.

- **Performance appraisal systems** must be positioned within the organisation. This will empower the organisation to identify the contribution of each employee and department and to formulate objectives accordingly.

- **Acknowledgement and rewards to employees** must be done according to the contribution that each employee makes inside the organisation.

- **Supportive working relationships** lead to the improvement of internal communication and the organisation's ability to deliver services. In addition, supportive working relationships must be established to create an environment that nurtures consideration, concern, support and trust.

- **A receptive organisational environment** that is supportive of employees must be developed. The structures of an organisation must also be receptive towards internal marketing initiatives as well as their implementation within the organisation. These initiatives encompass teamwork, group cohesion, and multidisciplinary teams.

- **Internal communication** must be aimed at the participation of all departments within the organisation. This will ensure that all employees are aware of their role and function within the organisation.

The support of management and supervisors is required to ensure that internal marketing strategies are successfully implemented. Successful internal marketing starts with top management and encompasses the following three prerequisites:

- internal marketing must be incorporated as an inherent component of strategic management;

- the internal marketing process must not be opposed by the organisational structure due to a lack of management support; and

- top management must demonstrate a continuous support for the process of internal marketing.

In addition to the requirements stated above, the commitment of all employees in the organisation is required to ensure the success of internal marketing. This implies that all parties should focus on the achievement of shared objectives. In the supply chain, each party therefore contributes to customer value and internal service quality. Employees that are directly involved with customer contact or the delivery of support services must be knowledgeable regarding the mission, objectives, strategies and processes of the organisation to ensure that internal customer relationships are managed successfully. It is within the internal marketing environment that the motivation, self-confidence and commitment of employees to the objectives of the organisation are developed.

A satisfied employee is therefore a prerequisite for quality-driven service delivery to the external customers of the organisation. The organisation that is committed to the creation of a positive working environment, thereby ensuring that motivated and committed employees are supported, will be positioned to deliver a level of service delivery that will motivate customers to return to the organisation. The long-term satisfaction of customer needs is directly influenced by the ability of an organisation to build positive relationships with employees. Satisfied employees lead to external customer satisfaction as well as an organisational performance level that motivates investors to invest in the organisation.

Summary

This chapter focused on the importance of internal marketing in the area of CRM, and how organisations go about building relationships with their employees. The chapter started by examining the perspectives that comprise internal marketing, which are reflected in the model of internal marketing. Functional co-ordination and co-operation are essential to the success of a CRM programme, and the chapter examined how the various functions of an organisation and their interactions affect one another. In addition, attention was paid to aspects such as the objectives of internal marketing, the four types of internal market groups and different customer segments of internal marketing, as well as the different roles that employees can play within the organisation and how internal marketing can take place. The chapter concluded with a focus on the guidelines for the successful implementation of an internal marketing programme.

DISCUSSION QUESTIONS

1. Define the term 'internal marketing'.
2. Briefly discuss the concept of internal marketing.
3. Explain the two dimensions that make up the concept of internal marketing.
4. What benefits does an internal marketing strategy have for an organisation?
5. List and discuss the different components of internal marketing.
6. Identify and briefly explain the different objectives of internal marketing.
7. Briefly explain internal marketing as a management strategy.
8. Identify and explain the different internal market customer segments of an organisation.
9. Provide guidelines to an organisation on how it can implement an internal marketing strategy. Make sure that you clearly indicate to management the aspects on which they have to focus.

Mini case study

The influence of internal marketing on internal customer satisfaction in the South African retail banking sector[42]

The South African banking sector remains highly concentrated as a result of the years of economic isolation during the 1980s.

There are currently 36 banks operating in South Africa, comprising 20 registered banks (of which 5 are foreign controlled), 14 branches of foreign banks and 2 mutual banks. The five largest retail banks, namely: Amalgamated Banks of South Africa (ABSA), First National Bank (FNB), The Standard Bank of South Africa (SBSA), Nedbank and Investec hold 90 per cent of the South African banking assets with ABSA, FNB, Nedbank and SBSA owning the bulk of the retail banking system. The remaining banks tend to focus on specific activities, regions or communities.

Given the homogeneity within the retail banking industry, there is very little differentiating the banks and imitation of any innovation is inevitable. For this reason a market-driven strategy that enables retail banks to deliver superior quality is essential as service quality is the only real differentiator and key to building a competitive advantage. Service quality is regarded as a driver of corporate marketing and financial performance and has been recognised as a key strategic issue for organisations operating in service sectors. Banks believe customers will be loyal if they receive greater value than from competitors and should therefore focus on improving service quality as a core competitive strategy.

Service organisations need to ensure that they can deliver on promises made to customers in all service encounters, labelled in marketing literature as 'moments of truth'. Contact employees have one of the most challenging yet rewarding tasks as the way they behave directly affects the service encounter. However, it is not these individuals alone who 'wow' the customer. Behind the scenes are a myriad of players all working together in a co-ordinated fashion to create the ultimate service experience. Since human interaction is required to deliver the service, it is necessary to have quality employees in place to do so. The employee is pivotal in creating and sustaining quality as the quality of the service rendered, is inseparable from the quality of the service provider. Irrespective of where technology leads, quality comes from people. For this reason, many service organisations, banks in particular, have resorted to placing increased focus on the attraction, retention and satisfaction of quality employees in order to create a sustainable competitive advantage. Attracting top calibre employees is a challenge for banks in South Africa and even though the labour pool may be large, finding the right quality of employees can prove to be an expensive and time-consuming process. Given these challenges, banks in South Africa have been placing an increased focus on recruiting at graduate level leading to the establishment of Graduate Development Programmes (GDPs).

GDPs were started by the Big 4 banks with the view of offering graduates dynamic, fast-paced environments in which to learn new skills, participate in a range of projects, and make an important contribution to the bank.

Each year a number of top calibre graduates are selected across numerous fields of study to enter their one-year development programmes. They are recruited with a specific position and business unit in mind, but spend a number of months rotating through different areas in order to obtain a better understanding of how the bank operates. These banking GDPs are specifically designed to help graduates succeed in complex environments and to build the talent pipeline by providing an in-depth training programme inclusive of coaching. One of the biggest challenges faced by banks is the satisfaction and retention of their GDP employees. Banks generally experience high attrition rates amongst this group of employees mainly due to job dissatisfaction. This results in significant costs for the banks as high attrition rates drive up training and recruiting costs. They also increase the potential for customer service complaints or quality problems, and create massive continuity problems for long-term projects. Because of high turnover, organisations are required to hire more aggressively, resulting in a steady loss of cost efficiencies. Since banks invest a substantial amount of money into the GDPs, a healthy return on investment looks dim. Employee satisfaction therefore becomes a key factor to business success. Employees are the backbone of any business success, specifically in the service sector. They need to be developed, motivated and retained at all costs to support the organisation and help to make it globally competitive. Given that employees are key to ensuring that customers are satisfied, which can lead to increased profits, achieving a competitive business advantage depends on understanding and acting on what it takes to maximise employee satisfaction.

Employee satisfaction is defined as the way an employee feels about his or her job. Employees who are more satisfied tend to be more effective and productive in the organisation. Satisfied employees believe that their organisation provide customer service that is reliable, responsive and empathetic, and that employees are knowledgeable and able to instil confidence in customers.

Employee satisfaction and internal service quality have positive relationships with organisational commitment, specifically affective commitment. Given the importance of employee satisfaction for service quality and employee retention, it is essential for organisations to understand the drivers behind employee satisfaction. The following have been identified as the main drivers of satisfaction. These drivers are role fit and clarity, reward and recognition, career advancement, training and development, performance feedback, interaction between other employees and management, satisfaction with leaders (supervisors and senior management), empowerment, assessing the level of stress and pressure in the work environment, the appearance and layout of the internal environment, the level of decentralised decision-making and the organisational culture. Should any of these factors not meet with the individual's expectations, job dissatisfaction is likely to ensue. Organisations should therefore start asking themselves how they can manage their recruits more effectively and how they can address the issues of job dissatisfaction experienced by these GDP employees. A way of addressing these issues and improving satisfaction levels is through a well designed internal marketing programme.

By developing a clearer internal marketing orientation, banks in South Africa could better understand the needs of their GDP employees and develop more effective ways of addressing their needs by placing a greater focus on the development and implementation of the internal marketing mix elements to create value for these internal customers. In this way the banks could satisfy and retain the GDP talent pool, benefiting from their creativity, innovation and technical savvy as well as their contribution to organisational success, whilst maximising their return on investment given the substantial financial commitment which accompanies the recruitment and development of graduates. If organisations were to use mechanisms such as internal marketing, it could contribute to higher levels of employee motivation, commitment and satisfaction resulting in happier employees increased productivity and affective commitment resulting in improved employee retention rates.

MINI CASE STUDY QUESTIONS

1. Why is internal marketing an important strategy for banks in South Africa to retain their GDP employees?

2. Is there a relationship between internal marketing and employee retention in the banking sector?

3. Why are GDP employees perceived as the internal market of a bank?.

4. Why is it important to retain GDP employees in the South African banking sector? What benefits does a retention strategy have for these banks?

5. What is implied with the following statement:

   By developing a clearer internal marketing orientation, banks in South Africa could better understand the needs of their GDP employees and develop more effective ways of addressing their needs by placing a greater focus on the development and implementation of the internal marketing mix elements to create value for these internal customers.

6. How can South African banks strengthen GDP employee relationships through an internal marketing strategy? Be critical in your assessment.

One-to-one marketing and mass customisation

Learning outcomes

After studying this chapter, you should be able to:

- explain the term one-to-one (1:1) marketing and differentiate it from traditional marketing;
- identify and explain the advantages of 1:1 marketing for the organisation;
- discuss and apply the steps in the 1:1 marketing process;
- define the term customisation and differentiate between mass customisation and personalisation;
- discuss the preconditions for mass customisation;
- explain three approaches to follow for customisation.

Introduction

In the previous chapter, the marketing of an organisation to its internal stakeholders, its employees, was discussed. It is now important to turn attention to the specific marketing approaches used for developing and maintaining relationships when products and services are offered to specific customers. There are two parts to this chapter: the first deals with 1:1 marketing and the second focuses on mass customisation. The 1:1 marketing approach seeks to identify individual consumers of a product, while mass customisation seeks to adapt products, services and production to meet the specific needs of these identified customers. It is evident that simply focusing on the customer is no longer adequate for organisations to ensure their success; building relationships with customers is much more complex.[1] The first step in creating successful customer relationships involves establishing a 1:1 relationship, after which the second step of mass customisation follows.[2] This twin logic of 1:1 marketing and mass customisation binds organisation and customer.[3] These two steps are regarded as inseparable and both are needed to derive the full benefit from relationship marketing (RM) and customer relationship management (CRM) actions.

Marketing
Definition of 1:1 marketing

One-to-one (1:1) marketing works on the principle of marketing to and targeting a customer individually. Traditionally, the concept of marketing has revolved around selling as many products to as many customers as possible. The use of market segmentation (see Chapter 3) made it possible to sell a single standard product to as many customers as possible, because the marketing method was adapted to suit and attract each segment of customers differently. 1:1 marketing seeks to sell as many products as possible to one specific customer over a period of time and across different product lines.[4] In other words, relationship marketing activities are utilised to deal with customers individually, one customer at a time.[5] This requires a change in mindset, in that the focus is not the number of customers that the organisation seeks to reach with the product; rather, it is the number of products that each individual customer buys that counts. This is known as **the share of customer** (as contrasted with market share in traditional marketing). Hence, 1:1 marketing does not mean interacting on a 1:1 basis with every customer, but rather evaluating each customer and determining a marketing strategy based on the profitability of the group or customer.[6] A differential marketing strategy can be created through an organisation's knowledge on how to customise offerings that suit individuals' needs on a one-to-one basis.[7] Therefore, customers and their activities relating to purchasing products/services should be monitored.[8] An example is given in Box 5.1.

5.1 INCREASING SALES OF FLOWERS THROUGH 1:1 MARKETING

If a florist shop (or other retailer) advertises, it is able to increase the number of products sold. Suppose, however, a florist sends a postcard to customers reminding them of a number of different aspects: 1) that a special event or day is coming up soon; 2) which flowers each customer purchased and sent to another party on this occasion the previous year; and 3) that a telephone call to a specific number will get flowers delivered this year. This would indicate that the florist has a record of all transactions and that it wants to keep the business of its existing customers. It does not mean that new customers are not important; it is, rather, encouraging existing customers to use the service again.[9]

> Learning (and using what is learned) from customers would ensure that organisations not only attract, but also keep, maintain, develop and retain valuable customers.[10]
>
> Thus, this florist focuses on 1:1 marketing, aiming to increase the number of products purchased by every single customer or group of customers.

Contrasting 1:1 marketing with mass marketing

Mass marketing is the marketing that has traditionally taken place where the market consists of people who are relatively similar (ie who are in the same market segment) and who are exposed to high levels of advertising.[11] Mass marketing calls for pushing product/service options (and hoping enough customers embrace these for it to be worthwhile) to increase the number of customers.[12] For these reasons mass marketing is regarded as inflexible.[13]

From Table 5.1, it is clear that mass marketing refers to marketing to the 'masses', where the marketing efforts are aimed at increasing the number of customers. In contrast, 1:1 marketing focuses on increasing the number of products sold to each individual customer.

Table 5.1 Contrasting mass marketing and 1:1 marketing[14]

Mass Marketing	1:1 Marketing
Product managers seek to maximise the sales of their product ie to as many customers as possible	Customer managers seek to sell as many products as possible to one customer at a time
New customers are sought on a continual basis	New business from current customers is also sought
Economies of scale is the focus	Economies of scope is the focus. (This refers to the extent of the knowledge that the organisation has concerning a customer where, the more information an organisation has, the better the quality of the relationship with the customer.)[15]

Advantages/benefits of 1:1 marketing

There are a number of advantages that can be gained from the use of 1:1 marketing by an organisation.

The ability to track defections by customers: In the case of mass products, the manufacturer of a breakfast cereal knows the sales levels in a specific geographical area, but does not know the specific details of each sale. If a customer does not purchase the product for a specific reason (eg bulk cereal purchases for a local sports team), there is no way the organisation can keep track of such defections (ie customers not purchasing a product anymore) or the reasons for the defections. When a customer leaves an organisation it is often only noticeable months after the customer's inactivity.[16] It is only through 1:1 marketing that the organisation can track defections and attempt to find reasons for the defections.[17]

The ability to know customers more deeply and satisfy their needs more adequately: Information concerning the customer can be collected and used to develop products and services that satisfy the needs of the customer better.

Steps in the 1:1 marketing process

The 1:1 marketing process consists of a number of steps.[18]

Step 1: Identify individual customers and establish how they can be reached

It must be possible for the organisation not only to identify its customers, but to specifically identify its valuable and most profitable customers. In identifying such customers, it is necessary to have a great deal of information about them. It is not enough to have their ages, income and other demographic criteria; rather, database management needs to be used in order to collect detailed information. This would include a record of customers' purchasing behaviour as well as their preferences over a period of time. It may require the co-operation of customers to make this information available, as required by the learning relationship (also see Chapter 2 and section of this chapter on **Customisation and the learning relationship**). An example of an organisation that may want to start 1:1 marketing would be a gym that wants to know how often their clients make use of the gym facilities.

Step 2: Differentiate between customers by their needs and values

In order to make the 1:1 marketing experience meaningful, it is necessary that customers can be differentiated according to their needs and the values that make them unique. The differentiation will indicate the most suitable and appropriate strategies that can be used to reach various customers in different ways with the organisation's product.

The strategies selected will be derived from the information that has been collected about customers' habits and preferences. For example, a gym might identify that some clients use the gym to improve their fitness levels, others aim to lose weight, whereas another group of clients use gym facilities to meet friends. For each of these client groups the gym can develop different strategies to attract and maintain them as clients, based on their needs. If it is not possible to differentiate customers, then the need for 1:1 marketing and mass customisation should be questioned. For example, when selling bars of soap, 1:1 marketing and mass customisation might not be necessary. For this low-cost product, it is unnecessary to see which customers use different colours of soap and to design different strategies to attract customers preferring different shades of soap colours.

Step 3: Interact with customers to establish a dialogue

Creating customer dialogue is a vital part of building customer relationships. Without dialogue, no relationship can develop or flourish. The organisation has to determine the best ways of establishing customer contact in order to develop a meaningful dialogue with them. Organisations have traditionally advertised their product in the media or sent customers letters in the mail. Organisations saw this as developing dialogue but unfortunately customers do not perceive this as such. The way that customers have been able to communicate has been through the use of toll-free numbers, as well as writing letters. While this has proved useful to organisations, it does not constitute dialogue.[19] Ongoing, continuous interaction with customers is needed to ensure proper dialogue.[20] Club card and loyalty schemes can be useful in creating the forum for dialogue to take place (see Box 5.2), but in many cases they are used to sell products.

5.2 USE LOYALTY CARDS TO ENSURE DIALOGUE WITH CUSTOMERS

Clicks Club Cards[21] are mainly used to gather information on customers' buying behaviour and to offer an incentive for purchases after a specified time period, such as a 5 per cent discount on a customer's next purchase. However, the Pick n Pay Smart Shopper Card[22] could possibly also be used to stimulate dialogue between Pick n Pay and its customers. Once a Pick n Pay customer receives a Smart Shopper incentive the customer can decide to donate part of the incentive Rand value to a non-profit organisation (eg a charity organisation) of their choice. This will possibly stimulate dialogue between the organisation and its valued customers and, in addition to influencing purchase behaviour, Pick n Pay will gather more information about the customer and their values and possibly adapt some offerings/ marketing methods.

An organisation should have an information strategy in place to create opportunities for dialogue with customers to gather, as well as keep, record of their preferences.[23] To create dialogue, it is necessary that customers and the organisation be prepared to exchange views about much more than just customers' purchasing activities. In other words, an organisation's customers need to be willing to share information about, for example, their disposable income levels, family members' roles and behaviours in purchasing decision-making, and changed product and service preferences. Organisations, on the other hand, should provide details on possible strategies they consider implementing to satisfy specific and changed customer needs. Organisations could in such a way receive valuable input and feedback from customers regarding their marketing mixes and their possible successes. This requires a high degree of participation and commitment from both parties.

> Suppose a customer were to call a toll-free number of a large organisation. This could create the opportunity to exchange views and ask questions about the product's features, like its variations, sizes and packaging. The organisation can use the opportunity to gain information on the customer's preferences and the marketing methods that will most likely attract their attention and convince them to purchase the product. This could be done by asking the customer a number of questions during the course of the phone call.[24] Many consumers have however, abandoned traditional media such as written mail and telephone in favour of email and mainly social media.[25] Therefore, one of the best ways to increase dialogue is to make use of technology, such as websites using the Internet, social media networks (eg Facebook and Twitter), voice mails, emails with electronic questionnaires and SMSes.

Step 4: Customise the organisation's products

Once customers have informed an organisation about their perceived needs, it is necessary to ensure that the organisation has a product that can meet these needs. This forms part of the mass customisation process that the organisation has developed. It may involve customising the product or the service itself. Without this customisation process, the information that has been gathered is of no use and is not being adequately exploited. For example, if a clothing retailer gathers information about which of its 27 national stores a customer most frequently visits, but makes no attempt to differentiate its offerings stores according to specific customer needs, then the information gathered has no value.

Step 5: Make the relationship a continuous learning relationship

This step focuses on the long-term relationship building that takes place between the organisation and its customers. Relationships are not static and as such require continual inputs from both parties if they are to be regarded as mutually beneficial. (The learning relationship is discussed in detail at the end of this chapter in the section on **Customisation and the learning relationship**. It was also dealt with in Chapter 2.)

Having created a 1:1 organisation with a 1:1 view of each customer, it is necessary for the organisation to ensure that the products offered are customised to meet the needs of its various types of customers. As customer preferences change, the organisation needs to update customer information and adapt products and services offered accordingly. For example, a clothing retailer needs to adapt its offerings to its customer group that has progressed from being teenagers to becoming young adults. Moving from one life stage to another would surely change these customers' clothing preferences. Therefore, for this customer group, the organisation needs to adapt its products, and the way in which it offers them.

Mass customisation

Whether or not to adopt the approach of mass customisation is the second critical decision when focusing on building and maintaining customer relationships. Mass customisation is also an approach that affects the entire organisation. It is important to realise that customisation does not only refer to the customisation of products, but also to the customisation of services.

Definition of mass customisation

Mass customisation can be defined as 'the process of providing and supporting profitably individually tailored goods and services, according to each customer's preferences with regard to form, time, place and price'.[26] From this definition, a number of comments can be made about what customisation means to the organisation.

Providing and supporting: It is not enough to provide only the customised product or service, it is also necessary to provide adequate support to the customisation process in order to keep customers' needs satisfied and to ensure that customisation is successful in the long term. This would require the provision of after-sales service and a warranty/guarantee service. For example, when sailing boats are specifically manufactured according to the individual needs of a customer, after-sales service is also offered. This means that the boat manufacturer will support the aspirant sailor with gear, sailing tips and advice as well as make manufacturing adjustments to the boat if required.

Profitable: Without the profits that can accrue from implementing customisation, there is no point in continuing with it. This implies that the customers should not be offered an unlimited number of options of products and services, as this would not be profitable for the organisation.[27] Therefore, the organisation should consider offering only certain options for customisation. For example, it might not be profitable for a furniture manufacturer which offers customised dining room suites to promote free delivery of all customised suits to any designation around the world. It could, however, be profitable if the extra costs incurred to customise the products are covered by a delivery charge.

Individually tailored: Customisation implies that products are designed individually to suit a market of one.[28] If customers are different and have different needs, each individual customer will receive different offers and therefore changes to products/services should be made to suit the needs of the individual.[29] This means that the product is designed specifically to satisfy individual needs that have been identified as part of the 1:1 marketing process.

Goods and services: Both products and services can be customised. Products such as motor vehicles and clothing can be customised to suit the requirements of the customer. For example, the patterns and colours of a motor vehicle's seat covers can be changed according to a client's preference. In the case of leasing an asset or rendering a financial service, adjustments can also be made to suit the needs of the customer. For example, specific banking methods can be personalised for each client, such as a personalised greeting appearing on the screen of an automated teller machine (ATM) each time the client uses the ATM.

Customer preferences: These preferences must be unique so that the organisation is able to develop a product that can satisfy them. If the needs of different customers are too similar, it may not be profitable to customise any item in the product line. (As with the example of selling soap bars given earlier).

Form, time, place and price: Customer needs could differ as to the nature of the desired product, when and where the product is required and/or the price the customer is prepared to pay for the product. The customisation process has to allow this change in form, time, place and/or price to take place.

A further definition can be given that places the concept of mass customisation in a slightly different light. Mass customisation can be regarded as

> *the use of flexible processes and organisational structures to produce varied and often customised products and services at the low cost of a standardised, mass-production system.*[30]

> *Mass customisation can also be defined as a method whereby custom-made products/services are provided to customers at prices consistent with mass production.*[31] *Put another way, mass customisation provides tailor-made products/services at prices that customers are willing to pay.*[32]

The goal of this process is to create a range of products and product options from which the customer can select, and to customise a product from within the range. Mass customisation should provide the benefits of the mass-production system, with the benefits of individualised need satisfaction (see the example that follows).

> Levi Strauss makes use of mass customisation in the sale of its jeans. A customer's requirements (size, style, colour, etc.) are recorded at a Levi's outlet and the information is electronically sent to one of Levi's plants where a custom-fitted pair of jeans is produced.[33]

Mass customisation can also be differentiated from customisation. Customisation is when one product is adapted and delivered to a customer, while mass customisation is when the customisation of products becomes routine for the organisation.[34] In other words, mass customisation occurs when organisations customise offerings on a large scale and quickly.[35]

Customisation and personalisation

It is further necessary to differentiate between customisation and personalisation. Personalisation is defined as

> *the process that enables communication, products and/or services to bear the name of the customer, [thus] adding value to the customer as they position themselves with others.*[36]

Examples of personalisation include putting a customer's name on diaries, caps and clothing, as well as on communications such as letters sent to the customer. Having a name on a letter or on an item does not necessarily mean that the personalisation is worth a great deal to the customer. For personalisation to be favourably perceived by the customer, it has to have value. This means that some personalisation is more valuable than others, depending on the perceptions and expectations of a particular customer.

An example of personalisation is the letters we receive that attempt to sell us roofing, or painting or a variety of household services. We ignore and discard many of these letters, as they do not have value for us as customers at a particular point in time. They might be personal, but they are not personalised.

Building relationships with customers involves much more than sending customers personalised mail or having trained call centre staff.[37] When comparing personalisation and customisation, it is evident that unlike personalisation, customisation has a consistently positive influence on customers' service quality and satisfaction levels.[38] If personalisation is to have a high degree of value to the organisation and, by implication, to the customer, it needs to be combined with customisation.[39] In that way, the customer is prepared to pay for the additional value that has been created specifically to satisfy their unique needs.

Value ⟶ Pay more

Preconditions for mass customisation[40]

It is clear that customisation is an area that requires critical decisions to be made by the organisation. Not all products can be customised to the same extent. Before embarking on customisation within the organisation, care needs to be taken that this is the correct step for the organisation to take. Thus, the organisation needs to answer the question: Should we be customising the product? In order to do that, a number of preconditions need to be examined.

Individual needs and preferences

In many instances, it would appear that customer needs are the same, but closer examination will indicate that their needs are, in fact, different. If there is no significant difference between the needs of people, customisation is not needed. If people's need differ, they will require a product that differs, albeit slightly, to satisfy their different needs. This requires a great deal of research on the part of the organisation to ensure that the nature of the differences in the needs has been determined and that these needs can be profitably satisfied through customisation. As mentioned before, to customise soap bars by having slightly different sizes and colours of soap bars available to different customer groups is probably not worthwhile and will prove to be an unprofitable strategy. However, it is reasonable to assume that different people have different preferences and needs when purchasing a motor vehicle. Preferences and needs possibly differ concerning the vehicle's type, use, size, colour, interior features, price, etc. Therefore, mass customisation in industries such as motor vehicle manufacturing and furniture design and production might be useful and profitable.

Assembling unique offerings

It must be possible for the organisation to develop a unique product offering and for this to be offered to the customer. However, if the organisation is unable to manufacture such a product, it cannot be offered in the marketplace. Another option is that the customer can assemble the unique product, if this cannot be done by the organisation, see the example from IKEA that follows.

IKEA provides furniture that customers can assemble, once they have selected the components that they would like. This gives the individual customer the freedom to select only the components they wants, thereby satisfying their unique needs.

Customer appreciation

Customisation has to satisfy the needs of customers and they will show their appreciation in the support they give to the organisation. The aspects that are customised by the organisation are those that are regarded as important by customers. It is also important to mention that customer appreciation comes from customer readiness for mass customisation; an organisation's amount and approach to customisation will depend on its customers' readiness for customisation. Examples of offerings that will be appreciated by customers include the fabric and design of seats in a motor vehicle, the customisation of which will provide added need satisfaction and so will be supported by customers. However, customers may not appreciate the customisation of other features in vehicles, such as the colour of the fabric used in the boot of the car.[41]

Adaptable technology and processes

The organisation has to have the machinery and equipment that can allow for customisation, eg that will allow the customer to order a specific fabric or seat design and incorporate it into the manufacturing process of the motor vehicle. This technology does not only refer to the ability to manufacture the product, but also to collect information about customers, to interpret the information that has been collected and thus to offer meaningful customisation options that will provide satisfaction to customers and increased profits to the organisation.

Support of intermediaries and suppliers

If an organisation is to implement a mass customisation programme, it will also require the support of the suppliers of raw materials and intermediaries in the distribution channel. There is a need for organisations to apply supplier integration, and therefore to align the development of supplier management and customer relationships.[42] Customisation requires changes in the ordering system, which requires greater adaptability and flexibility from suppliers. Therefore, the flexibility of manufacturing, as needed with customisation, depends on an organisation's supplier network.[43] Intermediaries in the distribution channel have to be prepared to make the customisation options available to the customer, and this may require additional technology and training of retail staff (see the example below).

> Assume that a motor vehicle manufacturer is giving customers options regarding interior seat design and fabric. This will mean that the retail outlet (intermediary) must have the technology to record the preferences of its customers; the suppliers must be prepared to supply different amounts of fabric and parts for the manufacturing of the seats as indicated by customers. If existing suppliers are not prepared to supply differing volumes, the manufacturing organisation may decide to use other suppliers who have greater flexibility.[44] In the same way, if any intermediary cannot record customer preferences or is not willing to offer the customised product to customers, the organisation should consider other retail outlets as partners.

In addition to the above preconditions, there are two more requirements for a mass customisation programme.[45]

- First, the organisation's readiness for such a programme as reflected in the employee attitudes, organisational culture and resources available for the mass customisation programme. In other words, it should be determined whether the organisational structure is conducive for mass customisation.[46] Specific emphasis should be placed on the financial resources of the organisation.

- Second, the competitive environment within which the organisation functions. This refers to the extent of the competition experienced by the organisation. The competitive environment may require that the organisation customise its products in order to sustain its competitive advantage. In other words, a competitive advantage would be obtained if it is the first in its industry to offer customised products. On the other hand, if competitors already offer customisation possibilities to customers, the organisation would also need to offer this option in order to remain competitive.

Approaches to mass customisation

Once it has made the decision in principle to mass customise, there are a number of different approaches that an organisation can take. An organisation can use the differentiation or customisation of its products/services as a basis for creating a competitive advantage.[47] It has to decide the extent to which it wishes to customise the product, service or non-product aspects, as well as the communication sent to the consumer regarding the product. Each of the options has a different effect on the organisation, with some having a limited effect and others a major effect on the way in which the organisation's functions relate to each other. So the decision has been made to customise, but the question is now: What should we customise? Three distinct options exist for organisations (also see Figure 5.1 below):

- **Option 1:** Standard product, standard service and customised communication.

- **Option 2:** Standard product, customised service and customised communication.

- **Option 3:** Customised product, customised service and customised communication.

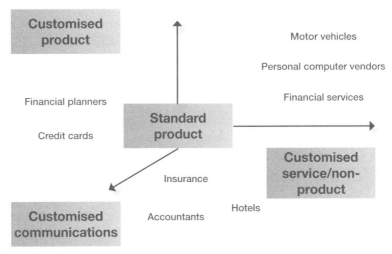

Figure 5.1 Approaches to customisation[48]

Option 1: Standard product, standard service and customised communication

In this option, the organisation keeps the product and the nature of the service standardised, but adapts the communication, customising it to the customer whom it is attempting to reach. In this instance, the organisation is personalising the communication and some organisations attempt to customise in this way. The impact of this personalisation is limited in that it does not affect the entire operation of the organisation (an example of an e-retailer follows on page 126).

Many e-retailers track the products purchased by their customers and adapt their communications to customers accordingly. Bookseller Amazon. com informs its customers electronically when titles by the same author(s) of previous books they purchased are released. Amazon.com is also able to suggest other authors that it believes the customer will enjoy, based on previous orders and communicates this directly to the customer using emails.

Option 2: Standard product, customised service and customised communication

In this option, the product is kept standardised, but the service offered and the communication are customised to the customer's needs. Here the organisation has the ability to adapt aspects of the service offered as well as the communication, but the core product remains the same. Hotels often use this option of mass customisation. The core product that the hotel offers remains constant, while the specific aspects of the service and communication change depending on the needs of the client. For example, breakfast room service is automatically offered if the client prefers this service. In addition, the hotel adapts the way of communication to the client, for example, by emailing the client details of special offers that are running during seasons that the client prefers to visit.

Option 3: Customised product, customised service and customised communication

In this instance, the organisation is able to customise the product, the service and the communication that are directed to the customer (see the example from the motor industry below). This places a great challenge on the organisation, as it has to be able to deliver the options that it offers to its customer. This implies that the organisation's inter-functional co-ordination and co-operation have to be at a high level.

In the case of a motor vehicle, for example, the customer is able to choose the components of the product (product customisation) and the leasing arrangement that they wants (service customisation), and the communication is aimed specifically at him/her, for example via telephone calls (communication customisation).

Selecting the appropriate degree of customisation

In customising the products, service components and communication, a decision regarding the extent to which each of these areas can be customised needs to be made. An organisation needs to examine various factors when deciding on the degree of customisation that it will offer. There are five main areas that need to be examined before implementing customisation, in order to determine the degree of customisation.[49]

The organisation's mission (the mandate fit)

The mission and vision that the organisation has committed itself to in the marketplace require investigation. The mission reflects the reason for the existence of the business and so it describes the way in which the organisation operates. In compiling its mission statement, the organisation is indicating the reasons for which a certain degree of customisation is required (an example is given in Box 5.3).

5.3 MISSION STATEMENTS GIVE DIRECTION FOR CUSTOMISATION IDEAS

The mission statement for a financial services company might be as follows:

> To develop comprehensive financial services to our clients through their life cycle by developing relationships based on mutual trust and the harnessing of best-of-breed products, services and technology to ensure the highest level of client service.'

This will reflect the degree of customisation that the organisation regards as appropriate for the industry in which it functions. In other words, this financial services company will customise their offerings to such an extent (degree) that they see fit to accomplish their mission statement specifications of mutual trust, best-of-breed offerings and technology with the highest level of service.

Woolworths' mission statement reads as follows:

> We, as passionate retailers, understand and lead our customers through excellence and a deep knowledge of our products and services and the world we live in.

The 'Woolworths difference' is displayed through the organisation's values: quality and style, value, service, innovation, integrity, energy and sustainability.[50]

Its mission statement and values clearly shows Woolworths' focus on customisation as they aim to be 'different', by living up to expectations as set by their mission statement and proclaimed values.

Customer feasibility

The organisation has to carry out research into the needs of customers and the components of the product that they would like customised. Research will indicate the nature of the customisation customers want and the importance of this customisation to them. In order to do this, focus group research or behavioural segmentation can be used. This will enable people who exhibit similar behaviour to be conveniently grouped together. Each group's members would indicate their preferences with respect to the product, as well as the components of the product that they value. If customers do not value customisation of the product, customisation will not be worthwhile. However, if specific components of the product can be adapted to specific client preferences, customisation will be a valuable offering.

Competitive advantage

One of the ways in which organisations can show a competitive advantage is through the implementation of customisation. Mass customisation can provide competitive advantage in three main areas:[51]

- Customers have wanted customisation for many years, but organisations have not been able to provide it or have been unwilling to provide it.

- Many organisations have yet to regard a 'segment of one' (where every single customer is actually a separate market segment and should be treated as such) as being viable and, as a result, they have not developed a plan to deal with such a segment.

- Mass customisation is difficult to implement successfully and as a result, organisations have not made a great deal of progress in implementing such a strategy.

In order to gain competitive advantage, it is necessary to examine the actions of the organisation's competitors and determine how the organisation wants to go about counteracting these actions in the marketplace. It is also necessary to determine the extent to which the competitors have employed customisation, as well as the extent of their success with it.

Operational feasibility

Once the organisation has determined that there is the need among its customers for customisation, and that this will provide a sustainable competitive advantage, it is necessary to ensure that it is possible for the organisation to actually carry out this customisation, ie whether the organisation has the ability to customise its products in the way that customers want. The machinery and equipment must be able to cope with the pressures that customisation will place on them, as will the staff employed in this function. Any changes that have to be brought about will have a cost implication, which can affect the profitability of the organisation and hence the desirability of the customisation.

Financial feasibility

The financial feasibility or profitability that the customisation will bring to the organisation needs to be considered. Before customisation is implemented, it is essential that the organisation calculates the costs associated with it, as well as the potential benefits that can accrue to the organisation as a result of the customisation.

Benefits will be in the form of increased sales, as customers will be able to select the customised components, products and/or services that will best satisfy their needs. This will have an impact on their life-time value contribution to the organisation. This will also create the opportunity to bring out new variations of the customised product in the marketplace. It can also attract new customers to the organisation, increasing sales.

The costs associated with customisation are found in the changes in the technology that have to be made, the training of staff that has to take place and the changes in supply arrangements. The costs, both capital and operational, associated with customisation are very large. If mass customisation would lead to unsatisfactorily large additional costs for an organisation, a mass customisation strategy might not be worthwhile.[52] The organisation should implement customisation at the level that it can afford and make the necessary adjustments.

Customisation and the learning relationship

The learning relationship (also see Chapter 2) is a term used to describe a relationship between the customer and the organisation where the organisation gets 'smarter and smarter' with every contact made with a customer.[53] Learning from customers can ensure links and ties with customers which may result in long-term profitable customer relationships.[54] In other words, learning-based and evolving relationships are formed between the organisation and its customers.[55] This means that customers are continually teaching the organisation which products they like and the nature of their consumption patterns. A learning relationship is a continuous connection with interactions between organisation and customer, to enhance collaborative efforts to continuously meet the customer's changing needs.[56]

This relationship works in that customers tell the organisation what they want through interaction and feedback. The organisation uses this information to adapt product specifications to satisfy the needs of customers, and then remembers the specifications.

For an organisation to create a learning relationship with customers, there are two requirements that have to be met:[57]

- The organisation must be a successful customiser of its products. It must have the technology to be able to design further customisations, while also having the capacity to remember the preferences of its customers.

- Customers must be prepared to put in the effort to teach the organisation their specifications and preferences. An organisation's ability to form learning relationships with customers will depend on its ability to source information about customers.[58]

Unless the organisation continues learning about its customers (and vice versa), the relationship will not continue developing and growing, and the benefits that may accrue to the organisation will be reduced.

Summary

The purpose of this chapter was to examine the concepts of 1:1 marketing and mass customisation, and the relationship that exists between them.

After having defined 1:1 marketing, the difference between it and the mass (traditional) marketing approach was examined. The steps that make up the 1:1 marketing process were also identified and discussed.

Mass customisation was defined and contrasted with personalisation as a strategy. In order to implement mass customisation, there are a number of preconditions that have to be met. Each of these preconditions was examined, as well as its effect on the customisation process. A number of customisation approaches or strategies were discussed and the aspects to consider when selecting the most appropriate customisation strategy were clarified. The chapter concluded with a brief discussion on the necessary learning relationship between an organisation and its customers.

DISCUSSION QUESTIONS

1. Explain the term '1:1 marketing'.
2. Explain the difference between the terms 'market share' and 'share of customer'.
3. Explain the term 'economies of scope'.
4. Explain the difference between economies of scope and economies of scale. Why is this an important difference in the case of 1:1 marketing?

5. Explain the difference between mass marketing and 1:1 marketing.

6. Discuss the steps in the 1:1 marketing process and apply it to a practical example.

7. Explain the term 'mass customisation'.

8. Differentiate customisation and mass customisation from personalisation.

9. Discuss the preconditions that are necessary for mass customisation to be implemented by an organisation.

10. Explain the three mass customisation strategies that an organisation can consider.

11. Explain the factors that affect the decision as to what extent an organisation should consider customisation.

12. Explain the relationship between customisation and an organisation's competitive advantage.

13. Explain what is meant by a learning relationship. How does it impact on the customisation of the product/service of an organisation?

Mini case study 1[59, 60, 61]

The motor vehicle industry in South Africa is very diverse. A number of manufacturers have local plants and they are supplemented by those who provide motor vehicles that have been imported from foreign sources. Motor vehicle sales tend to be driven by the economy, because of the price of vehicles and the fact that they are acquired using credit facilities. It is these credit facilities that enable sales of motor vehicles to continue. Credit facilities are not only crucial in the sale of new cars, but the bulk of the financing granted on motor vehicles is on used (second-hand) motor vehicles. The actual motor trade sales increased by 16.4 per cent year-on-year in January 2011 and used vehicle sales accounted for 12.2 per cent of this increase. In addition, during the last quarter of 2011, used vehicle sales gained ground compared to new car sales. As at April 2013, used vehicle sales were also up 9 per cent compared with a year earlier.

The used vehicle market has changed in a number of ways. The negative perceptions associated with used cars is changing, as seen in the use of terms such as 'pre-owned' or 'pre-loved' to describe used cars. The way in which these vehicles are acquired is also changing. The use of technology makes it possible to search for vehicles online by using the internet, and credit approvals can also be done online.

Customers wanting to purchase used vehicles are evaluated, by vehicle finance organisations, using the same criteria. Financing a vehicle up to five years old has the same degree of risk as for a new vehicle, while the risk associated with financing older vehicles increases. As a result of this risk, the time period over which older vehicles are financed is reduced.

MINI CASE STUDY 1 QUESTIONS

1. Is it feasible for an organisation financing used vehicles to make use of a 'segment of one' in its marketing? Motivate your answer adequately.

2. Is it a good idea for an organisation financing used vehicles to implement mass customisation? Motivate your answer adequately.

3. Explain three ways in which an organisation financing used vehicles could customise its service.

4. Explain how an organisation financing used vehicles can develop a learning relationship with its clients.

Mini case study 2

Cape Jungle Kids – customised jungle gyms[62]

Making sure there is something for everyone!

Cape Jungle Kids, local Cape Town manufacturer of children's jungle gyms (wooden, outdoor play structures), offers their clients the freedom to cater for their own needs. Cape Jungle Kids starts by providing a basic jungle gym that consists of a platform where four components can be added. The client selects which and how platforms are added. A client is charged for each individual component added, according to the client's individual needs and preferences.

Clients can select from the organisation's basic set of floor layouts and choose to add components from a variety of components on offer. However, a client can also design their own layout which suits their needs, space and budget. For example, clients can link platforms or design around their outdoor trees to create their own jungle gym structures. Components and changes to components which clients can incorporate into their jungle gym designs include the following: swings, slides, different colour shades of paint, different structure sizes and heights and different materials to be used, for example rubber swings versus plastic swings.

To facilitate the customised designing and manufacturing, Cape Jungle Kids also encourages clients to provide sketches or photos of their desired designs. Before the jungle gym production commences, Cape Jungle Kids offers to visit a client's site to see whether the designed jungle gym is appropriate for the site.

An added bonus of being a client of Cape Jungle Kids, is that the organisation is the most professional timber jungle gym builder in the Western Cape and guarantees their products for a year.

MINI CASE STUDY 2 QUESTIONS

1. Which approach/option to mass customisation is used by Cape Jungle Kids? Motivate your answer.

2. Is Cape Jungle Kids relying on traditional marketing or 1:1 marketing? Motivate your answer. In addition, provide an extract from the case study to motivate your discussion.

3. One of the steps in the 1:1 marketing process is to differentiate between customers by their needs and values. Do you think it is possible for Cape Jungle Kids to do this? Why? Provide practical evidence in your answer.

4. Is there evidence in this case study that Cape Jungle Kids attempts to interact with customers to establish a dialogue? Provide extracts from the case study to support your answer.

5. Provide a practical example of how Cape Jungle Kids can implement personalisation in the offering of their jungle gym products.

6. Which approach/option to mass customisation is used by Cape Jungle Kids? Motivate your answer.

7. Provide two practical ways in which Cape Jungle Kids can specifically customise its service.

Business-to-business (B2B) marketing

Learning outcomes

After studying this chapter, you should be able to:

- contrast business and customer/consumer markets;
- identify the conditions that are appropriate for the development of relationships between organisations;
- explain the factors that impact on the efficiency of the organisation;
- contrast the three types of relationship exchanges that exist within business-to-business (B2B) marketing;
- comment on the relationships that organisations have with their business partners (suppliers, intermediaries and competitors);
- explain how relationships can be built with co-venture partners;
- explain how e-commerce can be used as a tool in B2B marketing.

Introduction

One of the most important relationships that an organisation can have takes place with other organisations. There are a number of different roles that other businesses can play within an organisation and it is therefore necessary for the organisation to develop relationships with them.

For example, the way that consumers listen to music has changed. It is no longer necessary to purchase a CD but many people listen to music via a service known as Spotify on their mobile phones. This service is valuable to consumers, but for this service to be offered, it is necessary that the mobile phone provider and Spotify Ltd develop a relationship that provides maximum benefit for the consumer.

B2B markets and their composition

Consumer and industrial products

Consumer products are those products that are purchased by consumers for final consumption. Examples of these products include toothpaste, chocolates and beer.

Industrial products are those products that are purchased by an organisation with the intention of using them to produce other goods and services. A number of different types of industrial products can be identified.[1]

- **Mining products:** These are products that are taken from the earth, such as coal and iron ore, and that will be processed further.

- **Part-processed materials and components:** Further processing is generally necessary to use these products further, such as flour in baking products. Components are often assembled without any further changes being made to them, such as spark plugs and buttons.

- **Installations:** This includes capital equipment, buildings and heavy machinery, which are all expensive and which require large sums to be invested.

- **Accessory equipment:** This is equipment that is needed to make it possible to produce a final product, although it does not form part of the final product.

- **Operating supplies:** These are used either directly or indirectly in the production process, for example, cleaning supplies, stationery and lubricants for machinery.

Differences between consumer and business markets

Businesses deal with final consumers, yet one of their most important contacts is with other organisations. While it is necessary to develop relationships with both parties, the nature of the relationship is different as they involve different things. There are fundamental differences between doing business with consumers and doing business with other organisations. These differences are linked to the nature of these businesses and are reflected in Table 6.1 on the following page.

Table 6.1 Final consumers and business consumers: a contrast[2]

Final consumers	Business consumers
Goods are purchased for final consumption, and include speciality, shopping and convenience products.	Goods are purchased for production purposes and include components, accessory equipment and installations.
There are numerous consumers who individually are not able to exercise an influence on the organisation.	The market structure differs in that there are a few large consumers who exercise a great influence over the product.
Generally, use is made of intermediaries such as wholesalers and retailers.	The distribution channel for B2B activities is usually direct from the supplier to the organisation.
Consumers repurchase for a variety of reasons, which are as diverse as the people themselves.	There are a variety of purchasing situations such as straight re-buying, modified re-buying or new task buying.
Consumers make decisions regarding the suitability of the products to be purchased.	Purchasing decisions are usually made by a number of people who all have input into the final decision.
Customers are influenced by a wide variety of factors such as demographics and psychographic factors.	Organisations have a range of factors that they evaluate including price and quality on offer.
Close relationships are less likely to develop, as customers are more fickle and more likely to switch brands.	Close relationships are more likely to develop, as organisations are recognised for their importance.
Little likelihood of reciprocity of purchase.	Reciprocity is relatively common between organisations.
Mutual value creation is based on characteristics that are personal to the customer such as size and fit.	Mutual value creation is possible, as the businesses work together (as in the case of Intel and computer manufacturers).
Products such as low involvement products are one-way relationships.	There is higher interest in the relationships, though routine purchases may also be one-way relationships.

The nature of CRM in B2B markets

The question to ask is whether the supplier or any other business wants a relationship with the manufacturing organisation. For a relationship to develop, it is necessary to ensure that the relationship is wanted, and then go about developing this relationship. Examples of relationships include those with bankers, venture partners and competitors of the organisation.

Appropriate conditions for relationships between organisations

Six essential conditions can be identified that influence the development of a relationship between organisations.[3] These conditions are interdependent and together impact on the desirability of the relationship.

1. **Asymmetry:** This refers to the situation where one organisation can exert power over the other organisation. This would encourage the 'dominated' organisation to develop alternative links that will reduce the power being exercised by the more powerful organisation. This would enable the organisation to alter the balance of power.

> Assume Company X is the sole supplier of a specific raw material in South Africa. This will give it a great deal of power in the marketplace, as there is no other supplier that other companies can use.

2. **Stability:** Relationships can be developed to decrease the instability experienced within the external environment. Organisations enter into long-term contracts in order to ensure a stable environment with respect to prices and delivery agreements.

> Many transport companies enter into long-term contracts with other businesses because of the size of the financial investment that transport requires. This means that a vehicle is purchased specifically for a specific contract and the transport company agrees to carry out the work at a specific price.

3. **Legitimacy:** Being associated or having a relationship with a large, well-known organisation may improve the reputation of the smaller organisation. It can also reduce the checks that need to be carried out on such a small company, such as credit checks. This can increase the desirability of the relationship.

> For a small business, getting a contract to supply a well known retailer such as Woolworths or Clicks may make it easier to obtain not only financing, but also better credit terms.

4. **Necessity:** Organisations are required to use certain services such as those of auditors and accountants. Organisations tend to use the same accountants and auditors for extended periods of time, thereby developing a relationship with them.

5. **Reciprocity:** This refers to the relationship that develops where one organisation buys the goods of the other and vice versa.[4] This enables both organisations to pursue common goals, so that both organisations benefit. This in turn contributes to the development of a relationship.

6. **Efficiency:** This is an internal contingency and refers to the way in which business is carried out in an organisation. There are three aspects that affect the efficiency within an organisation, as listed below.

a. *Types of costs associated with transactions*

A variety of costs can be identified when carrying out transactions. Co-ordination costs are those costs incurred in investigating other organisations to determine whether to do business with them, such as investigating their creditworthiness. Motivation costs refer to the lack of completeness that an organisation may experience when carrying out an investigation. Another type of motivation cost occurs when one party shows that it is not fully committed to the relationship, which implies that its promises may not be kept.

b. *The level of transaction costs*

The level of transaction costs is affected by a number of factors, including opportunistic behaviour, moral hazard and bounded rationality. Opportunistic behaviour refers to the situation where one organisation exploits the situation to its own advantage, as there are terms and conditions within the contract that have not been met. Moral hazard exists when the other party in the agreement monitors the agreement and so ensures that it is not exploited. (Should the other party attempt to do so, it will hesitate to do so, as it is aware of being monitored within the terms of the agreement.) Bounded rationality comes about with the inability to factor in all possible outcomes within a situation and so these situations have not been described totally within the contract.

c. *The dimensions of transactions*

Transactions have the following seven dimensions that affect their nature, which in turn affects the nature of the relationship between the organisations:

- **Asset specificity:** This is when a transaction requires a specific item in order to enter into the agreement. This will also affect the management of the contract over time, as the investment in assets will require that a certain price level be maintained.

  > In the case of a high degree of asset specificity, where an organisation has spent a great deal of money on acquiring the required assets, it will only do so if it is sure that it will win the contract from the other organisation.

- **Frequency of transactions:** If it is a regular supply arrangement, a traditional contract of agreement will be drawn up. Should the contract be a once-off contract of high value, the organisation may spend money on drawing up a specific contract in order to specify the actions of both parties.

- **Duration of transactions:** If transactions take place over long periods of time, the relationship that develops is a much deeper one, and so an understanding develops between the parties.

- **Complexity of the transaction:** When a product has been customised, costs can be added to the transaction by making minor changes or adjustments.

- **Monitoring of a contract:** Because it is not possible to predict every action of a party in a relationship, the contract has to be monitored in order to ensure that both parties fulfil the terms and conditions associated with their activities.

- **The measurement of actual performance:** This is required to determine whether the parties are performing as they are required to perform. The measurement of the actual performance has to be accurate, while also indicating the existence of any possible problems, should they exist. Measuring the actual performance must be done in a cost-effective way in order to maximise efficiency.

- **The interrelatedness (connectedness) of transactions:** Decisions on the purchase of one item can affect the purchase of another item and this makes the purchase decision a connected decision. Not all decisions are connected and the degree of connectedness makes it necessary to examine the decision-making variables connected with each decision.

> Thinking about the relationship between Spotify Ltd and any mobile phone company, these seven factors all play a role. To be able to make music available to mobile phone owners, it is necessary that both parties have the necessary copyright licenses in place, which requires a financial investment by both parties. They also have to agree how the financing of the agreement will work. As it will be a long-term agreement, a regular contract will be drawn up. As it impacts the mobile phone company's customers, it is important that all the terms and conditions be clarified before the contracts are signed. Over time, both parties will monitor the agreement and functioning of the relationship. If necessary they will bring about changes and improvements to the situation.

Types of relationships in B2B

When building relationships with other business organisations, a decision has to be made concerning the nature of the relationship that will be developed. Three main business relationships exist. These three possible business relationships could be placed on a continuum, with a transactional relationship on one end of the continuum and a collaborative relationship on the other end.

Transactional exchanges refer to the anonymous purchasing that takes place between people, as in the case of the purchase of stationery and cleaning materials. In the example of stationery, each person obtains what they want (the seller obtains money and the buyer obtains stationery). The transactional exchange centres on the timely exchange of basic goods at competitive prices.[5] These exchanges are formal and competitive bidding can be used to determine the best prices.

At the opposite end of the continuum are the *collaborative exchanges* that develop between organisations. This collaboration is such that both parties work together to form very close links and relationships so that both parties are able to derive the maximum long-term benefits from the relationship. This will include joint problem solving and information sharing, and there will be a high degree of commitment from both parties (as shown in the example below).

> In the example of a large cement organisation that transports its goods for export by rail, it has an arrangement with the rail company that rail trucks will be supplied at a particular time and at a particular price. Should both parties complete their tasks as originally specified, the cement company receives quality service while the rail company has an income from its client. If the cement company does not fill the trucks within a specified period, it is charged a higher price because of the new arrangements that are required from the rail company. If the trucks are not delivered by a certain time, the cement company can obtain a discount on the transport costs.

Value-added exchanges lie between transactional and collaborative exchanges on the continuum. Here the aim of the organisation changes from that of finding clients to retaining clients and so building a relationship with them.[6] This requires that the business investigates its client's needs and adapts its product to suit these needs.

As organisations move on the relationship spectrum, the nature of the relationship will change. In the case of collaborative exchanges, the development and maintenance of trust is vital, as is the commitment of the parties to the relationship. Relationship commitment can be defined as the belief by a partner that an ongoing relationship is important and so it requires maximum efforts to maintain the relationship.)[7]

Relationships with specific B2B markets

Suppliers

One of the key relationships that organisations build is with their suppliers. The supply chain illustrates the wider network of role-players – from those who supply the raw materials, to those who carry out the entire transformation process, through to the consumer.[8] Here, organisations do not compete with each other on an individual basis; rather, they compete according to the efficiency within the supply chain. This means that if an organisation wants to increase its competitiveness in the marketplace, it can do so through developing close relationships with suppliers of the raw materials and services, in order to make its supply chain more efficient.

The importance of suppliers to the organisation can be seen in a number of areas:[9]

- the quality of the product supplied, which affects the quality of the final product;
- the quantity of the product supplied, which affects the availability of the product in the marketplace;
- the price, which affects the final selling price in the marketplace; and
- the timing, which affects the product schedule according to which manufacturing can take place.

There has been a change in the marketplace as to how organisations treat their suppliers. In the past, organisations tended to keep their suppliers 'on their toes' and did not commit themselves too much, in order to avoid giving suppliers any power over them. This has changed to reflect a higher degree of collaboration and co-operation between the suppliers and organisations. Co-makership is a strategy that organisations are implementing in order to improve relationships with suppliers. Co-makership is the decision to limit the number of suppliers with whom the organisation will do business.[10] This results in closer relationships developing with the suppliers, as there is a greater degree of commitment and involvement between suppliers and organisations. This reduces the friction in the relationship and replaces it with a co-operative spirit that results in greater profitability for all parties.

The reason for this change is the understanding that greater benefits can accrue for both parties as a result of this approach. The organisation is able to provide more information about its customers and this enables the suppliers to provide products that are more suitable to the customers. This benefits both the suppliers and the organisation from a customer satisfaction perspective as well as from a financial perspective. This also enables the organisation to develop products with the supplier for introduction into the market.[11]

The importance of developing sound relationships with suppliers is seen in the amount of attention given and the money invested in developing information and other systems that can improve the delivery of products to the organisation from the supplier.

> It is not necessary to have a computer to access the Internet – smartphones have become important. An Internet retailer (Kalahari.net) has partnered with Cell C to sell a dual SIM Android smartphone for this purpose.[12] The gobii smartphone is 'cheaper but does not compromise on quality'.

Box 6.1 gives an example of a company that has invested in such strong relationships with its suppliers.

6.1 WOOLWORTH'S GOOD FOOD JOURNEY

Woolworths has a policy of aggressively sourcing local (South African) suppliers who meet their stringent requirements. The 'good food journey' that Woolworths is undertaking focuses on sustainability from an environmental perspective, while supporting suppliers who act responsibly towards their communities and the environment. An example of this is Fruits Unlimited.[13]

Another supplier to Woolworths is Handri Conradie, who supplies soft-eating dried fruit. He is of the opinion that suppliers will be successful if they are able to take advantage of economies of scale while also being efficient in their operations.[14]

In the case of CRM, one of the important suppliers is the supplier of the database management system that is used by the organisation. Through data mining and effective data management, an organisation can examine its customer database and so make sense of the information that it has collected. An example of this is given in Box 6.2 on the following page (see also Chapter 10 on technology that supports CRM).

Specific guidelines can be proposed regarding how to develop a relationship with suppliers. Many of the guidelines are common to relationships in general, such as communication, trust and commitment. Also, databases can be developed to the advantage of both parties, while sharing market and customer information can also improve the relationship.

6.2 COLLECTING AND USING INFORMATION FROM CUSTOMERS

In the case of banks and retail stores, they both have accounts and charge cards that provide them with information about their customers. The extensive information that they have must be interpreted if it is to be used to the advantage of the organisations. This information will not only clarify the nature of each customer and their activities, but it can be used to refine the supply chain. This may result in removing the suppliers of certain goods and replacing them with other suppliers, or suppliers of products that will better satisfy customer needs.

Intermediaries

Intermediaries are those organisations in the distribution channel who help the product get to the marketplace. They include retailers, wholesalers and agents who have contact with customers.[15] The key to the success of an organisation can be found in the supply chain, of which the intermediaries are an important part. To improve its relationship with intermediaries, the organisation needs to treat them as it would treat its best customers, and not just as part of the process. This means that all strategies that are used in dealings with final consumers are used in building relationships with intermediaries.[16]

The complication in the process comes from the fact that the goals of the intermediary and the organisation may be different, making the relationship more challenging.

Keys to managing the relationship with intermediaries are as follows:[17]

- Planning undertaken by both the organisation and the intermediary can help to improve the relationship. This can support the intermediary, who tends to have a less-developed planning process (than the organisation).

- Channel-member profitability also needs the attention of the organisation. It can develop ways of improving profits, while the intermediary can alert the organisation to additional marketing opportunities.

- Respect and trust are further components of this process. As in any relationship, without trust between the two parties, the relationship will not develop and improve. This includes clear and open communication between the parties.

- The intermediary is the customer, but is often treated as if they were more of a nuisance than a customer. This would indicate that the organisation does not have power over the intermediary. But despite the fact that both the organisation and the intermediary are independent organisations, there is a high degree of interdependence between them.

- Keep the focus on the final customer. Despite both (the organisation and the intermediary) having specific goals that they wish to achieve, the focus needs to remain on the final consumers and the satisfaction of their needs.

Competitors

The concept of building relationships with competitors sounds strange to many people. Competitors are other organisations who sell similar goods and services to similar consumers.[18] Competitors are either direct competitors, or they are involved in selling a substitute product that will also satisfy customers' needs. Initially, the idea that you build a relationship with another organisation that is seeking to attract your existing customers, does not sound like good business sense. However, when organisations take on their competitors in the marketplace, a situation often arises that is not to the long-term benefit of anyone. This situation could include price wars, loss of reputation and the wasting of organisational resources. This conflict has the potential to undermine the entire industry, as the confidence of customers is also shaken, and the profits in the industry can also suffer.[19] If an industry is unregulated, cut-throat price competition may take place, resulting in bankruptcies among smaller organisations[20] (see Box 6.3).

6.3 THE EFFECT OF COMPETITION AMONG AIRLINE COMPANIES

The domestic airline industry in South Africa has been experiencing difficulties for some time with respect to profits and sustainability. New airlines have come and gone. Examples of these include (the original) Sun Air and Phoenix. The South African airline industry has seen a number of new airlines such as 1time and Kulula as well as Mango and Velvet Sky but 1time and Velvet Sky have since closed down. It has been suggested that the South African market could support another low-cost operator, and FlySafair was scheduled to introduce a service between Johannesburg and Cape Town in the second half of 2014.[21]

Before making a decision regarding relationships with competitors, the organisation must ensure that it is fully informed about the products and target markets of their competitors.[22] This will ensure that it can anticipate its competitors' actions and plan its own response in advance. Linked to this is the importance of ensuring that marketing information is continually gathered about competitors and their planned actions.

Collecting information concerning competitors will ensure that the organisation can determine a 'competitor profile' for each of its competitors. This will help determine how its competitors will react to its own strategies. From this competitor profile, the organisation will know which of its competitors are who will:

- fight to the death;
- engage in a counter-attack (and the form this will take); and
- ignore the actions of any competitor.

From the information gathered about competitors, it will be clear what their various' strengths and weaknesses are and how they can be exploited.[23]

Co-venture partners and strategic alliances

An alliance is defined as *an arrangement for organised and agreed relations between parties*, such as exists between customers, partners and competitors.[24] These alliances mean that co-operation takes place between the parties in the alliance.

> Examples in the airline industry of strategic alliances are numerous. Examples include British Airways and Comair, SAA and Lufthansa, and SAA and Qantas. Star Alliance is an example of such an alliance among airlines. Members include TAP, United Airlines, US Airways, Air Canada, SAA and Lufthansa. These alliances have been forged in the interests of both profitability and sustainability, while satisfying customer needs. Airlines are able to service routes which, on their own, would not be profitable.

Co-venture partners provide an organisation with the opportunity of exploiting a situation without having to carry all the risk and expense itself. It enables the organisation to exploit synergies that exist between the two parties. These relationships are not necessarily traditional relationships, as the partners may be involved in selling related products and services. By developing the partnership, access can be obtained to another group of customers. Organisations can also have help in obtaining economies of scale, as well as in sharing risk.[25]

An example of creating partnerships is seen in the alliances Xerox has forged with other companies. In the UK, Europe and Africa, Xerox has allied itself with Rank, while in India and Japan, it has allied itself with Fuji and Modi.[26]

What makes a successful strategic alliance? Two critical success factors can contribute to a successful relationship:[27]

- **A close working relationship:** Without a close working relationship between the parties, long-term success is not possible. This means that the parties are required to communicate frequently and deal with important issues that affect both parties.

- **Integrating points of contact:** The approach that the organisations use must be flexible in that they must be able to incorporate changes in the environment and in circumstances that have been identified. The integration between the two organisations needs to be strategic, tactical, operational, interpersonal and form part of their culture. By developing these interactions, the organisations will be able to ensure that the relationship continues to develop and to achieve the goals that have been set by both organisations.

Managing relationships effectively

There is little point in establishing relationships with other businesses and then not managing them effectively. As with all relationships, it is necessary to put in effort on a continual basis to ensure that the relationship stays positive. This indicates that relationship management is a continual process with which managers are engaged.

There are four requirements that indicate the extent to which a relationship is being effectively managed:[28]

- **Awareness:** It is important that the manager has an awareness of the problems and opportunities that form part of the relationship, as well as of the expectations of the other party in the relationship.

- **Assessment:** This refers to the continual evaluation of the resources that the organisation has to offer in terms of resources that are needed to get to the destination that both parties are aiming for.

- **Accountability:** To ensure that relationships are maintained, it is necessary to establish reporting procedures regarding the state of the relationship, as well as the performance of the relationship.

- **Actions:** All actions must be evaluated in terms of their potential impact on the organisational relationship. This means that the consequences of any action need to be determined so as to ensure they do not harm the relationship in any way.

e-Commerce as a tool in managing business relationships

Probably one of the most widely used tools for managing business relationships is the use of e-commerce and electronic sites to facilitate interaction between the partners. It is estimated that 90 per cent of all e-commerce carried out online in 1999 involved B2B deals and they were worth approximately \$553 billion.[29] e-Commerce is not about the sales that can be generated, but must be used to make a connection with business partners. Before buying a product, 93 per cent of businesses start looking on the Internet for a product that could satisfy their need.[30] It is also not about a transaction, but is rather a process with which the organisation is involved. The e-commerce forum enables organisations to reach new markets at lower costs.[31] It is not just the Internet that affects organisational customers, but also social media and social networks. It is suggested that 37 per cent of buyers (decision-makers) look for information on social media and 48 per cent make use of social networks.[32]

There are a number of factors that need to be evaluated when examining a particular exchange (B2B site). These factors include:[33]

- **Reputation:** Being a reputable exchange means that organisations can make use of the exchange with a high degree of trust. Operating in an online environment is more risky for any organisation, so having a good reputation is very important for any exchange.

- **An efficient system:** It is important that the exchange is able to present detailed information in a way that enables both parties to get the type of information they need (as well as the amount of information necessary). The system must also be adaptable to changing environmental conditions in various industries.

- **A focused exchange:** Exchanges tend to focus on specific industries, so it is really important to ensure that the exchange is appropriate for the products and industry in which the organisation is operating.

- **Be value-adding**: Organisations make use of exchanges in order to add value to their operations and the exchange needs to be able to do that. This value could be related to ease of use, accessibility or flexibility, depending on the industry.

- **A compatible way of doing business:** Exchanges need to be aligned with the other activities and relationships that develop within the organisation or within an industry. Being involved in an exchange should not imply that a completely new way of operating is required.

See Box 6.4 for more information on exchange websites.

6.4 EXCHANGE WEBSITES: A NEW WAY OF DOING BUSINESS

Agentrics came about through a merger of WorldWide Retail Exchange (WWRE) and GlobalExchangeNetwork (GNX) in 2005. They describe themselves as a 'global provider of business solutions for the supply and demand chain'.[34] It was founded by the world's top retailers and strives to provide greater efficiency in the supply chain. Manufacturers associated with this website include Kraft, GlaxoSmithKline and Panasonic while their customers include Carrefour, Tesco and Walgreen's.

Summary

B2B is one of the most important relationships that an organisation can build with another party. It is important to take note of the differences that exist between final customers and business customers and the impact that this has on relationship building. Not all businesses want to develop relationships, and the situation must be conducive to the building of such relationships. Relationships can be built with a number of other businesses, including intermediaries, suppliers and co-venture partners. Tools used in this building process include e-commerce.

DISCUSSION QUESTIONS

1. Explain the term 'B2B'.
2. Explain the term 'industrial products' and their components.
3. Explain three main differences between final consumers and business consumers. .

4. Name six conditions that can be used to determine the desirability of relationships between organisations.

5. 'Organisational efficiency is a very important component of relationship building.' Explain this statement, indicating whether you agree with it or not.

6. Explain the term 'relationship spectrum', using a diagram to illustrate your answer.

7. Why do you think an organisation should build relationships with its intermediaries?

8. 'The relationship with competitors is a very important one to build.' Explain this statement, indicating whether or not you agree with it.

9. Discuss the nature of a strategic alliance. Illustrate the importance of this relationship.

10. Which critical success factors can determine whether an alliance is successful?

11. Which strategies can managers use to effectively manage a B2B relationship?

12. What is meant by e-commerce? How can it be used to develop relationships with other organisations?

Mini case study

Transport is an important part of any supply chain and decisions associated with transport are important for a product. Deciding on a logistics provider to transport raw materials, work-in-process or finished goods is important.

There are a number of organisations providing an integrated logistics solution, meaning that it includes warehousing, transportation as well as freight forwarding (specifically for imported products). One of these organisations is Unitrans Supply Chain Solutions (USCS), a subsidiary of KAP.[35] KAP is an international group that delivers both products and services to organisation in South Africa and throughout Africa. USCS is the largest single profit centre in KAP, contributing 38 per cent of the profit in financial year ending 31 December 2013 (an amount of R392 million).[36] USCS' customers include BP, Air Liquide Southern Africa and Rainbow Chickens. They have 160 depots throughout the country, they employ 11 000 employees in 10 countries using more than 3 000 vehicles.[37]

All these customers are business customers who rely on USCS to get their products to their customers. Whether it is fuel (gas or petrol) or chicken which will be used by both business and final consumers, they are relying on USCS to get their products to the market in the right condition at the right time (and to the right customers).

MINI CASE STUDY QUESTIONS

1. Assuming you are the manager of a fuel organisation such as BP, discuss the nature of the relationship that you would want with USCS.

2. As a of a supply chain organisation like USCS, how would you go about building relationships with the company's various key clients?

3. As a CRM consultant, you want to advise USCS to develop a relationship with its competitors, including the Imperial Group and Super Group. Motivate this suggestion to the USCS CEO.

Stakeholders in Relationship Marketing (RM)

Learning outcomes

After studying this chapter, you should be able to:

- explain the nature of stakeholders and their importance in relationship building;
- explain the term 'stakeholders' and differentiate it from shareholders in an organisation;
- identify the composition of a lateral partnership;
- discuss the importance of these lateral partnerships to an organisation;
- comment on the developments in South Africa regarding lateral partnerships;
- explain the importance of the following specific lateral partnerships to an organisation:
  - investors;
  - environmental stakeholders;
  - the community; and
  - the media;
- indicate how organisations can build relationships with lateral partners.

Introduction

The definition of relationship marketing given in Chapter 1 identified the building of relationships with customers as well as with other *stakeholders* and it is these stakeholders that are the focus of this chapter. We will see that building relationships with these stakeholders is critically important to an organisation and that the quality of these relationships affects the organisation and its profitability. This chapter will investigate the specific relationships that organisations should build and suggest ways in which they can be developed.

Stakeholders and CRM: a definition

When examining the groups with whom the organisation aims to build relationships, the term stakeholder is used to describe *any party or group who is able to influence (affect) or be influenced (affected) by the organisation and its activities.*[1] This definition indicates that the use of the word 'stakeholders' means more than just the shareholders (people who have invested money in the business). Stakeholders are thus interested in how projects are carried out (through the efforts of their employees), as well as the outcome of these projects (shareholders, community and government).[2]

Using the term 'stakeholder' has major implications for an organisation, as it means there are many groups with whom the organisation seeks to build relationships. This means that the organisation has to determine priorities in its relationship building and build them in an integrated way.[3] This can be difficult, as these stakeholders affect different parts of the organisation and so interact with different managerial groupings. For example, trade unions may interact with the human resources department (and managers) in the organisation, while suppliers interact with representatives of the purchasing department. Without a unified approach to building relationships with stakeholders, the organisation does not receive the benefit of these relationships. It will be clear from the discussion in this chapter that relationship building takes place within the context of the organisation's activities, missions and values. Building relationships with stakeholders is also not just the task of the marketing department, but includes the actions of top management.

Stakeholders have also been described as being 'strategically significant' to the organisation. This is due to the influence they can have on the functioning of the organisation, as well as on its survival.

The composition of stakeholders

There have been many attempts to represent the relationship between stakeholders who influence the organisation and the organisation itself. Examples of these attempts include the Six Markets model[4] and the Relational Exchanges model proposed by Morgan and Hunt.[5] The stakeholders identified in relationship marketing are shown in Figure 7.1. In this diagram, these stakeholders are identified as a 'lateral partnership' and they will be the focus of this chapter. (The other partnerships shown in Figure 7.1 have been discussed in previous chapters.)

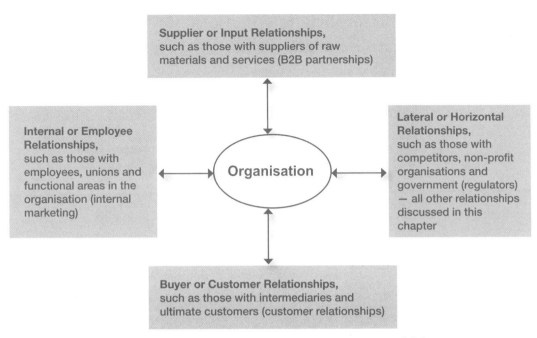

Figure 7.1 The stakeholders in Relationship Marketing[6, 7, 8]

Adapted from Morgan & Hunt, 1994; Peck et al., 1999; Christopher et al., 2002.

There are three important aspects to note in Figure 7.1:

- The organisation is central in the relationship-building process and is therefore placed in the centre of the figure.

- There is a mutually dependent relationship between the organisation and the stakeholders identified as 'lateral partnerships'. This is seen in the mutual influence that the parties have on one another. This means that the organisation not only influences a specific stakeholder, but that the stakeholder has an impact on the activities of the organisation.

- The groups of stakeholders influence one another, meaning that there is no stakeholder group that does not have an influence on (or is not influenced by) another stakeholder group. This is seen, for example, in the effect that the government has on the supplier and buyer partnerships. Supplier partnerships affect the lateral partnerships, while also affecting internal and buyer partnerships. Examples that are supplied in this chapter show how public and environmental concerns cannot be separated, but, in fact, have a mutual influence on each other.

The nature and importance of lateral (or horizontal) partnerships to the organisation

Stakeholders are important to an organisation, as their actions can affect the organisation. Without their support regarding certain key actions, the organisation will not be able to successfully implement a course of action.

> Take a car manufacturing company as an example. If the company wants to build a new plant in an environmentally sensitive area, the media have the power to influence the opinion of the public against this course of action. Further, protests by environmentalists will negatively affect public perceptions of the organisation. The shareholders may support the programme from a financial perspective, but veto it because of the actions of these other groups.

The global economic crisis of 2008 (and 2009) affected all countries and for many countries, the recovery is a slow process. These stakeholders are an important component in this recovery process in the long term.

Significant developments relating to lateral partnerships

The triple bottom line.

The term 'bottom line' is well known when referring to the profits of an organisation, but the term 'triple bottom line' (TBL) is now becoming commonplace. TBL refers to the scorecard where organisations have to report on an organisation's environmental (planet), social (people) and economic (profits) performance.[9] The 'planet' reflects how an organisation is doing in terms of the environment, the 'people' refers to the social responsibility of an organisation while the 'profits' refers to the economic successes that are achieved.

Economic reporting is more than reporting on financial performance, but needs to include supply chain, staff training and development, as well as economic value added.[10] This reporting can also indicate ways in which the organisation is saving money as a result of implementing these measures. Social reporting is not just about the social-responsibility spending of the organisation, but includes the interests of stakeholders such as communities and government.

The problem with having to report on the TBL is that many social and environmental effects cannot be directly measured in a currency format, but despite this, these initiatives and the reporting on them are critical to the stakeholders.[11] Despite its importance for stakeholders, there is also criticism of the approach not only due to the measurement issues (mentioned earlier), but also due to the compliance mindset associated with it.[12] This means that an organisation may decide that just have to 'do enough' rather than go beyond these measures.

The King reports

The King I report (named after its chairman, Mervyn King), was first published in 1994, followed by the *King Report on Corporate Governance* in 2004 (known as King II). The purpose of this report is to focus on corporate governance in organisations, focusing on how they should be managed. King II is focused on all public companies, banks and financial organisations, as well as certain public sector enterprises. It comments on the use of integrated sustainability reporting (another term for TBL reporting) to achieve a balance among the organisation's economic, social and environmental performances. The King report specifies the contents of this integrated sustainability reporting, while also providing for enforcement of the code of conduct governing this kind of reporting.

King III was released in September 2009 with the introduction of the new Companies Act in South Africa and became effective from 1 March 2010. Its focus is on the development of corporate governance, but from a broadened perspective than in the past.[13] The key principles of King III include:

- the importance of effective leadership, which includes the formulation of values and ethics within an organisation;
- the importance of sustainability, which includes social, environmental and economic aspects;
- the importance of innovation, fairness and collaboration as part of sustainability activities;
- social transformation and redress to contribute to sustainability, and to the benefit of society and the organisation.[14]

Broad-based black economic empowerment (BBBEE)

BBBEE and BEE (black economic empowerment) are strategies of government linked to its political transformation objectives in society. (This topic generates emotive discussion among citizens and the purpose of its inclusion here is to focus on its effect on relationship building.) The intention behind these government strategies is to promote the achievement of the constitutional right of all South Africans to equality by increasing the participation of black people in the economy, which results in a more equitable distribution of income.[15,16]

Based on this policy, scorecards and charters have been developed to guide the implementation of BBBEE. The effect of these codes is that an organisation has to examine its ownership (shareholders), management and suppliers who contribute to the organisation's success. The effect of this bill is that the organisation has to build relationships with parties that are different to those of the past and may require new approaches to relationship building.

Specific lateral partners who affect the organisation

Stakeholders have specific expectations of an organisation and these vary from stakeholder to stakeholder. Internal stakeholders (such as employees) would have different expectations from external stakeholders (such as shareholders or the community). Should these expectations not be met, the stakeholders will act in a way that indicates to the organisation that their expectations are not being met. For example, a shareholder may sell shares, the community may protest, while the government may develop legislation or regulations to change the situation. For example, investors would expect to receive a return on their investment while society would expect an organisation to act as a responsible citizen. Starbucks and Amazon were the subject of media and public criticism when it was published that they paid little or no tax in the UK, despite high levels of sales.[17]

Investors and financial stakeholders (shareholders)

In many cases, marketers do not pay much attention to shareholders, believing this to be the task of management or public relations practitioners. However, the development of relationship marketing has brought this group to the attention of marketers as a relationship group. There are some that believe this group is only important for companies that are listed on the stock exchange, such as public companies. It must be remembered that every organisation has investors, even if they are SMEs (small or medium-sized enterprises), and it remains their task to build relationships with this group. Further, with the transformation objectives associated with BBBEE, there are people owning shares who have never been involved in this way previously.

The role of the shareholder is to provide funds to the organisation, which are used in the development of the organisation's activities. The reason for investing in the organisation is the generation of returns on the investment made.[18] A number of financial methods have been developed and are used to measure the value that the organisation creates for its shareholders, such as economic value added (EVA) and shareholder value added (SVA).[19]

Despite the importance of shareholders, it has been suggested that organisations have problems when building relationships with investors. The main reason for this is investor churn, ie the constant change of investors, as people buy and sell shares in the company. It has further been suggested that the average public company in the USA has an investor churn of 50 per cent (or more) per year.[20] While it is suggested that investors need to have a long-term perspective, research in 2000 indicated that corporate shares were sold at a rate six times greater than in 1960. Even in the case of organisations such as McDonald's, shares are sold by shareholders every two years.[21]

The reason why shareholders invest in the first place, ie to generate profits in the short term, is often the cause of this. Should these returns not be generated, investors sell their shares and shareholder churn is the result. This trend may be changing, with shareholders in socially-responsible organisations being willing to accept lower returns over a longer period of time.

For a South African organisation, a number of target markets for investor relations can be identified:

- **Johannesburg Securities Exchange (JSE):** Whether an organisation is listed on the main board or on the alternative board (AltX), the JSE is an important stakeholder group.

- **Investors (present and future):** These are the people who have invested their money in the organisation with the intention of generating returns (in the form of share price increases and dividends).[22]

- **Employees:** These would be employees who have been given shares, sometimes as part of the organisation's BBBEE (or BEE) programme.

- **Customers:** The people currently buying an organisation's product may like the product so much that they decide to invest in the organisation, and so want information regarding its financial performance.

- **Suppliers:** Suppliers want to make sure that they will be paid and so knowledge of the organisation's financial situation is important to them.

In managing this relationship, it has been proposed that organisations make use of an investor relations manager, but this may not be adequate for the scope and importance of the task.[23] Not everyone is convinced that investor relationships are very important. It has been suggested that the only thing that is important to an investor are the financial statements reflecting profit and cash-flow situations. It has also been suggested that organisations hype very small successes and try to ignore the failures or negative events.[24]

It has been put forward that under the new Companies Act, shareholders will expect more from directors.[25] Should an organisation suffer financial loss while under the control of the directors, the Act increases the possibility that they can be sued by the shareholders.[26] Theo Botha is regarded as a 'shareholder activist' who requires the managers of organisations to explain their actions and the performance of the organisation.[27,28]

In building relationships with investors, it is advisable that the organisation should make use of the RACE (research, analysis, communication and evaluation) formula.[29] This formula consists of a number of key steps:

- **Research:** When wanting to build relationships with the investor, it is necessary to carry out research as to what types of investors have put money into the organisation, what their needs and perspectives are and what types of information they would like to have.

- **Analysis (and action):** Once the organisation knows what types of investors have put money in, it is necessary to examine closely their needs and their responses. These will be incorporated into the organisation's communications with investors. This will mean that the best course of action will be determined.

- **Communication:** This refers to the messages that are sent to the investors, as well as the integration of the messages with the activities of the organisation. The organisation has to communicate with its shareholders using media that reach them. This would include the Internet (through the investor relations tab), as well as the financial media.

- **Evaluation:** Here the communication is evaluated to determine whether a specific medium actually reaches the target audience, while also determining the quality of the communication with the market. The relationship quality and the behaviours of the investors that result from the communication can also be evaluated. Even if the investor sells their shares, the quality of the relationship that existed at the time they did so can also be evaluated, as the needs of the shareholder will determine when the shares were sold, and this is important information for the organisation to know.

Environmental stakeholders

With any manufacturing organisation, there is always the question of environmental issues. Environmentalism and the focus on global warming have placed the environment on the agenda for all organisations.

Environmental stakeholders are not equally important to all organisations, as their importance depends primarily on the nature of the organisation's activities. This makes the environmental stakeholders critical to manufacturing organisations, petrochemical and mining companies, among others.[30]

The power of environmental stakeholders differs throughout the world. In the more developed economies, the power of these stakeholders is higher than in developing economies. Generally, however, these stakeholders are beginning to exercise more power and influence over businesses' activities. Members of the public are also aware of the importance of the environment and so are also being influenced by these groups. This has resulted in a greater degree of activism, which can cause damage to the organisation's assets.[31]

> The effect of poor environmental management can be felt on the bottom line of the organisation. Iscor (now Mittal Steel) was sued in 2002 by the residents of Vanderbijlpark for causing pollution in the area. The residents in the area are still affected by the situation.[32] A number of asbestos mining organisations have settled class action suits against them in UK and South African courts to compensate workers for the illness they contracted while employed by these organisations. Millions of pounds are being paid to claimants.[33]

The community

Organisations are established in areas where, by implication, there is support from the community. One of the components of the mission of the organisation may be the role of the organisation in the broader society and providing support to communities. This support takes the form of tacit acceptance of the functioning of the organisation and the provision of labour to the organisation.[34] Research carried out in 2002 has indicated that 30 per cent of the UK public has boycotted a product or company for ethical reasons in the previous year.[35] This means that organisations have to take into account what the community and the public think are important and integrate this into their actions. It has been suggested that communities have become more important rather than less important.[36]

Relationships with communities have to be built continuously and cannot be left to deteriorate and only get attention when the organisation wants something from the community.[37] This is seen in the 'think globally, act locally' philosophy of organisations.[38]

Government, local authorities and regulatory bodies

This refers to bodies that are created to oversee the activities of the organisation and affect organisations in geographical areas or within an economic area (such as the European Union or the Southern African Development Community).[39]

This group of stakeholders affects all organisations to a varying extent. All organisations are required to pay their taxes and are affected by the actions of the local authorities. However, not all industries have regulatory bodies that affect their operation.

> An example of a regulatory influence can be seen in the communication industry. ICASA (the Independent Communication Authority of South Africa) has been created to regulate the telecommunication and broadcasting industries to the benefit of the public.[40] ICASA's mandate is based on the policy of the government to provide access to basic communications to all people in the country at an affordable price. ICASA's task thus includes licensing radio stations, enforcing compliance regulations and managing telecommunication frequencies. Service providers such as Telkom are required to get ICASA's permission to change their prices, as this affects accessibility to the service.

The introduction of the Consumer Protection Act also impacts the way in which organisations market their products and services to consumers and the way in which specifically marketing communication is done. It came into effect on 1 April 2011 and affects all transactions. The Act requires that marketing is not 'misleading, fraudulent or deceptive'.[41] The Act has far-reaching effects on marketing activities, including on loyalty programmes. The Act affects the terms and conditions under which these programmes operate, as well as the benefits offered to customers, as in the case of limits associated with the exchange of products and services for points.[42] The legal aspects do not fall within the goals of this text, and it is suggested that readers acquaint themselves with the Act.

Media

The media in their various forms are vitally important to an organisation with respect to how the organisation communicates with the general public and the community. The media are a powerful tool when an organisation is attempting to build public opinion and can affect the reputation of the organisation among the members of the public.

Establishing a good relationship with the press and media representatives can be done by the organisation itself (and specifically the public relations practitioners), or it can use an external PR firm to build these relationships. Which method the organisation uses depends on its specific requirements, as both can provide an advantage to an organisation. In general, building relationships with the media and their representatives is similar to building relationships with other stakeholders, as discussed below.

Stages in stakeholder relationships

It has been proposed that there are three stages in the development of stakeholder relationships.[43] These stages are illustrated in Figure 7.2.

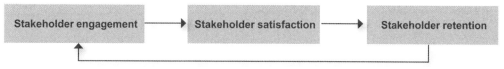

Figure 7.2 Stages in stakeholder development[44]

It is necessary to examine each of these stages in more detail. It must be borne in mind that an organisation can be at a different stage of development with different stakeholder groups, depending on the relationship-building activities that have taken place in the past.

Stage 1: Stakeholder engagement

Engagement refers to the activity of opening communication and interaction with a specific stakeholder. Part of this engagement activity involves an audit that the organisation conducts among each group of stakeholders so that it can identify the key issues associated with each stakeholder group.[45] This engagement will allow both parties to share ideas and opinions while exchanging views, and therefore allows for the development of a relationship. This is done through the creation of stakeholder councils and advisory boards.

Stage 2: Stakeholder satisfaction

Satisfaction comes about when the needs of the parties are met and stakeholder satisfaction implies that the stakeholders feel that their needs are being met by the organisation. Should they not be satisfied, they will withdraw their support. Stakeholder satisfaction can be measured by using satisfaction studies (as discussed in Chapter 3).[46]

Stage 3: Stakeholder retention

Retention is the organisation's ability to 'keep' its stakeholders as important contributors to the functioning of the organisation and the management of its various activities. Retention will allow for the creation of mutual value in the long term, to the benefit of both groups.

Strategies for stakeholder relationships

As has been indicated, lateral partnerships have an important effect on the relationship marketing strategy of the organisation. The question that can be posed is: What strategies can be used in the management of these relationships?

Communication is regarded as critical in building relationships with stakeholders. This group is large, making the use of mass media (as in the case of advertising) necessary.[44] In reaching these stakeholder groups, the cost-effectiveness of the medium that is chosen is key. While advertising does contribute to the perceptions and reputation of the organisation, public relations activities can be regarded as the most suitable method.[48] Irrespective of the specific method selected by a particular organisation, the integration of this communication activity is essential in order to ensure that a consistent message is delivered to the stakeholders.

The Internet has changed the way in which organisations communicate with people and communities. It has created the space for members of the public to connect and interact directly with others. The organisation can interact with these members of the public and so create a forum where concerns can be addressed.[49]

As has already been discussed, relationships develop when both sides 'win' or gain from the relationship. In the past, organisations have decided on a course of action, informed the stakeholders about what they were going to do and then defended their actions with question-and-answer sessions. This has not worked effectively and as an approach has been re-examined. A new approach that has been developed is the Issues Negotiation™ approach.

The Issues Negotiation™ approach works through five stages, as follows:

- **Stage 1:** Insight. Here the organisation seeks to understand the motivation of a particular stakeholder group. Without understanding the group's motivation, the organisation cannot effectively communicate with its members.

- **Stage 2:** Include. The focus of this stage is to include all the stakeholders in the decision and this may include inviting opponents of a particular project to take part, as well as friends.

- **Stage 3:** Explore. This means that both groups explore the various alternatives and the assumptions on which they are based. Understanding a specific groups' perceptions means that the quality of the communication to them can improve, which contributes to the positive relationships that develop.

- **Stage 4:** Negotiate. The purpose of negotiation is to find common ground. This may involve doing fact finding so that the issues can be correctly identified. It could be said that organisations should not make information available if it could be damaging to the organisation. However, previous situations have shown that keeping information out of the public eye does not improve the organisation's position, and, in fact, often it weakens it.

> ### Communicating with society
>
> An example of an industry that has suffered from failing to make information available to the public is the tobacco industry. Initially it denied that cigarettes were dangerous and even presented scientific information that 'proved' that smoking was 'good for you'.[50] Later research has clearly indicated that smoking is not 'good for you' and this has resulted in a number of court cases and huge damages being awarded against the tobacco industry in court.

- **Stage 5:** Progress. Progress will be reflected in the plan that the parties compile to reflect the decisions and actions of the organisation. At this stage, understanding has developed and continuous communication and growth in understanding has meant that the relationship has continued to develop.

Summary

The focus of this chapter has been the stakeholders who are interested in the outcomes of the organisation. The concept of 'lateral partnerships' was identified and the individual components of this group of partners were examined. From this examination, it can be seen that relationship building with these partners requires an integrated approach among the various parts of the organisation. We have also seen that not all the stakeholders are equally important to all organisations, yet an organisation is required to build relationships with all these stakeholders in order to ensure its survival.

DISCUSSION QUESTIONS

1. What is meant by the term 'stakeholder'?
2. Why is a stakeholder important to the organisation?
3. Why could it be said that stakeholders are 'strategically significant'?
4. What is meant by the triple bottom line? Why is it important to the organisation?

5. What specific groups of stakeholders can be identified? What are their expectations of the organisation?

6. What is the role of the shareholder in the functioning of the organisation?

7. Comment on the specific target markets for the investor relations (IR) of the organisation.

8. Are environmental stakeholders equally important for all organisations? Give reasons for your answer.

9. Comment on the influence that environmental stakeholders are able to have on the organisation.

10. How do communities affect the functioning of the organisation?

11. Comment on the effect on the organisation of the press (or other media) as a stakeholder.

12. A number of stages have been identified in the development of stakeholder relationships. Explain these five stages.

13. What specific strategies can an organisation use to build relationships with its stakeholders?

Mini case study

The Green Scorpions – the Silent stakeholders

The Environmental Management Inspectorate (EMI), or the Green Scorpions as they are also known, is an enforcement agency whose task is to enforce compliance with environmental regulations in South Africa. They have a wide range of powers to carry out their task. The EMI was formed in 2005 to investigate businesses and other institutions (including municipalities) that are suspected of committing environmental crimes such as pollution and any crime that affects the environment.[51] Between 1 April 2012 and 31 March 2013, they made 1 818 arrests for a variety of environmentally-related crimes, including dumping and rhino poaching.[52] In 2012 they received a note of congratulations from Greenpeace on the work done to combat environmental crimes committed specifically by ESKOM.[53] Members of the EMI come from SANParks, provincial parks boards, environmental departments as well as other parts of government.[54]

The establishment of the EMI

The EMI was formed through the National Environmental Management Act (NEMA) of 2008. It is a collection of inspectors from the three levels of government namely national, provincial and local government. The objective of the EMI is to ensure that the environmental legislation that organisations comply with the law, and if necessary, enforce this compliance.[55] Should they discover infringements of the law, they do not prosecute the case themselves but rather hand over the evidence to the National Prosecuting Agency (NPA) for their action. Prosecution is not the only option that they have – they can also fine offenders as well as issue enforcement notices. Should organisations ignore these notices, prosecution is a possibility.

The tasks the EMI carries out include the following:[56]

- If an organisation is suspected of breaking the law, the inspectors can investigate the alleged offence. It is possible for members of the public to report a possible offender to a call centre or via the website.

- At a scene where inspectors believe that an environmental crime is being committed, they are able to enter the premises and look for any evidence of criminal activity.

- They are able to search and seize items or articles that they believe are associated with the crime.

- The directorate also administers admission of guilt fines that offenders have to pay if they have committed an offence. If they do not admit guilt, the case is handed over to the NPA for prosecution.

Why the EMI?

Environmental issues continue to play an important role in the decision-making of organisations irrespective of the products or services delivered. Examples of these include whether the product is environmentally friendly (or can be disposed of in an environmentally-friendly way) as well as the extent to which office or factory buildings operate in an environmentally-friendly way.

Environmental issues have become more important in the light of climate change, carbon emissions and other serious global environmental threats. Organisations such as Greenpeace monitor environmental activities and report on developments around the world regarding environmental damage that is taking place.

What does the EMI do?

- Construction projects

  Prior to commencing a large construction project (such as the building of a road, power station or office park), it is necessary to conduct an environmental impact assessment (EIA) which shows what, if any, environmental damage will result from the project. Once the project has been approved, there are numerous environmental laws that construction companies have to comply with while they are building. The EMI carries out inspections during this time to ensure that the construction companies are complying with the applicable acts.[57]

- Water quality management

  South Africa is a relatively dry country, so water resources are valuable to its people and needs to be managed as efficiently as possible. This is a challenge for the government both nationally and locally at municipal level and water pollution needs to be kept to a minimum.[58] Pollution affects water quality and the effects of contaminated water on human health and the spread of disease is well known. This makes the EMI's job in the area very important. If an organisation were to dump contaminated water in rivers and streams, this would be a task for the EMI.

- Air pollution

  Not only is the quality of water important, but air quality is also important for the people of South Africa. Around the world, it is suggested that one quarter of the world's population breathe polluted air. This means an increase in diseases such as cancer, lung and cardiovascular diseases and an increased likelihood of premature death.[59] Research suggests that poor quality air results in each South African losing 67 working days as a result.[60] Currently statistics suggest that China is the country with the lowest air quality, while cities in India also have poor quality air.

  Vereeniging and Vanderbijlpark (south of Johannesburg) are known for the steel industry, but also for the smog and pollution which is associated with the factories in the area. While some organisations have spent a great deal of money to remedy these issues, the problem still exists, though to a lesser extent.[61]

- Waste management

  Modern life can be associated with waste. In 2000, it was calculated that each South African produced 0.7kg of waste per day.[62] Getting rid of waste is always a problem, with landfills filling up and space for more landfills running out. Most waste causes environmental damage. Hazardous waste (such as medical waste) cannot be put in an ordinary landfill – there are special requirements for how it is to be treated. Failure to dispose of this type of waste correctly is illegal and makes an organisation liable for fines and prosecution.

- Wildlife conservation

  A very real environmental threat facing South Africa is the poaching of certain wildlife species such as rhinos for their horns, elephants for their tusks or lions for their bones. This threat impacts not only the survival of the species but also the employment generated through tourism. A special task force has been created within the EMI to focus on the investigation of syndicates involved in the poaching of these animals and special courts have been created to assist in prosecuting those involved in this type of environmental crimes.[63]

What is the link between EMI and businesses?

Any organisation that is being socially responsible and reporting their activities using the triple bottom line would have nothing to fear from the EMI, as all their activities would be in line with the requirements of society with respect to the various environmental laws that have been passed. Those that have something to fear are those who are not acting in a socially responsible manner and hoping to 'get away with' breaking the law.

MINI CASE STUDY QUESTIONS

1. Why do you think the EMI could be regarded as the *silent* stakeholders?

2. Do you think it would be necessary for an organisation to build relationships with the EMI as a stakeholder group? If yes, what specific type/s of organisations would regard a relationship as important?

3. What specific relationship building activities do you think such an organisation could develop to build this relationship?

PART 3

The management of CRM

Planning a CRM strategy

Introduction

Businesses must realise that they need to build and maintain relationships with their customers in order to create a competitive advantage. In the next section we will see why it is so important to have good relationships with your customers.

Why businesses need relationships with customers

Businesses compete based on the relationships that they build with customers. Relationships also have an effect on the retention, satisfaction and loyalty of customers over the long term.[1] Improving customer retention rates has the effect of increasing the size of the customer base. A larger customer base delivers better business performance. Similarly, as customer retention rates rise, the average length of time a customer remains a customer (tenure), will rise.[2]

Lack of planning, undefined business goals and the absence of measurement are most often the reasons for CRM failure. CRM is not just about technology – it is a holistic approach to refocusing the business on customers. It is about the development of a customer-centric business culture that is dedicated to winning and keeping customers by creating and delivering value better than competitors.[3]

In South Africa over the past few years, the first wave of CRM has focused on implementing technology solutions and improving efficiency. However, business-focused CRM involves putting customers first: taking a fresh look at how customers are dealt with; finding out about and solving commercial problems; and changing the culture of the organisation, as a whole, to serve customers more effectively and profitably.[4]

The rationale for CRM is that it improves business performance by enhancing customer satisfaction and driving up customer loyalty. Satisfaction increases when the business communicates with their customers; when it manages the overall experience; when difficult situations are handled with empathy and in a dignified manner; and when service processes are implemented and controlled.[5] As satisfaction rises, so does the intention of the customer to repurchase. This in turn influences actual purchasing behaviour, which has a significant effect on business performance. Business performance can be measured in many ways, but the recent trend has been away from simple short-term financial measures such as return on investment (ROI). Four sets of key performance indicators (KPI) are used, namely financial, customer, internal and learning and growth indicators.

Grönroos, one of the founders of relationship marketing says:

> We know too little about how relationship marketing should be integrated best into the planning of a company. The only way to find out is through trial and error, and through research. Under these circumstances, it seems reasonable to start by adding CRM dimensions to the marketing plan in use, retaining its basic format.[6]

This chapter focuses on planning a CRM strategy. We firstly focus on factors influencing the success of CRM. Then guidelines or processes for planning for CRM will be suggested, which includes the development of CRM strategies to improve customer loyalty.

Factors determining CRM success

For organisations to meet the challenge of a relationship approach means having a culture of customer orientation and the staff resources (this includes their recruitment, training, remuneration, number and control), system resources (ie structures, procedures and priorities) and information resources to effectively implement the relationship approach. This also means understanding the classic relationship between an organisation and its customers, as well as their product needs, interaction modes and profitability over time. We referred to all these important factors in Chapter 1.

The question may be asked: 'How does an organisation create a customer-centric business philosophy and culture?' To successfully implement CRM in an organisation, there should first of all be a commitment from the executive or senior management.

Customer-centricity[7]

A customer-centric business shares a set of beliefs about putting the customer first. It collects, disseminates and uses customer and competitive information to provide better value to customers. A customer-centric business constantly adapts to customer requirements and competitive conditions. There is evidence that customer-centricity correlates strongly with business performance.

The main implementation barrier which an organisation that wishes to implement CRM will face, is, for example, resistance to change, which can be attributed to a negative attitude and a lack of knowledge among employees. Everyone should be knowledgeable about the business's mission, strategies and goals, as well as departmental goals. Training employees and thereby increasing their knowledge and influencing attitudes are important if a business wants to become customer-centric.[8] Prospective CRM managers can experience additional challenges, such as:[9]

- finding the best CRM examples to benchmark their project against in this emerging area where few suppliers have developed fully integrated CRM initiatives that have effectively planned the introduction of the most effective CRM system;
- envisioning the end state of CRM, and the investments and actions needed to achieve this end state;
- focusing on working with core customers to develop the transition plan from the existing relationship to the desired one – a particularly daunting challenge;
- determining how to really add value to core customers and doing this faster than competitors; and
- demonstrating the feasibility of the CRM concept by using pilot tests to show the effectiveness of the proposed CRM system prior to rolling it out.

Relationships should be specifically planned.[10] If executive management begins to understand the components (trust and commitment) and importance of the customer relationship through this planning process, it will start to place the relationship at the centre of the business and link its various strategies and capabilities to improving relationships with all stakeholders. CRM cannot simply be added onto marketing, with business otherwise proceeding as before; CRM has organisation-wide implications.

In order to compete effectively in an uncertain business environment, many chief executive officers (CEOs) hope that CRM will be a 'cure'. However, up to 80 per cent of all CRM initiatives fail to deliver on their promises. The main reason for this failure is not CRM itself, but a lack of planning, and the absence of clear goals and strategies. If implemented correctly, CRM can offer many benefits in less than three months.[11]

As mentioned earlier, CRM is an organisation-wide issue and the role of all employees is of critical importance. Management should create, continuously encourage and improve its understanding of, and appreciation for, the roles of the employees in the organisation. Employees should have holistic views of their jobs, and have the optimum mix of skills, knowledge and personal traits that contact personnel in particular need in order to implement CRM. They must be prepared (through training) both in terms of knowledge and skills if the organisation expects to earn loyalty by helping clients make wiser purchase decisions than they might make at competing organisations. The business should manage employees in order to ensure that their attitudes and behaviour are conducive to the delivery of quality services. Traditionally customers were thought of as people or organisations external to a business that are served in a way that their needs are fulfilled and that they are satisfied with the service provider's performance. There are internal service functions that are subjected to the same criteria of needs and performance as applied to external customers.[12] Monitoring staff performance and rewarding staff competence are also important factors in ensuring excellent service.

Developing a service culture is a means of creating and enhancing good interactive marketing performance needed for implementing a relationship marketing strategy. The employees involved in marketing have been called 'part-time' marketers. They have to learn to perform their tasks in a marketing-like way so that the customers will want to return.

Operational CRM[13]

Operational CRM focuses on the automation of the customer-facing parts of business. There are a variety of CRM software applications which enables the marketing, selling and service functions to be automated. The most important applications within operational CRM are discussed on the following page, namely marketing automation, sales force automation and service automation.

- **Marketing automation** applies technology to marketing processes. Marketing automation enables businesses to develop, budget and execute communication campaigns. Sales or service actions are initiated by a business in response to an action by the customer. The customer action triggers the business response. If a business customer emails a request for information, this might initiate a sales process that commences with a courtesy call to thank the customer for the request.

- **Sales-force automation** was the original form of CRM. It applies technology to the management of a business's selling activities. Sales-force automation software enables businesses automatically to record leads and track opportunities as they progress through the sales pipeline towards closure.

- **Service automation** allows businesses to automate their service operations, whether delivered through a call centre, a contact centre, web or face-to-face in the field. Service automation software enables businesses to manage and coordinate their service-related in-bound and out-bound communications across all channels.

The success of CRM is heavily dependent upon the alignment and integration of all related business processes. The integration of the different departments within an organisation can make the difference between the success/failure of a CRM initiative. For example, while many successful businesses have automated their front- and back-office and supply-chain systems, they will still need an extra information system to tie them all together.

If the organisation wants to develop better relationships with its more profitable customers, it needs to first revamp the key business processes that relate to customers, from customer service to order fulfilment. A CRM rollout will succeed only after the organisation and its processes have been restructured in order to better meet customer needs.

Information resources

Two important information resources are customer information and knowledge, and acquiring a CRM software system.

Customer information and knowledge

Information about customers is of paramount importance to CRM. It has become increasingly important due to the level of globalisation taking place and the speed of technological changes.[14] Information on the organisation's existing customers will form the core of customer data. The specific information held may vary by type of market. For example, a sophisticated consumer data system may use the postal code to differentiate specialist geo-demographic data or include lifestyle information that allows customer profiles to be developed.

Customer information is potentially an invaluable aid in decision-making. Moreover, the information collected for marketing purposes must, like the marketing function itself, be future-oriented. It must be possible to exploit customer data to drive future marketing programmes and the data provides the basis of a strategy to do this. The use of technology to help manage customer information is the focus of the next section.

CRM technology

The success of any CRM initiative depends largely on ensuring that the most appropriate facilitator with regard to CRM technology has been selected to assist the organisation in utilising CRM successfully. The system must be flexible and easy to customise, be available for individual or concurrent users, permit future functionality without additional modules having to be purchased and require a low level of expertise to maintain it, especially if maintenance is to be carried out internally (see also Chapter 10).

Decision support systems are used by CRM to obtain and use information that is relevant to specific decision-making situations and are made up of the following parts, namely:[15]

- **Data system**. It includes the processes used to capture and store data that originates from a number of internal and external sources.

- **Dialogue system**. It permits users to explore the databases by using the system models to produce reports that satisfy particular information needs.

- **Model system**. All the routines which allow the user to manipulate the data so as to conduct the kind of analysis desired.

Customer relationship management must be flexible enough to stay in touch with a changing audience (the customer). It must reflect different requirements in different industries. It must be accessible to external stakeholders as well as mobile professionals such as salespeople and field technicians. It must operate over any communication channel and it must integrate with other systems to provide a single view of, and for, the customer. Finally, it must be implemented in such a way that appropriate work practices and skills are deployed, because many of the requirements of CRM cannot be solved by technology alone.[16]

Those companies that have been successful with CRM initiatives have been successful by understanding the complete definition of CRM and by implementing a solution that builds and maintains the company's momentum.

These companies realise that technology, though important, must be accompanied by changes in the organisation itself.

Technology is not necessarily required for effective CRM

Consider a successful hair salon. The business owner and the staff work hard to provide personal, high-quality service, thus building a loyal customer base over time. Computers are not necessarily required for them to do this.[17]

CRM must start with a business strategy that drives changes in the organisation and its work processes, which are, in turn, enabled by information technology. In other words, a business must first have its business objectives in place before focusing on technology – not the other way round. A customer-centric business can reap significant benefits using CRM technology.

Successful CRM initiatives start with a business strategy and philosophy that aligns business activities around customer needs. CRM technology is a critical enabler of the processes required to turn strategy into business results.

Integrating customer data[18]

It is necessary to link all sales and servicing departments, and the front office through to back-office systems where a great deal of the information about customers and the history of their interactions are stored and updated. This linking is essential to deliver the right information to the right person, at the right time, in order to ensure that adequate support is provided to a particular client so as to maximise the value of the interaction for both parties. Linking the front- and back-offices is all about integrating the data from different parts of the organisation. This ensures that all pertinent information about that particular client and his or her importance to the organisation is accessible at the right point, is understood and is in a format that can be used both easily and effectively.

A business needs to integrate every interaction it has with the customer, whether it is a call to its call centre or a request via the Internet. These interactions also require interfacing with back-office systems such as central billing and data on products and services, as well as with all elements of the supply chain.

A CRM system must be capable of transforming all knowledge about key customers into valuable business intelligence in real time through any channel.

Through CRM processes, an organisation can synchronise its systems around service delivery to the customer rather than just synchronising data around itself. This will ensure that the business will be able to understand and predict customer behaviour, implement smarter customer strategies and maximise its own and its customers' profitability.

The quality of the data used in successful CRM applications is also critical. Corporate CRM systems fail because they provide reams of sales operational data that, in itself, is meaningless. These front-office systems must be integrated with analytical solutions that convert this operational data into real business intelligence.

A business must actually plan how it will create, implement and manage a programme to ensure the building of relationships with its customers.[19]

The CRM planning process

In Chapter 1 it was mentioned how important it is for the business to build and maintain long-term relationships with its customers. CRM offers organisations the opportunity to build long-term customer relationships and to regard these relationships as a key marketing asset within the organisation. In balancing the need to develop customer acquisition and retention strategies, organisations can improve their profitability as customer retention increases. For example, a small improvement in customer retention rates from 85 to 90 per cent could result in net present value profits to increase from 35 to 95 per cent among businesses.[20] The role of customer retention in developing CRM strategies is therefore critical.

A business wishing to improve relationships with its customers, thereby improving profitability, could employ the planning process illustrated in Figure 8.1. The different stages in the CRM planning process will be discussed in the following sections.

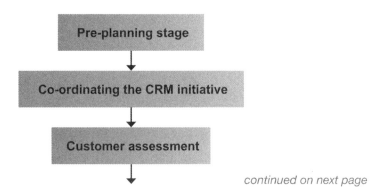

continued on next page

Figure 8.1 Stages in the CRM planning process

continued from previous page

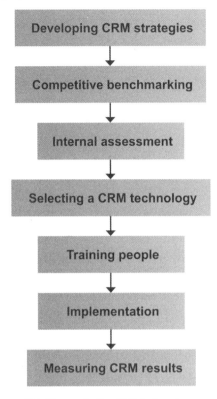

Figure 8.1 Stages in the CRM planning process

Pre-planning stage

The pre-planning stage enables the business to analyse the expenditure of time and effort and to decide on the various key components before the actual CRM planning process begins.[21]

An organisation must have a clear understanding of why CRM is needed. In order to justify undertaking this transformation, a compelling vision and an understanding of the underlying platform and critical goals are required. The organisation should think about and document ideas on how a new CRM philosophy will improve the business's competitiveness. Realistic goals and expectations need to be set and anticipated results considered.[22] The business will receive short-term benefits, although most of the benefits will be long term in nature (see the example on the following page).

> **Short term benefits of CRM**
>
> CRM can provide immediate 'cheap growth' just by uncovering opportunities to re-allocate sales resources from customers who are less likely to buy to those who are more likely to buy.[23]

The CRM vision and goals must have champions at all levels of the business, from senior management to frontline contact personnel. The sooner this support is secured and communicated, the better the opportunity for success. Project champions will play a vital role in day-to-day guidance and decision-making, and will act as referees when needed.

It is also necessary to reconcile the magnitude of the coming change with the organisation's readiness. If the business does not have the depth or breadth of resources for this transition, it is best to secure external resources required for CRM implementation early on and certainly before the project begins. The number and type of resources needed to achieve success must not be underestimated.

Co-ordinating the CRM initiative

The presence of a customer-centric organisational culture makes the introduction of a CRM strategy much less threatening to the business's employees. A customer-centric business will be resourced and organised to understand and satisfy customer requirements profitably. This will involve attributes such as identifying which customers to serve; understanding customers' current and future requirements; obtaining and sharing customer knowledge across the business; and measuring customer results.[24] The most efficient and effective way to co-ordinate and execute the many tasks required to embed CRM into an organisation's culture is to treat the transition as a project. It is important to appoint a project manager to lead the CRM change. This person should be someone who is accountable for achieving measurable results. The more senior and respected this person is in the organisation, the better. Leadership will help to prioritise the CRM project. It is not uncommon for businesses to be involved in a number of projects simultaneously. Prioritising major projects is a high-level decision. High-level ownership of the CRM project gives an overview of the progress of the overall project and the timelines and contribution of the components.[25]

Since the CRM implementation process will involve multiple development cycles, an overall road map that illustrates how each cycle fits within the overall plan should be created. A step-by-step, phased approach, establishing tangible milestones and metrics along the way, must be followed. Each project or department should have measurable short-term goals, as well as a long-term vision for the whole organisation. An organisation should be careful, however, not to let the plan dominate the planning. There will be unanticipated roadblocks and tasks that will necessitate adjustments being made.

Finally, clear roles and responsibilities must be established for each team member, based on the project plan and goals, with the timing and the criteria for success being crystal clear.

Customer assessment

This stage of the planning process looks at where the organisation is now with regard to its customers and relationship marketing. Every customer-centric organisation must define or refine its customer vision. What benefits can the business provide to its customers that would satisfy them and would foster loyal and profitable relationships? To answer this question, the business must be open to criticism and the views of its customers.

In customer assessment, the profitability of the total number of its current customers needs to be established. Customer profitability is largely dependent on customer satisfaction, customer retention and customer loyalty (these factors were also discussed in Chapter 2).

Customer satisfaction, retention and loyalty

Customer satisfaction is the customer's fulfilment response to a consumption experience, or some part of it. Customer satisfaction is a pleasurable fulfilment response, whereas dissatisfaction is not a pleasant fulfilment response[26] and is measured by the rate at which customers are kept – the customer retention rate. This is expressed as the percentage of customers at the beginning of the year that still remains at the end of the year. The more satisfied the customers are, the longer they stay and thus the higher the retention rate. A retention rate of 80 per cent means that, on average, customers remain loyal for five years, whereas one of 90 per cent pushes the average period of loyalty up to ten years. As the average of 'life' of a customer increases, so does the profitability of that customer to the firm. To conclude, as the retention rate increases, so does overall profitability (see Box 8.1 on the following page).

8.1 IT PAYS TO RETAIN CUSTOMERS[27]

A cost study of service companies found that customer retention has a more powerful effect on profits than market share, scale economies and other variables that are usually associated with competitive advantage. More specifically, it was established that companies that reduce customer defections by five per cent can boost profits by between 25 per cent and 85 per cent.

The service companies have experienced profit increases of anything from 30 per cent to 125 per cent. This latter result was achieved by a financial services company that succeeded in increasing its retention rate from an industry average of 90 percent to 95 per cent. Over a period of six years, its market position rose from 38th to fourth in its industry.

Measuring the profitability of customers

Once a firm has recognised the importance of building customer relationships, it needs to decide which customers it wants to build closer relationships with in the future.

As businesses move towards one-to-one marketing, they need to develop a longer-term view of the value of their customers. Effectively, relationship marketers need to predict the future purchasing behaviour of key customers to arrive at their customer lifetime value (CLV). CLV measures a customer's profit-generation for a business.

To calculate the CLV, three sorts of information are needed:

- the anticipated lifetime of the customer relationship in months or years;
- the profit in each future period adjusted for any customer-specific capital costs, such as marketing and customised services; and
- a discount rate.

Figure 8.2 shows how these relate to each other.

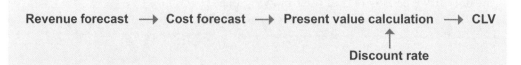

Figure 8.2 Information needed to calculate the CLV

CLV analysis suggests that the value of a relationship with a customer can be increased either by increasing the amount of profits (by increasing the revenue from the customer and/or decreasing costs to serve), or by extending the relationship lifetime. Customers at the beginning of their relationship lifetime will need a different CRM strategy to those approaching the declining stage of their relationship lifetime. For most businesses the concern will be to identify those customers or market segments that have the highest CLV potential. They are not concerned with the past. What matters is the future. Banks understand this principle well; they have identified students as potentially high value customers over a lifetime, even though in the short term they may be unprofitable. Revenue from customers grows over time as they buy more and existing customers are cheaper to serve than new customers, because the supplier and customer have built a relationship with each other over time. Existing customers generate referrals and they pay higher prices than new customers, because they are less sensitive to price offers from other suppliers.

Developing CRM strategies

In recent years, marketing managers have tried to measure and maximise the lifetime value of each and every customer. If a company truly understood each of its customers' CLV, it could maximise its own value by boosting the number, scope and duration of value-creating customer relationships. Some cutting-edge marketing strategies are available for maximising customer lifetime.[28] Each of these strategies plays a unique role in optimising shareholder value, customer equity and overall profitability. Each strategy also works in combination with other strategies to increase overall impact on the business's value.

To treat different customers differently, it is necessary to group them into value-based tiers, ie groups of customers with similar values to the organisation. In this way, the most valuable customers, the ones that have the most potential to grow, as well as the unprofitable ones can be identified. It is necessary to look at each group more closely, and profile its members by their needs and preferences.

Next, a specific set of strategies for retaining and growing the best customers must be defined. The organisation should recognise that these customers are the key to its success. On the other hand, cost-reduction strategies should be devised for the least profitable ones, or for customers who cost the business more than they contribute to it.

	Short-term customers	Long-term customers
High profitability	**Butterflies** • good fit between company's offerings and customer's needs • high profit potential *Actions* • aim to achieve transactional satisfaction • not attitudinal loyalty • milk the accounts only as long as they are active • key challenge is to cease investing soon enough	**True friends** • good fit between company's offering and customer's needs • highest profit potential *Actions* • communicate consistently, but not too often • build both attitudinal and behavioural loyalty • delight these customers in order to nurture, defend and retain them
High profitability	**Strangers** • little fit between company's offerings and customer's needs • lowest profit potential *Actions* • make no investment in these relationships • make profit on every transaction	**Barnacles** • limited fit between company's offerings and customer's needs • low profit potential *Actions* • measure both the size and share of wallet • if share of wallet is low, focus on up- and cross-selling • if size of wallet is small, impose strict cost controls

Figure 8.3 Selecting CRM strategies

After analysing the customers' lifetime value or future profitability and the projected duration of their relationships, the organisation can place each of them into one of four categories, as shown in Figure 8.3.[29] The four quadrants of the matrix suggest how customers can be sorted on the basis of customer longevity and profitability for the firm. While there may be long-standing customers who are only marginally profitable, there may be short-term customers who are highly profitable. Hence, it becomes clear that the relationship between loyalty and profitability is by no means assured.

Each of the segments in Figure 8.3 is discussed in the following sections, and an appropriate strategy for each is indicated.[30]

Strangers

Strangers, as the name suggests, are the least profitable customers for the firm. A characteristic of a stranger would be their lack of loyalty. Strangers are not profitable. When the customer shows no sign of making a significant contribution in the future, it may be best to terminate the relationship. The decision to terminate such relationships cannot necessarily be made by the employees responsible for maintaining customer relationships, as shown in the example from the banking industry below.

Role in banking relationships[31]

A study in the banking industry found that personal bankers can be effective in maintaining and enhancing relationships with customers allocated to them, but do not play any role in identifying and establishing relationships. Given that few bankers in the survey could accurately calculate relationship profitability, the task of identifying relationships that ought to be terminated cannot be undertaken by such bankers. This is possibly due to a lack of training in this field. This uninformed basis is not an appropriate one on which to make decisions about allocation of time, effort and resources.

For customers in the other three quadrants of the matrix, the choice of strategy will make a material difference to the segment's profitability.[32]

True friends

True friends are those customers who look as if they will be profitable in the future. They are the most valuable customers of all. They fit in well with the business offerings. They are also steady purchasers, buying regularly, but perhaps not intensively, over time (see the example below from a mail-order company).In managing these true friends, firms should provide consistent, yet intermittently spaced communications. Firms should strive to achieve attitudinal and behavioural loyalty among these customers.

A mail-order company found that the true friends tended to return goods at a relatively high rate, reflecting their comfort in engaging with the company's processes. They are also steady purchasers, buying regularly, but not intensively, over time.[33]

In managing these true friends, the greatest trap is overkill. A mail-order company, for instance, found that intensifying the level of contact through by increasing the number of mailings was more likely to put off a loyal and profitable customer than to increase sales. People flooded with mail may throw everything out without looking at it. Sent less mail, however, they are more likely to look at what they get. Indeed, the mail-order company found that its profitable loyal customers were not among those who received the most mailings.

What is more important is that businesses need to concentrate on finding ways to bring their true friends' feelings of loyalty to the fore, by satisfying them because 'true' believers are the most valuable customers of all.

In a banking study it was found that customer satisfaction in retail banking correlated highly with branch profitability. Highly satisfied customers had balances that were 20 per cent higher than satisfied customers and, as satisfaction levels went up over time, so did account balances. The reverse was also true: as satisfaction levels fell, so did account balances.[34]

Butterflies

These customers are profitable but not loyal. However, although staying for only a short term, they offer high profitability for the business. They enjoy finding the best deals and avoid building a stable relationship with any single provider. In this instance, the business may wish to harvest or optimise cash flow from the customer with a view to spending the cash to develop other customers.[35]

Barnacles

Barnacles are those customers who, despite being long-term customers, offer low profitability to the business. In other words, these customers do not generate satisfactory return on investments, due to their small size and low volume of transactions. The business needs to decide how it will treat these customers. The business will have to decide whether it is worthwhile to continue with the relationship or whether to terminate it. If it is predicted that the customer will not be able to make a contribution in the future, it is be best to let them go. An example of a strategy to deter barnacles is given below.

> **Barnacles disciplined**
>
> Banks, for example, prefer the average customer to use automated teller machines (ATMs) for routine transactions. If banks must maintain the traditional teller services for customers, the benefits of the technologies and processes in which they have invested will not be realised. They therefore charge customers for teller services for routine transactions. Their customers are being disciplined financially to encourage them to use the ATM in future.

There is no one right way to make loyalty profitable. Different approaches will be more suited to different businesses, depending on the profiles of their customers and the complexity of their distribution channels. Whatever the context, no business should ever take for granted the idea that managing customers for loyalty is the same as managing them for profits. The only way to strengthen the link between profits and loyalty is to manage both at the same time. Fortunately, technology is making that task easier every day, allowing businesses to record and analyse the often complex behaviour of their customers. The next section deals with a process that can help with this: competitive benchmarking.

Competitive benchmarking[36]

Competitive benchmarking is a continuous process for evaluating organisations' products, services and work processes that are considered to be best practices, for the purpose of organisational improvement (see Box 8.2). One of the key components of the competitive benchmarking process is the selection of benchmarking partners, such as regulators, customer advocacy groups and sponsors. A common misunderstanding about benchmarking is that it is only a matter of identifying and learning from the best-in-class businesses. This is not the case. Benchmark groups are networks of businesses that expect mutual gain from their participation. Benchmarking groups can have a significant impact on the creation of customer value. Many industries are regulated, for example, financial services, railways, electricity and airlines. A close relationship with regulators allows businesses to ensure that they are not in breach of regulations or legislation. Customer advocacy groups promote and protect the interests of consumers. Although sponsors are generally not playing such a significant role in the for-profit context, they play an important role in the not-for-profit context. Sponsors are looking for commercial gains from sponsorship, for example, influencing consumer attitudes and behaviour and rewarding employees.

8.2 INTERNAL BENCHMARKING[37]

Avon Cosmetics established an internal benchmarking study to identify and share best practice within and across the business's geographical sales regions. The objective was to improve branch productivity through a range of process improvements. Some of the outcomes were changes to the way in which managers were trained in the use of the business's information technology (IT) system, an improved call management system and regular meetings between customer service supervisors to share ideas and experiences.

Internal assessment

A business should determine the kind of relationships that would be best for it and whether CRM is appropriate. Some of the factors that need to be considered during this internal assessment process are discussed below.

Is CRM appropriate?

Integral to the internal assessment process is an understanding of the core business in which the organisation is engaged. Thus, a business must ask itself whether or not it should focus on the needs of individual customers. In certain types of business, it may be more profitable to focus on mass production and mass service.

Sometimes mass production is more profitable[38]

Some businesses are in the business of producing high-volume goods at the lowest possible price and CRM will distract such a business from its single-minded focus on being the low-cost producer in its industry. Yet even for this business, CRM may still have an important role, such as in the business's relationship with distribution channel intermediaries.

In some industries, the lifetime profitability from individual customers is not high enough to warrant an all-out CRM effort. For example, supermarket chains secure a very modest return on sales, usually less than two per cent. Here, the lifetime revenue potential of an individual customer and the costs of bonding to each one of them, may be uneconomical for both the retailer and the consumer products business company that produces a single brand or just a few products. In these situations, it may still pay the business to cater for market segments and local or regional market preferences. The business could also focus on frequency marketing by providing inducements for the customer to shop at the store again or to repurchase the brand, rather than adopting CRM as a strategy.

Business culture

In order to implement CRM successfully, a crucial requirement is that the culture of the business must emphasise self-respect, respect for others and a commitment to mutual and active listening. If these are lacking, then the culture needs to be revisited before proceeding with the CRM project. In this process, the initiative needs to come from executive management.

Executive management support

A CRM initiative needs to be supported by top or executive management (as stated in Chapter 1). If top, or executive management is incapable of forming relationships, then no meaningful relationships will be formed.

Capacity of the business

Another aspect that needs to be assessed is the capacity of the business to undertake CRM. Do the employees possess the necessary skills and knowledge? Other resources of the organisation, such as technologies, systems and processes and whether or not the business can afford to change and adapt its technologies and processes also need to be considered.

Process alignment[39]

Once customers and suppliers make a commitment to each other, they may begin to look for opportunities to align their processes. The goal of process alignment is to reduce the costs of maintaining the relationship. Two processes are aligned, namely quality-control processes and the order-fulfilment processes. In the case of the alignment of quality-control processes, the following processes on both sides of the relationship will take place, namely:

- quality standards will be established by the customer;
- quality conformance against best-in-class will be benchmarked by the supplier; ·
- the supplier and customer will agree on a strategy for quality improvement; and
- a quality-assurance programme will be introduced by the supplier.

The order-fulfilment process involves the customer establishing an acceptable inventory level and issuing an order for inventory replenishment when that limit is approached. The supplier fills the order and invoices the customer who will pay the invoice. In both of the above process alignment costs can be reduced and the relationship between the business and its customers can be maintained. The next section focuses on the selection of a CRM technology (see also Chapter 10).

Selecting a CRM technology

If an organisation is looking to select a CRM provider, it is necessary to first take a long and very analytical look at the organisation's own business processes and to take an equally long and hard look at the organisational culture as well as specifically, at all contact-personnel and management. It is in these realms that success or failure of any CRM programme or project will be born. The astute organisation will discover rapidly that the greater part of CRM lies in people and processes. Only when these are aligned, streamlined and optimised will the organisation begin to gain a 'feel' for its own hybrid technology requirements; and only then will the 'right' CRM vendor, service provider or application begin to become apparent. CRM must, therefore, be a business-driven imperative, not a technology-driven exercise.[40]

Customer expectations played a direct role in the emergence of CRM technology. Multichannel CRM presented a significant technical challenge. The technology required to support remote sales people is very different to the technology required to support a large, high-volume call centre. CRM technologies are more than just a simple suite of applications. CRM must be flexible enough to stay in touch with a changing audience. It must reflect different requirements in different industries. It must be accessible to external stakeholders and mobile professionals such as salespeople and field technicians. It must operate over any communication channel and it must be implemented in such a way that appropriate work practices and skills are deployed.[41]

Training people[42]

If people do not want CRM to work, it will not. It is important for CRM champions to be located at different levels in the business. People's skills, knowledge and attitudes required for successful CRM performance may need review and upgrading. These will vary according to the level of CRM implementation. The knowledge and skills required include how to segment customers, design experiments and interpret experimental data using statistical procedures. People may need to be trained in these and other competencies. Chapter 9 focuses on the implementation of CRM in a business.

Summary

In this chapter, we suggested broad guidelines for planning a CRM strategy. The factors determining CRM success were highlighted and the relationship between loyalty and business performance was also outlined. The stages in a CRM planning process, including developing CRM strategies to treat different customers differently, were then discussed.

DISCUSSION QUESTIONS

1. Explain and illustrate the factors determining CRM success.

2. Discuss the relationship between loyalty and business performance.

3. Before a CRM strategy is chosen for the different groups of customers, an organisation should determine their current and future profitability.

   a. Explain the different customer segments that can be identified in this way.

   b. Illustrate the different CRM strategies that could be used for each identified segment.

Mini case study

A mobile banking innovation from Kenya is going to be 'exported' to Europe. M-Pesa, as this innovation is called, is a service that one can use in order to send money to someone else. This has changed the way business has been conducted in East Africa. M-Pesa or 'mobile money' in Swahili, was introduced in Kenya in 2007 by Safricom, the country's largest mobile telephone company, in partnership with Vodafone, the holding company of Vodacom. M-Pesa has 18 million clients – nearly two thirds of all Kenyans use it and the next target market is Romania, because of the fact that more than a third of the population of Romania does not have access to traditional banking services.

The idea is to tap into the market of seven million possible clients, who are still only using cash in their transactions.

MINI CASE STUDY QUESTION

In the case study of M-Pesa, how would you say this new innovation of 'mobile money' will impact on the loyalty of customers towards commercial banking?

Implementing CRM in an organisation

Learning outcomes

After studying this chapter, you should be able to:

- explain three prerequisites for the implementation of any strategy;
- explain why implementation is important for any strategy and the specific challenges in the case of a CRM strategy;
- explain the term 'customer leader';
- explain the importance of technology in the implementation process;
- explain the role of corporate culture in the implementation of a CRM strategy;
- explain the importance of change management and resistance to change within an organisation;
- explain the importance of control within the strategy implementation process and specifically in the case of a CRM strategy.

Introduction

After the goals and objectives for the CRM strategy have been developed, it is necessary to devise the process for implementing this strategy. Without implementation, the objectives will be no more than words on paper, without any reality. The changes required to enable implementation to take place form the focus of this chapter. These changes take place in the organisation, but the organisation cannot ignore the needs of the customer in the various components that are discussed here. For example, in the case of communicating with the customer, the customer has expectations as to how they would like to receive communication from the organisation.

Prerequisites for the implementation strategy

An organisation needs to have a number of prerequisites in place before attempting to implement a CRM strategy, as given below. Without these prerequisites, implementation is more difficult. Many of these are similar to the implementation of any organisational strategy.

A shared vision: It is not enough to have a corporate vision; it is necessary to share the vision with those that will be required to implement the vision. This vision cannot be imposed on the organisation's staff, as this breeds resentment among them. The chief executive officer (CEO) has to obtain the co-operation of the staff so as to create a sense of ownership and commitment to the vision.[1] This vision is not a document that is kept hidden, but rather something that is an integral part of the way in which the organisation does business. It is knowledge that all the staff members have and need to be reminded of, in order for it to affect their behaviour and for a CRM strategy to be implemented.

Decentralisation of authority and management: This has to do with the place of decision-making within the organisation. When authority is decentralised, decisions are made at the lowest level in the organisation, by the people who actually interact with customers. When these members of staff are made responsible for decision making, they are able to show initiative in dealing with customers, so that relationships with customers are improved.

The support of top management: It is the task of the members of top, or executive management to direct the activities of the organisation. Without their support in all its forms, the CRM strategy will not be a success. Their support includes the allocation of resources, the development of objectives, the management of reward systems and the development of the organisational structures that support the strategy.[2] Their support is necessary because the implementation of a CRM strategy has far-reaching effects throughout the organisation. Their support can result in overall support at lower levels for the strategy, while also assisting in reducing the degree of resistance to change within the organisation.

It is necessary that executive management communicate their intention of implementing the CRM strategy to all levels of staff, thereby giving the strategy the support necessary. This is not to imply that criticism of the strategy is to be suppressed; rather, it indicates that criticism needs to be valid and, where necessary, it can be incorporated within the strategy as it is adapted over time.

The importance of the implementation phase in a CRM strategy

The success of any strategy is determined by whether it attains its objectives or not. This is no different in the case of a CRM strategy. In order to make a success of the CRM strategy, implementation needs to be carefully planned by management.

There are a number of challenges in the implementation of a CRM strategy:[3]

- The scope of any CRM strategy is very broad. This means that it impacts on the entire organisation. This requires changes to be made throughout the organisation and it is necessary that these changes be well-managed as they are implemented.

- There is a very real possibility that there will be resistance within the organisation to both recognising the need for and the implementation of a CRM strategy. It will require a great deal of leadership and managerial skills for this resistance to be overcome, in order to make the implementation a success.

- The skills that are required to implement a CRM strategy place a great deal of pressure on the managers within the organisation and where these skills are in short supply, this may place additional stress and pressure on managers.

One of the techniques that can be used in implementing strategy is the appointment of *sponsors* or *influencers*. These people are specifically selected for their ability to influence the perceptions of others in the organisation, while also being able to lead a team of people coming from divergent departments. They will then be able to appoint others (change agents) to assist in the implementation of specific aspects in the various departments (or divisions) within the organisation. This will make it possible to bring about the required changes throughout the entire organisation that are required for the successful implementation of any strategy.

There are a number of key factors that are important for the implementation of a CRM strategy. These include development of a customer leader, changes in technology as well as changes in processes.

The development of a customer leader

One of the key components to the implementation of any strategy is identifing the person who will provide the inspiration and direction for its implementation. The task of the customer leader (or champion) is to take a group of people, mould them into a team and motivate them to achieve a number of objectives.[4] Use of a champion within organisations has been documented in the literature.[5] This person or team has a 'change mindset' and is always looking for better ways of doing things for the benefit of the organisation and its staff. A CRM strategy affects all the parts of the organisation and hence requires this inspiration throughout its functions to facilitate the implementation process. The role of the leader is to get buy-in from the parties involved in the implementation of the strategy.

The characteristics of an effective leader in an organisational context have been widely debated and researched. Effectiveness can be described from a number of different perspectives, such as the skills that leaders have or the behaviour that they exhibit. In the case of CRM, the leader has a slightly different role to play, namely that of making the employees of the organisation customer- and CRM-oriented.

It is suggested that a specific management and leadership concept exists for managing customers and the relationships that are created with customers. This concept seeks to build a technological environment that attempts to integrate the marketing, sales, service and supply-chain functions to enable the staff to provide superior customised and personalised service to customers. It requires specific leadership skills to implement the CRM strategy in the organisation, which is known as customer relationship leadership (CRL). This customer-oriented leader has the task of aligning the organisation (and its employees) to the goals of the CRM strategy that has been developed for the organisation.[6] This would mean that the customer-oriented leader has to ensure that the goals set for CRM are consistent with the goals of the organisation, while also ensuring that the employees have clarity concerning the goals of the CRM strategy.

The selection of a CRM strategy can have major implications for an organisation, so correct implementation of the strategy is required. CRL seeks to integrate the key components of the CRM process so as to maximise the returns from the CRM strategy.

The components of the CRM strategy include customisation, after-sales service and the development of personal relationships with customers. The customers are the core of the model, as they are the reason for the existence of the organisation. The CRL philosophy identifies technology, organisational environment and innovation as the keys to implementation. There thus needs to be an integration process between the components of the CRM strategy on the one hand and the key implementation aspects in the CRL strategy on the other. This alignment is necessary if the organisation is to have a complete view of their customers.

What does this mean for an organisation? To gain the best view (or picture) possible of the customer, I need to supply customers with the products, provide the best after-sales service and have deep, meaningful relationships with them. This is done through the technology both parties use as well as the organisational culture and innovation which makes it possible to develop these relationships.

In order to implement CRL, changes in a number of key areas are needed, namely in the areas of technology, processes and people.

Changes in technology

The recent changes in technology have brought about significant modifications in the way in which business and specifically CRM, can be done. For a leader in the organisation, it is vital that changes be brought about in technology to make it possible to implement the CRM strategy. The effect of technology is strategic within the organisation, especially in the case of CRM. The technology will enable the organisation to not only stay up to date with its customers, but also to collect additional information with every transaction that takes place. The technologies that have been developed for specific CRM applications are known as information and communications technologies (better known by the abbreviation ICT). These technologies enable the implementation of CRM within the organisation. There are two main aspects to these technologies, namely the front-office applications (which are integrated with the customer database) and the customer contact and access channels.[7] ICT is an integral part of the success of the CRM strategy and involvement of the information technology (IT) department contributes to the success of the programme (see also Chapter 10).

Implementing new technology

New technology causes confusion in the minds of staff and so a great deal of care needs to be taken when deciding which software will most adequately satisfy the needs of the CRM strategy. Examples of technology that can be introduced are the Internet, as well as CRM software that is able to track and update the customer database. Examples of these include customer support and service (CSS) software as well as sales force automation software. New software is continually being developed that can be used to collect and interpret customer data, plus evaluate the customer behaviour being exhibited. Adoption of the new technology may be a problem, but this change management process has to be managed by the leader. The development of software specific to the organisation can also be considered, depending on its needs.

Training in new technology

When the new technology has been selected and purchased, it is important to train the staff in using the technology to its full capacity. This means that not only is the initial training vital in making staff able to use the technology, but it is also necessary to continue with the training as more advanced applications are introduced. Training courses can be customised to meet the specific needs that the staff experience.

The challenge that technology presents is that it is real-time technology; as such it is required to support decision-making as it provides information immediately. These decisions are made continually, not on a once-off basis as they may have been made in the past.[8] This also places pressure on the technology to be reliable and stable. This means that the information that it provides should be consistent and that the system should not 'crash' on a regular basis.

One of the technologies that needs to be developed is the use of various social media in the CRM programme. Social media (such as Facebook, YouTube and Twitter) are valuable as tools as they enable two-way communication between the organisation and the consumer. This enables the organisation to know what customers are thinking and feeling immediately. It also provides a platform for consumers to interact with the organisation. These media are powerful as the comments and conversations are visible to everyone and thus impact other consumers.

Integration of technology within the organisation

In large organisations with many divisions, the technology used by the various divisions is often not complementary. This means that the systems used in one department are not accessible to other departments. It also means that the customers are inconvenienced, as there are no standard forms available for their use and they are required to submit new applications with all their details, rather than just to alter the existing information.

The example that follows illustrates not only the importance of technology within CRM, but also that the leader is required to integrate these various systems to the benefit of the customer.

What happens without integration?

In the case of a financial institution, a division, such as home loans, may use a different technology to the credit card division. This means that if a person wants to increase their credit limit, they are required to submit proof of identity and income, etc. which another division of the bank already has in its possession. This creates the impression that the bank is highly inefficient and it is frustrating for the customer.[9]

Changes in processes

Processes refer to the way in which things are done to enable the strategy to be implemented successfully and CRM requires that the processes be customer-centric.[10] Processes need to be developed around the customer and their needs, and they can be used to govern the relationship that is created between the organisation and the customer.[11] The processes that are referred to include the expectations and commitments that are part of the relationship, the roles that the various parties play in the relationship and the time that will be committed to the relationship. It may also be necessary to change the processes for different customers, ie whether they are B2B (business-to-business) customers or whether they are individual customers.

Processes refer not only to those things that affect the customer, but also to the way in which relationships are managed within the organisation, which includes the organisational structure and the corporate culture that exists. The organisational processes include the automation of the selling process, which can assist in tracking both the sales and the process of the order.[12] CRM strategy requires changes in the processes within the organisation in a number of different areas, as outlined below.

Implementing changes in organisational processes

Here we refer to the changes that need to be made to the organisation's internal processes, such as administration procedures, in order to implement a CRM strategy. These processes need to be integrated with the technology chosen for the CRM strategy.

> Forms and documentation may not always be compatible with the new technology. The database may require the inclusion of fields that are not part of the documentation, in which case those capturing the data need to omit these items. Such items may, at a later stage, determine key actions that are required within the strategy. This may include customer information that has not been collected. Ideally the customer needs to input data directly. This eliminates errors in processing as there is no transfer process.

A further organisational process that may change has to do with the institution of a management team to manage the CRM strategy. A CRM strategy team is suggested as a method of governing the relationship between the organisation and its customers in terms of the new CRM strategy being implemented. This team would involve a group of people, including the management of the organisation and key customers.[13] This team has the task of expressing and clarifying the rights of all the parties in relation to the new system, including those of the customer.

This may require the organisation to give up a degree of control over the marketing activities in the organisation, which is not necessarily a popular idea and may be subject to varying degrees of resistance. It is suggested that the membership of this team be temporary in nature and that meetings take place on a quarterly basis to facilitate the relationship.

Implementing changes in corporate culture

Corporate culture is a key determinant of the long-term success of CRM strategy implementation. Corporate culture refers to the common characteristics that exist within the organisation that express the traditions, values, customs and practices that characterise the people who work there.[14] The culture is largely intangible, yet it reflects the way in which things are done within the organisation. The corporate culture of an organisation can be seen in the shared values, the norms of behaviour that are exhibited, and the symbols and symbolic values that are reflected within the organisation.[15] The purpose of the culture is to bring together a group of diverse people and bind them together so that they can strive towards achieving common goals. The culture of the organisation is determined by the management, specifically the top, or executive, management.

Corporate culture in action

A practical example of corporate culture can be seen in the dress code for work. There are organisations where employees coming to work in shorts and T-shirts is perfectly acceptable. This is a reflection of the corporate culture that exists. There are also many other organisations where this style of dressing would antagonise the management, as it goes counter to these organisations' culture. It is the culture that determines whether a particular style of dressing or type of behaviour is acceptable within a specific context. Another example of corporate culture are words and phrases that are used.

Four types of corporate culture can be identified:[16]

- **Power culture:** Usually found in smaller organisations, this kind of culture is defined by a central person, a power source. This person (or group of people) has the power, hence the organisation tends to be political in nature and employees tend to display a tendency to power, politics and risk taking.
- **Person culture:** Here, the individual determines the culture and the culture of the organisation is subordinate to the individual. Control mechanisms,

such as budgets, will only be successful if there is consensus regarding their use.

- **Role culture:** As a bureaucracy, there is great emphasis placed on the role played by each person within the organisation. The power source is the position that the individual holds.

- **Job culture:** This is linked to the implementation of a specific project, where the team is required to complete a specific task by co-operating with the other people who are concerned.

The corporate culture can either be an obstacle or a catalyst in the process of strategy implementation. If the culture is supportive, it will make the implementation of the strategy more successful (and much easier), while if the strategy is an obstacle, changes in the culture will be needed if the strategy is to be implemented successfully.[17]

The ideal situation comes about when the strategy and the corporate culture are in agreement, which means that the culture is supportive of the strategy selected. This means that there are no underlying impediments to the implementation process. Should aspects of the CRM strategy be in conflict with the culture, it will be necessary to bring about changes to the culture if the strategy is to be a success. This is a long-term process and one that does not take place easily.

The implementation of a CRM strategy may have an impact on the culture of the organisation. The CRM strategy is one that has a high customer focus and this may require changes in employees' behaviour towards customers. It may also require longer working hours, or hours that are more convenient to the customer, while being more inconvenient for the staff.

Changing opening hours to suit the customer

Woolworths food stores are open until 8 pm at night. This is to enable their customers to shop at hours that are convenient to them. However, this means that the store is open at hours that are inconvenient to staff, which has necessitated a change in shifts, as well as a willingness among staff to provide service at different hours from those that are regarded as the norm.

Cultural change is brought about by top management and is a long-term process.[18] This change takes place as a result of the changes brought about by staff, as well as through deliberate actions of the top management of the organisation. Leadership, and especially the development of a customer leader, can affect the corporate culture and change it towards that of a customer orientation.[19]

Without this change in corporate culture, the necessary support for the strategy may not exist, making its long-term success questionable.

Implementing training programmes

In order to implement a high-customer-focus strategy such as a CRM strategy, it is necessary that training be conducted among the staff so as to enable them not only to deal with the situations presented by the customers, but also to use the CRM technology efficiently. Both of these require effective training programmes for all staff. It means that the staff need to be trained at times suited to them and on topics that they feel are important, not necessarily as determined by the organisation and the training department. This may mean the development of smaller courses or where only parts of the courses are presented to satisfy a specific need. Extensive consultation with staff will be required for this to be implemented. Training enables the organisation to receive the maximum benefit from the programme being implemented.

Developing organisational structures that support the CRM strategy

It may also be necessary to adapt the structure of the organisation to reflect the change in strategy. The structure that is developed within the organisation is one that needs to support the strategy, and much has been written concerning the strategy-structure relationship, as well as the nature and types of structures that can be used. Care needs to be taken in the selection of an organisational structure and, under certain circumstances, it may be necessary to make adjustments to the strategy to increase its effectiveness.

Various factors affect the selection of an appropriate organisational structure. These factors can be divided up into three main categories:[20]

- **Internal factors:** These refer to those issues that are found within the organisation that can have an effect on the structure. Examples of these factors include the skills levels of the staff, the motivation and leadership styles, as well as the culture of the organisation.

- **External factors:** These factors refer to the environment of the area/city, region and country in which the organisation operates, as well as the international environment in which it operates.

- **Market factors:** These refer to the competitors that can be identified in the environment, the organisation's customers, the product (or service) complexity and the technological changes that can be identified.

After examining these factors, the organisation will be required to select an appropriate organisational structure. The aim of the structure will be to attain the goals of the organisation, which is the implementation of the CRM strategy. This new strategy will require different levels of responsibility from employees, as well as different skills and leadership.

Changing the way in which people work

One of the most important aspects in implementing any strategy is to bring about changes in people and the way in which they do their work. Part of trying to implement change is dealing with people's inherent tendency to resist such change. This resistance to change comes about from the fear of the unknown, as well as the uncertainty that accompanies any change. It is seen in people's reluctance to implement new methods, systems and ways of working, or in their tendency to make more errors.

Reasons for resistance to change are diverse and they include:[21]

- **Inertia:** This implies that staff are content with the current way in which things are done and they are reluctant to do things differently.

- **Time pressure:** If people are under time pressure, their resistance to change increases, as they are required to put more effort into getting the job done in a shorter time.

- **Surprise:** If the changes are unexpected and there has been little psychological preparation for them, resistance is more likely.

- **Peer pressure:** Where a group is cohesive, its members will stand together regarding their opinion of the change and this can increase the degree of resistance to change.

- **Self-interest:** Resistance to change comes about when it is not clear how the person will be affected by the change being proposed. Resistance reflects insecurity regarding people's future with respect to changes that are taking place.

- **Uncertainty:** This creates a situation where employees are not sure about their position or how change will affect them. Too little information and communication will increase the levels of uncertainty regarding the various aspects of the changes that are being considered.

It will be necessary for the leader to counter resistance to change if the implementation of the strategy is to be successful. Strategies that can be used to counter resistance to change include education of the staff regarding the proposed changes in strategy; communication regarding the nature of the changes; and encouraging the participation and involvement of all staff members in the implementation process itself.

The change process will have to be managed by the organisation's leaders in order to ensure that the desired changes are implemented by employees and that they have bought into the changes and are prepared to implement them fully.

The importance of communication in the implementation of CRM

Communication within the organisation is essential in the implementation of the CRM strategy. It is not only communication with customers (externally), but also communication internally with all of the staff in the organisation. Without the communication of information to employees, there will be increased resistance to change, lower degrees of participation in the change process and a bad motivational effect on staff.

The relationship with customers is managed through communication with them through a two-way flow of information. This is done through the organisation communicating with each customer in their preferred way, whether it be the telephone, email or SMS.[22] It is essential that when a customer initiates contact, they are channelled to those employees within the organisation most suited to dealing with the issues being raised. The employees who deal with the customer need to record the communication and need to be trained in handling the complaints and comments made by the customer.

Control of a CRM strategy

A strategy is not implemented without first making decisions regarding how to determine its success. Any strategy will have key areas that will determine whether it was successful in achieving its goal. The CRM strategy is one that requires a great deal of investment on the part of the organisation and it is necessary to determine if it has been successful. The success of any strategy is determined by the objectives that have been set for the strategy.

Indicators of the strategy's success include:[23]

- revenue increases that occur as a result of the strategy, as well as the associated decline in costs;
- the acquisition of new customers;
- the customer experience and perceptions of this experience;
- good retention rates of existing customers;

- high revenues and profitability for new customers in comparison to existing customers;
- acquiring competitors' share of business; and
- acquiring competitors' share of core customers' business.

Each of these indicators can point to the aspects of the programme that have been successful, and which of these aspects need to be changed or improved.

It has been suggested that a fairly high percentage of CRM implementations fail. In 2009 approximately 47 per cent of programmes did not attain the goals set for the plan.[24] These programmes were not necessarily a total failure, but they did not achieve their objectives. Reasons for this include unrealistic expectations and IT systems failing to meet expectations.

Summary

In order to implement a CRM strategy, it is necessary to have the right technology, the right processes and the right people. The implementation process depends on first having these three key components in place, and then fully implementing the CRM strategy. These three components need to be adapted where necessary to ensure the success of the CRM strategy. It is also necessary to pay attention to the way in which the process will be controlled in order to determine whether the strategy has been successfully implemented.

DISCUSSION QUESTIONS

1. Why is implementation important in a CRM strategy?
2. Why is leadership important in a CRM strategy?
3. What is meant by CRL?
4. What are the components of CRL?
5. In what three key areas are changes needed if the implementation of a CRM strategy is to be successful?
6. How can technology affect the implementation of a CRM strategy?
7. How do changes in processes affect the implementation of a CRM strategy?
8. How can leaders overcome resistance to change?
9. Why is communication important in the implementation of a CRM strategy?
10. How can the implementation of a CRM strategy be controlled?

Mini case study

Steve's Stationers

Steven de Waal operates a stationery company in Johannesburg. He started the business in 1978, opening a store in the downtown central business district (CBD). His primary market was the businesses in the CBD, but there was also a significant percentage of sales to passing trade.

Over time, Steven opened more branches of the business in shopping malls in various parts of Johannesburg. Each of the stores had significant corporate support in its specific area. There are currently 11 stores around Johannesburg and Steven has planned to open new stores in other centres around South Africa.

An investigation into Steven's business has indicated that the corporate sector makes up 70 per cent of the business conducted. These corporate clients spend an average of R3 900 per month on stationery supplies.

The stationery market is very competitive. Not only are there many small stationery stores, but stationery is also sold in supermarkets, while there has been a concerted effort on the part of some wholesalers to sell more stationery, using price discounting specifically to do so. It is in this competitive market that Steven trades.

An examination of Steven's corporate clients indicates that 20 per cent of clients contribute 80 per cent of the profits of the organisation. The remaining 80 per cent of clients cause the greatest amount of administration work for the staff in Steven's stationery store. Many of these clients do not pay their accounts on time and it requires extensive follow-up for the monies owing to be collected.

Steven is the CEO of the business and there is a geographic structure within the organisation. Each store has a branch manager and it is each manager's responsibility to contact the functional manager regarding their stock and staff requirements. Each store has a computer system, but this is not connected by means of a server or network system. The marketing manager has a number of sales representatives who visit the various businesses in order to gain orders. Each order placed is delivered within 24 hours.

Steven has decided that a CRM strategy is required to improve profits in the corporate market. He is aware that 80 per cent of profits tend to be generated by 20 per cent of the customers, so wants to use this knowledge to the benefit of the organisation.

MINI CASE STUDY QUESTIONS

1. Formulate the objectives for Steven's CRM strategy.

2. Explain the technology that Steven will need to use to implement the CRM strategy.

3. Explain the changes in processes that will be required to implement the strategy.

4. Explain the changes in people that will be required to implement the CRM strategy.

5. How will Steven determine whether the strategy has been successful?

Technologies and metrics in CRM

Learning outcomes

After studying this chapter, you should be able to:
- explain the importance of technology in facilitating the CRM process;
- identify the various technologies that support and impact on CRM;
- explain the importance of metrics in managing the CRM process;
- identify selected metrics that relate to CRM.

Introduction

Customer relationship management (CRM) has become almost totally reliant on technology. Quite a number of the aspects that make up CRM, for example facilitating and building relationships with customers, could not function without information technology or technological support. This chapter will explain the importance of technology in the CRM process, identify the most important technologies that support CRM and finally explain the key metrics used to manage and evaluate the CRM process.

As well as using technology to facilitate CRM, it can also be used to keep track of the organisation's CRM efforts. This is important for two reasons: it justifies the money being spent on implementing CRM; and it highlights what is effective and what is not (ie it enables the organisation to become more efficient in its CRM activities). Obviously, the activities that are effective need to be expanded on, while those that are ineffective need to be addressed in some way – either done away with completely or revamped to ensure that they are effective. Thus, the second part of this chapter addresses some of the key metrics that are used in the CRM field.

The CRM context

In order to deal with technologies and metrics in this chapter, we need to briefly revisit two issues that are crucial to an understanding of CRM. The first relates to the strategic versus tactical perspective of CRM, while the second relates to the customers' experiences and their 'touch points' with the organisation.

CRM has two main perspectives: a strategic perspective and a narrower tactical perspective.[1] As a strategic perspective, CRM is a mindset; a way of life. It is about understanding and becoming closer to and more personal with each customer. The strategy puts the customer at the centre of the organisation. The tactical view of CRM tends to look at how technologies and processes can be used to build this relationship with the customer.[2]

In the case of the strategic view of CRM, most of the effort is put into managing customer relationships with the organisation. The strategic view is a holistic outlook that seeks to maximise stakeholder value by developing long-term customer relationships that bring with them sustainable profitability at lower cost.[3] This outlook is built on the premise that it is cheaper to maintain an existing customer than to find a new customer.[4] On the tactical front, however, the focus is more on using technologies and processes to track, analyse and understand customers, and to place this knowledge in the hands of frontline staff as well those staff that develop the systems, process and products that serve the customer.[5]

Regarding the second issue, it is important to know that CRM is a customer-centric approach. This approach acknowledges, amongst other things, that customers may have many different 'touch points' (ie various interactions) with an organisation and their experiences of these touch points contributes to shaping their overall view of the company. Generally positive experiences translate into a positive view of the organisation, while generally negative experiences may translate into a negative view. Clearly, this positive or negative view impacts directly on customers' future purchasing and the long-term relationship they are likely to have with the company. This understanding of touch points is important because various technologies are used at a tactical level to facilitate, in a positive way, the interaction between customer and organisation at these touch points.

We will draw on the above points later in this chapter. We now focus on highlighting some of the key technologies that are used to support CRM.

Technologies to support CRM

There are many technologies used to support CRM. These fall into two main categories, namely hardware and software technologies, and include online applications, promotional technologies, social media, call centre and telephony tools, handheld devices, and remote kiosks and dispensing machines. The single technology that serves as the cornerstone for almost all CRM activities is the computer. It is really only since the development of the computer that CRM has taken off. Desktop computers came into being in the early 1980s, while the transition from transactional marketing to relational marketing took place in the 1990s.[6] If one thinks about it logically, this makes sense. In order to build a relationship with customers, it is necessary to know who they are, record their transactions and individual peculiarities, and then analyse such information to better customise future promotions and marketing offerings aimed at these customers. Doing this by hand is almost impossible. It needed computer processing power to be able to capture, analyse and interpret this data and this was only possible some time after the first desktop computer appeared in 1981.

Increased computer processing led to a rise in CRM

Once desktop computers took hold and became more commonplace in the 1990s, so CRM slowly began to take off. As computers became faster and smaller, it became possible to expand CRM efforts further afield. For example, laptops and netbooks (smaller, less powerful, but more mobile versions of laptops developed for Internet access 'on the go') have made it easier to gather data in the field. Today, various handheld computing devices, combined with the World Wide Web (referred to as 'the web'), have expanded the adoption and application of CRM exponentially. Examples of such devices include the tablet (a small, book-like computing 'screen' a bit bigger than a smartphone but with many computing and wireless connectivity features built into the device); the personal digital assistant or PDA (similar to a smartphone but without any telephone capability); and the smartphone (essentially a cell phone with advanced computing functionality and wireless connectivity built into it).

Furthermore, as computer processors have become smaller, it has become possible to embed such processors in devices such as fridges, motor vehicles, televisions (TVs) and hundreds of other everyday devices. This has made it possible to track customer usage of such devices and even to control the performance of these devices remotely. With wireless communications, these devices can linkup with the Internet, enabling data to be captured and sent back to the companies that produced them so that they can better understand the use of the products in question and thereby improve them.

Clearly, it is not computers alone that have had the major impact on CRM that we see today, but rather the convergence of other technologies with computers, such as satellite communications, the Internet, wireless devices and cell technologies.

CRM software solutions

Computers, however, are actually quite dumb devices. They only do what the software that runs on them tells them to do. Software applications are where the solutions to CRM challenges and power lie. Today there are many CRM software applications that exist (see Box 10.1 on the following page for some well-known vendors). There are essentially five main categories, as listed below.

- **Enterprise solutions** are software solutions aimed at large corporations and usually built into existing enterprise resource planning (ERP) systems. Examples include SAP and Oracle.

- **Stand-alone or on-premise solutions** are software applications that are housed at the company and managed (sometimes even built) by its own employees.

- **Hosted solutions** (also known as on-demand CRM) are owned, maintained and hosted by a third-party supplier at a remote site and allow the client to access the services online (usually via the Internet) as needed. They provide a simpler, faster and often more affordable way for a business to gain value from software that would otherwise be too expensive to acquire.

- **Mobile CRM** are fully-featured software solutions accessible via smartphones, tablet devices, personal digital assistants and laptops/netbooks. They allow sales, service and support staff to access and interact with a full range of customer data while in the field.

- **Web-based (or customer-directed/self-help) solutions** allow customers to access and update their own data via the web and to request and/or access customer-related services from a company, wherever the customer may be.

The objectives of CRM software include to:

- track and manage all customer-related information in single desktop interface;

- provide access to a complete history of the customer (their personal details as well as their purchasing history and preferences);

- leverage the individual expertise of certain staff within an organisation through knowledge management;

- automate business processes to initiate actions;

- know which marketing campaigns are having the most impact on customers;

- standardise and automate the sales process where possible;

- track customer services interactions and measure levels of customer service;

- use corporate dashboards to gauge key performance indicators;
- consolidate various customer database silos into a single contact list.

10.1 WELL-KNOWN SOFTWARE VENDORS

Clarity soft	WebCRM	coAction
Infusion	RightNow	eSalesTrack
NetSuite	Parature	Marketo
Maximizer	Ivinex	Surado
Oracle	Landslide	Zoho
Pivotal	Infor	Salesnet
ProspectSoft	FrontRange	Soffront
Sage	Kana	VAI
Salesforce.com	Eloqua	Microsoft Dynamics
SAP	Consona	Amdocs

Telephony solutions[7]

Contact with customers is an important cornerstone of an organisation's CRM efforts and the telephone is a key tool in facilitating such contact. Most organisations today have a call centre of sorts, even if it is only one person handling customer queries. More often than not, however, companies have a small (or even large) department of individuals to handle calls from their customers, be it for marketing information, to query accounts, lodge complaints or to request assistance. Other companies may out-source their call centre services to third-party call centre operations that handle customer calls for a fee. Figure 10.1 and Figure 10.2 illustrates what typical large call centres look like. The individuals who operate the telephones are normally referred to as call centre agents and they make use of computer-aided telephony systems to receive and make calls.

Figure 10.1 Typical call centres[8]

Figure 10.2 Call centre operator[9]

At the core of any call centre (big or small) are the telephone lines and service agents needed to ensure that all calls are answered relatively quickly. There is nothing worse in the process of building customer relationships than to allow a customer to wait 10–20 minutes to get through to a number either because there are too few lines or too few people to answer the calls. The basic telephone system should also provide easy call forwarding, call hopping, call waiting, redialling, automated message taking, etc. Linked to the underlying telephone system is the computer-assisted telephone system that manages the calls between agents, enables calls to be recorded, and provides agents with assistance and access to databases so that they can serve customers better.

The purposes of such call centres are primarily to solve customers' queries (involving receiving in-bound calls) or to generate sales (involving the making of out-bound calls) both important touch points with the customer. In the case of customer queries, these may be many and varied. In such instances, the customer does not want to be put through to different individuals or departments in order to get their query dealt with. Instead, they want a 'one-stop' solution. However, it is unlikely that there will be a call centre agent who is familiar with all of the aspects of the company (bearing in mind that the agent may work for an out-sourced call centre firm). This is where the computer-assisted telephony systems become useful. Such solutions are inevitably computer-based and software driven.

Computer-assisted telephony systems tap into the CRM database systems of the organisation and place comprehensive customer details, as well as sales, service and communication history, in the hands of the agent. Call centre agents must be fully trained, not only to use the system, but also to follow the required process to assist customers with their queries. Such processes are often software directed; that is, the software dictates what the questions are that the agent should ask, as well as what answers to give the customer (these question-and-answer directions are called 'scripts'). Such software solutions are commonly based on artificial intelligence and are increasingly able to record and decipher natural language conversations. The simple act of being able to record a conversation is useful for later training, quality assurance purposes and to solve a dispute with a customer.

Telephony hardware that has helped to improve call centre performance includes wireless telephones that enable call centre agents to move around without disconnecting the customer, perhaps to visit another nearby agent or to do other work in order to be more productive. Hands-free headsets have enabled the agent to interact with a computer while still talking to the customer. Before the introduction of such devices, the agent would need to hold on to the receiver and jam it between their ear and shoulder – an awkward way to work if this is your fulltime job. Today, telephones are digital devices which mean that conversations can be recorded, stored, analysed and even forwarded to other, more appropriate, individuals within the organisation to respond to.

With the emergence of the web, call centres are increasingly being integrated with an organisation's online web-based services and some examples are given in this chapter. Thus, agents can direct customers to various webpages for more information and to access specific (often self-help) services.

Interactive voice-response systems

One frustrating feature of modern call centres is that the customer may have to work through a whole host of automated or interactive voice response (IVR) options when first calling the call centre number. The idea behind this call channelling is to direct the customer to the most suitable call centre agent (agents often specialise in providing assistance in specific areas). While this may seem sensible, it is frustrating for a customer needing to interact with impersonal automatic telephone responses for a long process before eventually making human contact. An example of Discovery Health's excellent customer service is given in Box 10.2.

10.2 EXCEPTIONAL CUSTOMER SERVICE BY DISCOVERY HEALTH[10]

For Discovery Health, exceptional customer service requires rapid payments of claims and seamless access to healthcare facilities. To address these needs, Discovery Health makes a continuous investment in developing new operational products and services as well as ensuring robust information technology. This service infrastructure shown in the table below supports the very high volumes and delivers consistent levels of service across the business (figures are for 2011):

Claims	
Claims volumes per month	3.7 million
Percentage of claims submitted electronically	88 per cent
Claims amounts paid for each working hour	R12 million
Percentage of rands paid directly to the healthcare professionals	94 per cent
Claims error rate	0.9 per cent
Average days from receipt to processed	0.21 days
Average days from receipt to paid (members)	1.85 days
Call centre	
Number of calls a day	33 500
Percentage answered within 20 seconds	84 per cent
Percentage of calls abandoned	1.8 per cent

Voice-over Internet protocol

Internet technology has made it possible for individuals and companies to make and receive calls over the Internet instead of using either traditional telephone landlines or cell phones. This type of telephone call is called voice-over Internet protocol (or VoIP). The major benefit of VoIP is cost saving. Sending and receiving VoIP calls is much cheaper than using landlines or cell phones. Other benefits relate to the fact that VoIP is a digital medium that uses computers and the Internet as the main communication channel. This makes it possible to record and store messages, automate the sending and receiving of calls, and to link these calls to other digital media such as video. Thus, it is the flexibility of VoIP that, when added to the enormous cost savings, makes this technology so powerful for delivering customer service. Essentially the same benefits that a telephone and/or cell phone bring to a company can also be achieved using VoIP.

Cell phones

The modern-day cell phone (also called a 'mobile') is also a form of telephony. The power of the cell phone is that it is mobile (the user carries the phone with him/her most of the time and can therefore be reached at times even when they is not near a landline telephone). Another benefit of the cell phone is that it is digital and can therefore be connected to and controlled from a computer. This makes it possible to send and receive messages generated by computers and to control the storage and recall of messages.

Text messaging

Text messaging – also known as short messaging service or SMS – enables a user to create a small text message (usually up to 160 characters in length, but today, several messages can be linked together as a single communication) and to send this text message from one cell phone to another. The benefits of text messaging are that it is cheap, relatively easy to use, can be sent from and received by a computer, can be stored and can even incorporate multimedia features such as pictures and short videos (this function is normally referred to as multimedia messaging service or MMS rather than SMS). Texting is also a good alternative way of reaching someone whose cell phone is turned off. Texting is timesaving and relatively affordable. It is also less intrusive than calling someone. When the recipient receives a text message, they can view the message whenever it suits them.

Furthermore, texting is a great way to communicate with customers when you do not necessarily want to be caught up in long conversations with them. For example, if a customer has just bought something from your store or business and they have given their cell phone number to you, sending them a short text message to thank them for their support is an effective way of enhancing customer relations.

Texting can also be used to:

- let a customer know that an activity that you have undertaken on their behalf (a repair, for example) is complete;

- allow customers to track where an order, repair or parcel delivery is in the process;

- check whether a product the customer is interested in is available at the store;

- request a price quotation for a product;

- allow customers to rate a company's service or provide a short review of a product;

- enable customers to request alternative products and pricing to the one they have selected;

- inform customers of store policies and/or store hours/locations;

- remind customers of an event or outstanding account;

- wish them well on their birthday (again, fostering good customer relations);

- inform customers of the introduction of new products or services;

- provide feedback that a customer requested;

- provide a means for a customer to submit information or to lodge a complaint;

- schedule an appointment; and

- provide a form of confirmation for the customer for payments made or actions taken (such as an article handed in for repair).

Another major benefit of text messaging is that an SMS sent from a customer's phone can be used to activate an account, make a payment, open and close a door, start a machine, switch on a device or initiate any type of electronic activity.

Unstructured supplementary service data

Unstructured Supplementary Service Data (USSD) is a technology unique to Global System for Mobile communication (GSM) based cell telephones (the ones used in South Africa). It is a capability built into the GSM standard which supports real-time (or session-based) transmission of information over the signalling channels of the GSM network. USSD is similar to SMSs, except that the latter are a store-and-forward method of transmission and is therefore somewhat slower. In the case of USSD, the connection remains open, allowing a two-way exchange of a sequence of data. This makes USSD more responsive than services that use SMS and can be used to access or submit information to databases.

In operation, USSD is used to send text between the user and some application (such as a database). The primary benefit of USSD is that it allows for very fast communication between the user and the application. Most of the applications enabled by USSD are menu-based and include services such as mobile prepay and chat. How it works is that the user composes a message – usually rather cryptic – on the cell phone keyboard. The phone sends it to the cell phone company network where it is received by a computer dedicated to USSD. Some processing or database querying may occur on the computer. The answer from the computer (which could be information drawn from a database for a sales person in the field) is sent back to the cell phone. The answer can be seen on the cell phone screen, but it is usually with a very basic presentation. Messages sent over USSD are not defined by any standardisation body, so each network operator can implement whatever it decides is suitable for its customers.

USSD can be used to provide independent calling services such as a callback service (for example, cheaper cell phone charges while roaming) or an interactive data service (for example, stock quotes or sports results). It can also be used to query a database (for example to access customer information when out of the office) or to make cell micro-payments. Cell micro-payment systems, such as SWAP Mobile in South Africa, Mobipay in Spain, and M-Pesa in Tanzania, all use USSD technology.

Promotional technologies

In a discussion of the technologies that support CRM, we need to understand that one of the touch points that customers have with an organisation is with the promotional and branding efforts of the company. These are about the organisation promoting itself to customers in order to create a positive image of the company (ie the brand) in their minds. This promotion, or communication, is often the first contact the customer has with the company. It is usually a one-way, company-to-customer (or push) type of communication.

Technology plays an important role in the promotional and branding efforts of most organisations. Technologies used for promotional purposes include, amongst others, radio, television, print, billboards, kiosks, telephony, the web, social media, email, and cell phones. While most of these are seen as 'everyday' technologies, they remain technologies that play a role in building relationships with customers on the promotional front. Bear in mind that these same technologies may be used for other CRM purposes beyond promotion. For example, websites and social media have become key channels to allow the customer to communicate back to the company. Using such technologies, customers can request assistance, provide input, pay accounts or complain about a problem they are currently experiencing. These are all different touch points for the customer and are different from the promotional touch point referred to earlier (albeit that the technologies used are the same).

Marketing managers need to understand the promotional technologies that are available to them and how best to use these technologies in the CRM process. Although many of the technologies have been around for some time, they are changing and improving all the time. For example, in the past billboards were massive boards on the side of highways and streets onto which were pasted large-format posters. Changing these billboards took effort and required a long lead-time. Today, many of these billboards are digital and can portray a dynamic message or even a video. In the past, if a marketing manager needed to change a message quickly for some reason it was quite difficult, if not impossible, to do. However, with the new electronic and digital billboards, a message can now be updated or changed completely within minutes, even from a remote location. This provides the marketing manager with additional flexibility that was not available before.

Similar advances have been made with other promotional technologies. In the field of television, for example, with the advent of DSTV and the personal video recorder (PVR) customers now have the power to record TV programmes and play them back later, fast-forwarding over advertising messages. Marketing managers need to consider whether it is still worthwhile using TV advertising to reach their customers, given that customers can choose to fast-forward over the advertisements. However, the move to high definition (HD) TV makes it possible to portray advertising messages at a level of quality and clarity that was not possible before. For products where it is important to show a richness of colour, this move to HD TV is very beneficial.

Print advertising provides another example. Today, it is possible to print messages on a wider variety of materials and to incorporate special features such as luminous print so the message can be seen at night. This places new promotional opportunities in the hands of the marketer. Also the introduction of the Internet, the web, social media and other online technologies has made incredible promotional opportunities available to marketing managers that were not possible 20 years ago. Such online technologies have become so important today that we discuss them separately. See the section on Online technologies on page 226.

Marketing managers must constantly keep an eye open for new developments in promotional technologies and consider how such developments could enhance their promotional touch points with customers. Clearly, not every development is usable. Marketing managers need to decide which will best suit their needs.

Sales force automation technologies

One of the first contact (or touch) points that organisations have with customers are often via the sales person. This might be in a store or at the customer's premises or at a trade show or almost any place where the sales person might meet a prospective customer and where the customer is ready to learn a bit more about the company and its products. Sales staff are often also called upon to solve problems before they can sell. For example, upon encountering a sales person, the customer may say to the sales person that they is still waiting for an answer on an account query they have lodged and so they are unwilling to buy anything else from the company until the query is addressed. Thus, before the sales person can begin selling they first have to solve the query on hand. If they refer the customer to a colleague in the company, the problem may take yet more time to be solved and result in a lost sales opportunity. It would be a very powerful if the sales person could solve the problem there and then.

Thus, sales force automation (SFA) should strive to achieve four goals, it should:

- have a marketing function;
- have a data capture function;
- empower the selling process; and
- enable the sales person to solve problems.

There are several technologies that contribute to, or form the basis of, SFA. Clearly, the computer is one. Today, laptops/netbooks and, increasingly, tablet devices, smartphones and PDAs are being used by sales staff to capture information, demonstrate products in video form, access customer data and to connect to head office for input or approval. As we have mentioned before, computers alone have no meaning and it is the software solutions that are hosted on computers that actually put power in the hands of the sales force. Ideally, the sales person would want to have access to software that automates the business tasks of sales, including order processing, contact management, information sharing, inventory monitoring and control, order tracking, customer management, sales forecast analysis and employee performance evaluation.

More specifically, SFA software generally includes a contact management system which tracks all contact that has been made with a given customer, the purpose of the contact and any follow up that may be needed. This ensures that sales efforts are not duplicated, reducing the risk of irritating customers. SFA software also includes a sales lead tracking system, which lists potential customers often obtained from third-party, paid-for phone lists or customers of related products. Other elements of an SFA system can include sales forecasting, order management and product knowledge. More developed SFA systems have features where customers can actually model the product to meet their needs through online product-building systems. This is becoming more and more popular in the automobile industry, where patrons can customise various features such as colour and interior features such as leather versus upholstered seats. An integral part of any SFA system is company-wide integration among different departments. If SFA systems are not adopted and properly integrated with all departments, there may be a lack of communication which could result in different departments contacting the same customer for the same purpose. In order to mitigate this risk, SFA must be fully integrated across all departments that deal with customer service management.[11]

We have already mentioned some of the CRM software that the sales force may also tap into, but sales force-specific software includes, amongst others: Sage ACT!; Goldmine; Sales Cloud; OracleSalesOnline; Microsoft Dynamics CRM; SalesForce; SugarCRM; SalesNet; Salestrakr; LeadMaster; Maximizer and NetSuite CRM+.

Kiosk and dispensing machine technologies

Today, many organisations make use of remote information, teller and dispensing machines to deliver services, information and even products to customers. For some companies such machines are peripheral to the company's work, for others they are at the core of the company's marketing and sales activities. For example, cool drink vending companies, such as Amalgamated Beverage Industries (ABI) (marketers of Coca Cola in South Africa) have thousands of vending machines located in offices and buildings around the country. Such vending machines are one of their key selling channels. These vending machines are also a major touch point for the customer and an issue in the customer's experience of the company. If their experience with the vending machine is a negative one (for example, they put their money in the machine, but no cool drink comes out) it will have a direct impact on the customer's relationship with the organisation (they may feel that the company is 'stealing' from them).

Similarly, if a bank's automated teller machine (ATM) is slow or not working it will affect the customer's experience of the bank and so weaken the relationship the bank has with the customer. A faulty automated information kiosk in a shopping mall may provide a frustrating experience for the customer and this takes something away from the relationship between organisation and customer. Conversely, machines that function well and provide remote and well-distributed services for customers will contribute to building a better relationship with the customer. Thus, organisations need to take special care to ensure that such machines are always working that they and provide the expected service.

Technology is changing all the time, and we need to be aware of future advances and their potential, see Box 10.3 for some examples.

10.3 OH, I LET MY FRIDGE DO MY SHOPPING!

Increasingly, communication between electronic devices is happening wirelessly (cell phones, for example, are primarily wireless devices). By building wireless technology into various everyday machines, it is possible for the machines to be controlled by cell phones, laptops, desktop computers and other wireless devices. For example, in Japan consumers can buy cool drinks and sweets from automated vending machines using the wireless technology capability of their cell phones or even their laptops. It is now also possible to use your cell phone or smart card to gain access to buildings or to pay for entrance to sports stadiums, all using wireless technology. Wireless technology in fridges, for example, can determine what products you are short of by scanning radio frequency identifiers. These are devices embedded in the packaging of products. Fridges can send a message to your cell phone encouraging you to purchase these out-of-stock goods or can even initiate the purchase themselves (in practice, it may be some time before this becomes commonplace). The opportunities to use wireless technology for customer service and support are still largely unexplored, mainly because the novelty of this technology.

Database mining and marketing

Companies often gather large amounts of information from and about their customers. Unfortunately, this information often lies in these databases unused. A database is an electronic storage space for organised information usually found on a computer's hard drive. Instead, what companies should be doing is to proactively capture and analyse this information. Such a process is called data mining or database mining. These findings should then be used to strengthen their relationships with their customers (database marketing). Database marketing is thus the more comprehensive concept, although these terms are often used interchangeably in the literature.[12]

To give a very basic example, just by recording ID numbers or birth dates, organisations can send birthday wishes to their customers. This has a very positive effect on the company-customer relationship, ensuring that the customer feels wanted and important. It is a small, easy-to-implement action that strengthens customer relationships.

Take another example. Imagine a customer who has been with a cell service provider for a very long time (say 12 years). Based on the information the firm has in their database about this customer, the service provider awards them VIP status and offers them special offers (perhaps a few cents off all future calls). This will ensure that most of these long-term customers remain loyal to the same service provider. If the company does nothing, these customers may feel unappreciated and be more willing, or inclined, to move to an alternative service provider.

Online technologies

With the introduction of the Internet and the web which really took root in the early 1990s, these 'online' technologies have had a massive impact on marketing and business in general. In the sections below, we discuss how these online technologies have impacted on CRM.

The web

The Internet and the World Wide Web (or just 'The Web') are increasingly being used by companies to build customer relationships in a myriad of ways. For example, websites serve as an easily accessible way of learning more about a company without having to visit its offices in person. In addition, websites can also:

- facilitate home purchasing, thus making the shopping process easier for busy or working home keepers (for example, companies such as Pick n Pay and Woolworths allow customers to make all or some of their purchases online and to have the goods delivered to their homes);
- enable customers to lodge complaints and provide other feedback on the company, thus facilitating fast communication between the customer and the organisation;
- allow customers to access a wide range of information about the company and its products;
- allow customers to track deliveries, thereby keeping them in the loop;
- provide customers with links to a wide range of supporting information to enable them to make the right purchase decision;
- keep customers informed about special offers, events, new products, withdrawn products and other related information;
- enable customers to view their accounts and make account payments;

- allow customers to have contact with the company wherever they are and at all times of the day and night (24/7);

- provide an alternative channel to reach the firm's contact centre;

- access purchase-policy information, warranties, guarantees, contact details, company location and opening hours; and

- create a community where customers can share experiences and communicate with others to learn about the company, product and relevant business sector (for example, visit www.tripadvisor.com to see how an organisation provides an online information-sharing community for travellers and holiday-makers).

On the one hand, websites serve as a marketing channel for the organisations they represent and they are increasingly being used as virtual stores where customers can shop and buy products. On the other hand, websites also serve as an interactive communication channel for customers to ask questions, state their views, share opinions and, if necessary, to complain. As a marketing and shopping channel, the web offers powerful touch points for the customer when doing business with a company. As a communication channel, the website remains a touch point, but now provides the customer with an easily accessible 'voice' to speak back and complain (or compliment) if necessary. Customers can also ask about products, share their views and provide feedback. The web is a 24/7 media-rich environment and is easy to use. These are all factors that facilitate and enhance communication between customer and company. The web also facilitates the automation of many tasks (such as paying accounts, or lodging a service request.). The fact that there is a computer monitor between the customer and company provides some protection to the customer who might otherwise be intimidated by having to speak face-to-face with a person in the complaints or customer service department.

Organisations, unfortunately, still pay too little attention to their online efforts and are often too engrossed in the physical world. Yet, the website is itself a touch point that may be the source of negative experience for the customer. As customers increasingly make use of the web as their primary contact with companies, so they may become frustrated with badly designed and user-unfriendly websites. Therefore, companies need to pay attention to the functionality and user experience of their websites. They need to understand that if this virtual environment is not user-friendly and does not meet customer expectations, it will become a barrier to business and, like a rude sales person, it will represent a form of poor customer service. Finding creative ways to deliver good service online and to keep the customer happy and 'linked in' to the organisation is another online challenge for the company.

Electronic mail

Electronic mail (or email) is a communications technology that is generally linked to the Internet and the web (as you use the Internet or the web to send or receive emails). Email is probably one of the most common means of business communication in the modern world. The main benefit of email is that it is a very cheap form of communication. In addition, an increasing number of customers have email addresses. Email is quick and easy to use and, like the other technologies mentioned before, it is a digital medium. This means that emails can be stored, forwarded to others, replied to and may even include digital attachments such as documents, graphics, videos, audio files or other electronic files. In this way, email becomes a very 'rich' communication medium. Email may be used in conjunction with call centres and websites to extend the reach of a company and to offer an alternative way to communicate with customers.

Emails can also be sent automatically to potential customers. However, if the recipient did not agree to receive the email, this is known as junk email or 'spam' and can become a source of irritation to the customer. Automated responses can be generated in response to incoming emails received from customers. The benefit of email is that it is very quick and easy to use to launch a marketing campaign: the organisation generates a single promotional email which they then send to all of their customers. Email programmes will even automatically include in the email the customer's name and other details taken from the company's database, making it a very personal promotional campaign.

As far as automated responses are concerned, certain software can 'read' the contents of emails to check for keywords and send automated responses that provide customers with pre-prepared answers to frequently asked questions or refer them to web links where they can access more information. This auto responder software ensures that customers receive immediate feedback to their queries, thereby enhancing service quality, the customer experience and the overall customer relationship.

Social media

Notwithstanding the impact that the Internet, or more specifically, the web has had on marketing and facilitating the company-customer relationship, a new development in the online realm is having an even more profound effect, and that is the social media. Social media can be defined as the various forms of electronic communication channels through which users create online and peer-to-peer communities to share information, ideas, personal messages and other content such as videos.[13] The channels referred to include Facebook, Twitter, LinkedIn, MySpace and blogs (web logs or online 'diaries').

The power of social media is that it facilitates instant communication firstly between customers and secondly between customers and the company. This means that if customers are unhappy, they can immediately share their complaint with a community of family, friends, colleagues and peers. A 140-character 'tweet' (on Twitter) to several thousand friends could prove very harmful for the transgressing organisation. Unfortunately, there is very little that organisations can do to stop this form of communication – companies have 'lost control' of their marketing.[14] The best that they can do is to engage as openly and honestly about the issues at hand. The only effective way to deal with this real-time inquisition is to provide a better customer service – companies no longer have a place to hide.

Clearly, web and social media strategies need to be incorporated into the customer relationship-building process, a few ideas on how to do this are suggested below.

- **Get the customer experience and customer service right.** A company can listen and state their case as much as they want to, but if the experience they are offering is not up to scratch nothing that they do on social media or in the online realm will set that right! In other words, you cannot build a relationship with someone if you do not meet their needs.

- **Become involved.** If organisations are not using social media, they will not know what is being said about them.

- **Engage.** Start communicating with customers. This is not just one-way communication, this is interactive communication. Give your customers a chance to share their views and state their opinions and then listen to them. Management does not know what is best; customers do. At the very least, use this channel to identify the touch points that count and share the experiences that customers have from their point of view. This will be invaluable input in your future customer-orientated efforts.

- **Respond.** Do not just listen – do something about it; get involved in a conversation. If you get your customers drawn in, they will feel as though they are part of your organisation. In this way you are building a relationship with them.

- **Improve.** Customers will want to see changes. Try to enrich their experiences and tell them about the changes, even if they are small changes. Make customers feel that they have contributed in some way. If there are reasons why you cannot do it the way in which they suggest, share this with them (assuming it is not competitive information). If they understand your plight they may be willing to accept it (or they may even come up with alternatives).

- **Get your staff involved.** Social media is in the hands of everyone. If your staff are using social media positively, this can only benefit your company. Through bringing staff into the process, they can take ownership and may become disciples of the customer experience themselves.

- **Inform.** Use social media to inform customers and staff of what you are doing. Do not miss the opportunity to inculcate your brand with all of your communications.

- **Honesty.** Do not lie; your customers will catch you out.

- **Innovate.** Use this social media realm as a way of innovating your customer experience and setting yourself apart from the competition.

In this section we have highlighted a number of key online technologies that are helping to shape the customer relationship space, but it is not a definitive list. Other types of technologies can also be considered, as outlined below.

Other technologies to consider

We live in a technological world in which a myriad of technologies drive what we do and shape who we are. Think of the impact of the motor car, the aeroplane, the cell phone, and even the five-bladed shaving razor. When two-bladed razors came out, most men were amazed, then came three and now five bladed razors. Every day new technologies are entering the marketplace and marketing managers need to keep abreast of the latest technologies and consider how these new technologies could be used to support the customer and carve out a competitive niche for the company.

We have already discussed a number of technologies, but there are others. For example, fax-on-demand (FOD) is about delivering information quickly and easily by means of fax machines, initiated at the request of a customer. A customer with access to a fax machine may call a given FOD number and when the call is answered the customer need only press the start button on their fax machine to have the information faxed to them from the FOD machine. In this way, the customer can access relevant information (brochures, price lists, etc) in an automated way, without having to interact with company staff members. They can also do this any time of the day or night. Although FOD remains a useful tool, it is being replaced by Internet-based technologies.

Smart cards are another form of technology that could cement the relationship an organisation has with its customers. These are cards similar to credit cards but with the ability to store information about the customer on a computer chip embedded in the card. This makes it easy when dealing with a customer to get quick access to his or her personal and account details. It is also possible to store 'electronic money' on this chip, for example by inserting it into an ATM and downloading 'cash' onto the card. The card can thus be used for purchases. These types of cards are often used to identify selected clients and are promoted as a prestige feature (ie only top or selected clients are issued with these cards).

In the next section, we examine the role of CRM metrics in keeping control and managing the customer relationship with the organisation.

CRM metrics

Metrics are quantitative measures used by management to track performance and to identify good performance and problem areas. Metrics are increasingly being used by management to 'tweak' the performance of organisations. In this section we deal with some of the key metrics that you are likely to encounter in CRM.

The metrics you ultimately decide to use will depend to a large extent on the objectives of your CRM campaign. For example: Are you focused on creating more loyal customers (that is, more customers in total who are loyal to you, as well as individual customers who are more loyal to you than before)? Is customer profitability the key for you or is the life-time value of your customer more important?

Because CRM is focused on the many customer touch points that exist within a company, there are many metrics that could be used to measure the performance at each of these touch points. For example, one such customer touch point might be the promotional activities of the organisation and the organisation may want to measure the success of its promotional efforts. To this end, the organisation might use measures such as the number of campaigns launched, customer retention rates, cost per interaction by campaign, the number of customer referrals, etc. Another customer touch point may be with the sales staff, in which case the type of metrics that could be used include the number of prospects reached by sales staff, the number of sales calls made, the closing rate of sales staff, and the average revenue per sale. On the service side, metrics might include the number of cases handled by agents, the average time to resolution, customer satisfaction levels, and complaint time-to-resolution.[15] In fact there are anywhere from 30 to 50 different metrics that are relevant to the CRM context.

These metrics generally fall into the following broad categories:[16]

- brand performance measures;
- promotional performance measures;
- sales force performance measures;

- call centre performance measures;
- despatch and logistics performance measures;
- customer asset management measures;
- customer behaviour measures;
- service centre performance measures;
- field service performance measures;
- website performance measures;
- social media performance measures.

You will note that these performance measures all tend to be customer-facing measures and are closely associated with the typical touch points one finds within a company.

In this section we highlight a select number of typical customer metrics that one is likely to encounter in CRM. It is important to stress that this is not a definitive list. The purpose of the selected metrics is to allow you to gain some insight into the nature of the metrics and to show that different metrics have different purposes and benefits, and may also have different drawbacks.

The selected metrics that are introduced in this section are:

- number of customers;
- total value of sales per period;
- average value of customer purchases per period;
- number of transactions per period;
- average number of purchases per period per customer;
- average spend per purchase;
- churn rate;
- customer acquisition cost;
- customer lifetime value;
- customer satisfaction.

Number of customers

Although it may seem strange to consider this as a metric, it is actually a very important one as customers are what a business is all about. Without customers, the company has no business.

Formula

Number of customers = the number of people or businesses that purchased from the company in a specified period of time, normally a year.

Comments

Knowing the number of customers a company has is the first step in growing the business. Simply knowing the number of customers is already good information, but it would be even better if the company knew the names and profiles of its customers.

In reality, it is actually quite difficult to determine the number of customers a company has. In the case of cash customers the company may never actually learn the customer's name, but the number of till transactions or cash receipts will give a clue as to how many customers it has.

While it is important to count customers only once, even if they may have purchased more than once during the period in question, in the case of cash customers the company will seldom know if a customer has purchased more than once. It is also important for a company to clearly define what it means by 'customer'. For example, when Microsoft negotiates an educational licence with a university for the university's staff to use its operating system, is this one customer (the university) or many customers (the individual staff members)? Similarly, when a gym sells a family membership with, for example, the father paying the account, is this one customer or several? A customer may take many different forms varying from an individual or a group of individuals, to a legal entity such as a business or division of a business, a government department or even a church or other non-profit entity.

Total value of sales per period

This is a common metric that is used as input into many other metrics, usually per product category.

Formula

Total value of sales for a particular entity (in Rand) for a given period (usually a year) and usually for a particular product category and/or customer type.

Comments

This is a key financial measure recorded as part of the company's accounting procedures. As a financial measure it is useful in indicating the success of the company. Growing sales normally means a growing business and increased profitability, but it also depends on how these sales are achieved. If they are cash sales then this should translate into a positive cash flows, a good situation to be in.

On the other hand, if sales are mainly on credit then this may translate into a negative cash flow situation and reflect a company that is struggling.

As a marketing metric, this figure is less revealing as it represents sales of all types (credit, cash, etc.) over the period in question for the entity in question (the entity might be the business as a whole or a division of the business or a branch or store).

The problem with this metric is that as a total figure it provides no insight into the sales of often very different products. Consider a large corporation that sells consumer electronics, chemicals as well as industrial equipment. If the total sales are R1 billion, this does not provide any insight into the fact that R100 million of total sales may be attributed to the sale of machines for two industrial factories (ie two customers); R600 million may be attributed to the sale of consumer electronics, some of which are sold via 20 wholesalers, some of which are sold direct to some 10 000 walk-in and online customers, and some of which are sold to a single foreign importer; while R300 million may be attributed to the sale of chemicals to 100 large customers. The only way to make meaning out of this figure is to break it down into its component parts, usually according to product category and payment type. With this background, the metric has more meaning.

Average value of customer purchases per period and entity

The purpose of this metric is to determine what the average purchase value is per customer for a particular period and for a particular entity. It is usually only useful if calculated for a particular type of product category.

Formula

Average value of customer purchases per period and entity (usually for a particular product category and/or customer type) = total value of sales per period and entity for the product category in question ÷ number of customers (for a particular product category).

Comments

This is a useful metric (at a specific product level) as, for each product in question, it tells a company on average how much product each customer is purchasing and how much money the customer is spending on that particular product. It does not indicate how often the customer is purchasing or what the average value is per purchase transaction, but it provides insight as to how important this purchase is relative to the customer's other purchases.

If the company can gain some insight through primary or secondary research into the average income of customers, then this metric could indicate how important this particular purchase is relative to the other purchases the customer makes. For example, if it is already a significant share of the total income of customers, then it may be difficult to increase sales per customer (ie they may already be maxed out and the focus should be on increasing the number of customers); however, if it is a relatively insignificant share of total income then it may be the possible to increase either the number of purchases per customer or the value of each purchase.

We have highlighted that this metric will really only be meaningful if it is measured per product category and per payment and customer type. For example, if a company sells a particular product that is purchased directly by a limited number of industrial customers, but also by individual customers, then it may be worthwhile breaking the metric into these two groups. Also if the company sells a number of different products, each of these should be analysed separately with further sub-division according to customer type (such as industrial versus online versus consumer, and/or cash customers versus credit customers, etc).

Number of transactions per period

This is a useful metric that provides additional insight into the selling activities of the company, but one that is not always possible to capture.

Formula

Derived from sales records usually per product category and/or customer type.

Comments

In some companies, especially in the case of cash sales, purchases may not be recorded at all. Also, this metric is often not calculated because transactions are captured: (a) in many different ways (for example cash sales, credit sales, export sales, lay-by sales, barter sales); and (b) they are for very different products that are not comparable (such as products versus services, or chemicals versus industrial machinery). This metric is most useful if it is calculated for similar products (for example men's clothing versus women's clothing) and for similar types of customers (such as industrial versus online versus individual consumer, and/or cash customers versus credit customers).

Average number of purchases per period per customer

The purpose of this metric is to establish on average how many purchases a customer makes each period.

Formula

Average number of purchases per year = (total sales for period ÷ average value of a sale) ÷ number of customers.

Comments

It is likely that this metric will need to be calculated by product type, as the average value of a sale may differ dramatically from one product to another. Also, customers are buying different categories of products. This metric indicates the number of customer interactions with the company per period.

Average spend per purchase

This metric attempts to measure how much each customer spends per purchase, bearing in mind that a customer may buy several different products at each purchase occasion.

Formula

Average spend per purchase = (total sales ÷ number of customers) ÷ average number of purchases per period per customer.

Comments

For some companies it is important to get an idea of how much their customers are spending each time they buy. For example, think of a restaurant: it would be useful for the restaurant to know how much each sit-down customer spends on average; if they know this, the figure can also be used to calculate the lifetime value of a customer.

Churn rate

This metric attempts to measure the percentage of a company's existing customers who deliberately stop buying from the company or choose to buy from another company in a given period.

Formula

Churn rate = number of customers who leave the business in a given period of time ÷ the total number of customers at the end of the period.

Comments

Churn is also sometimes referred to as the customer defection rate.

One minus the churn rate is the retention rate. Most models can be written using either churn rate or retention rate. If the model uses only one churn rate, the assumption is that the churn rate is constant across the life of the customer relationship.

Customer acquisition cost (CAC)

This metric calculates the average marketing and sales costs associated with acquiring a new customer.

Formula

Customer acquisition cost = total marketing or advertising investment/cost aimed at acquiring new customers (ie a specific campaign) ÷ number of new customers as a result of this marketing or advertising campaign.

Comments

This is a useful metric to determine whether the amount spent on marketing or advertising to new customers is reasonable, but it may need to be considered in conjunction with other metrics such as cost per lead, conversion rate and customer lifetime value. Some companies simply take their total marketing spend and divide it by the number of new customers acquired in a particular period, but this is not accurate as some of the marketing spend will be used for public relations, brand building and other marketing expenses aimed at existing customers (for example getting them to spend more).

Bear in mind that you will need to clearly define what constitutes an acquisition expense as opinions differ. For example, it is suggested that rebates and special discounts may not represent an actual cash outlay, yet they have an impact on cash (and, presumably, on the customer's purchasing activities). Also bear in mind, that before customers actually buy from a company, they normally first become interested or potential customers (ie prospects or leads). Therefore, it may be necessary to first calculate a cost per lead value, followed by a conversion rate to determine the customer acquisition cost.

Customer lifetime value (CLV)

This metric calculates what the present value of a customer is assuming they continue to buy from the company for their lifetime; that is how regularly do customers buy from a company and what is their average spend each time they buy.

Formula

CLV = [(average value of a purchase – the average costs to service each purchase) × (the estimated number of times a customer purchases from the firm per year × the number of years that the firm expects to keep the customer) – the cost of acquiring a new customer + (the cost of acquiring a new customer × the number of new customers referred by the first customer)] × a customer adjustment factor; or CLV = margin × (retention rate ÷ 1 + discount rate – retention rate).

Comments

CLV (also known as lifetime value (LTV) or lifetime customer value (LCV)) is a fairly recent concept that argues that a customer's value should not be viewed just in terms of their past purchases but rather in terms of the potential they have to purchase from the company in the future.

CLV has become an important way of judging the health of a firm and it is important to measure how long, on average, customers remain customers of the company.

CLV goes hand-in-hand with the concept of relationship marketing in which companies strive to build a long-term relationship with their customers because of this lifetime value and because it is cheaper to convince an existing customer to buy from the company than to convince a new customer to buy from them.

The customer adjustment factor is an estimate that is usually provided by management which is a figure greater or less than 1. A figure higher than 1 suggests that the CLV will grow with time, while a figure less than 1 will 'shrink' over time (the customer adjustment factor can be adjusted to include the discount rate).

Customer satisfaction

This metric attempts to establish a measure – an index – of the customers' satisfaction with the company.

Formula

This is a multi-dimensional metric that requires customers to be surveyed to determine their levels of satisfaction. Five to ten questions are best.

Alternatively, there are other satisfaction models one could use such as the ACSI (American Customer Satisfaction Index) formula which is:

Customer Satisfaction Index (0–100) = ((Satisfaction – 1) × 0.3885 + (Expectancy – 1) × 0.3190 + (Performance – 1) × 0.2925) ÷ 9 × 100)[17]

The very proprietary Net Promoter Score (NPS) is another competing model. Net Promoter is a registered trademark of Satmetrix, Bain and Reichheld. Based on responses on a zero- to 10-point scale, customers are grouped into promoters (9 or 10), passives (7 or 8) and detractors (0 to 6). The percentage of detractors is subtracted from promoters, thereby obtaining a Net Promoter Score (NPS). The exact formula is not available publicly.

Comments

Generally, a firm would use a survey instrument (questionnaire) and analyse the data collected using methods such as factor analysis and regression analysis. In the USA the standard ACSI methodology can be used by firms to compare themselves with industry/geography benchmarks, which include historical trends. Be aware that customer satisfaction, customer loyalty and customer commitment are often used interchangeably, but that customer satisfaction is more about the experience of the customer, whilst customer loyalty is more about the customer's behaviour.

Summary

In this chapter, we have introduced the various technologies that play a role in facilitating CRM. These technologies include computers, software, telephony systems, promotional technologies, automated kiosks, tellers and dispensing machines, sale force automation, online technologies including email and social media, as well as fax-on-demand and smart cards. We emphasised the importance of marketing managers keeping track of and evaluating the latest technologies in order to determine what is relevant so that the organisation can keep itself at the forefront of CRM technologies.

The second part of the chapter examined the role of metrics in measuring CRM performance. It recognised the fact that there are many touch points for customers in an organisation and that each touch point should have metrics that measure performance at that particular touch point. A number of examples of CRM metrics were provided to give some idea of the nature of these metrics and the benefits and drawbacks associated with each. This is not a definitive list of metrics.

DISCUSSION QUESTIONS

1. Explain the importance of technology in managing customer relationships.
2. Define enterprise solutions and give an example of a company that would use this tool.
3. Do you think that call centres play an important role in an insurance company like OUTsurance? Why or why not?
4. Define and explain the purpose of interactive voice response systems.
5. Do you think that cell phones are a useful tool for companies which need to manage their customer relationships? Why or why not?
6. The use of social media platforms, like Facebook and Twitter, for communication and CRM purposes is becoming more popular. Log on to the Internet and find two Facebook pages for sit down restaurants, for example, Ocean Basket and Spur.

Mini case study

Reward loyal customers!

Roger Mpofu is a customer of a leading cell service provider in South Africa. In fact, Roger has been a client of the company that was bought by the current company. Roger has had his cell number for many years; almost from the day that cell phones come onto the market. During this time, Roger entered into a second cell contract for his wife. He has also purchased a third cell contract for SMS messaging service. Thus Roger has three accounts with this company and considers himself a good loyal customer, who has paid his accounts each month without fail.

Roger does not consider the service provider to be the most competitive company on the market and after each two-year period when he is asked to renew his contract, he often struggles to find a competitive package that meets his needs. Roger is somewhat choosy about the phones that he wants. On occasion he has asked the sales agents to allow him to upgrade without cost to a better phone but they are not willing to do so. Unwilling to accept the phones that were on offer for his particular level of contract, when his previous contract came to an end Roger chose to live with his current phone and not to upgrade.

Recently, however, a phone that Roger has had his eye on for some time came onto the market. Roger asked whether he could obtain the phone on his current package and the answer was no. He was told that he would have to pay a substantial additional fee per month to upgrade his contract to include the phone in question. He would also have to pay an additional fee for a data package to use many of the facilities that the phone offers. Roger asked the sales agent whether the company could not consider a special dispensation in this regard as an incentive. He suggested, for example, either reducing the monthly surcharge for the new phone or perhaps including the data package free or at a reduced rate. Roger argued that he has been a loyal customer, but that the company has never acknowledged or rewarded this loyalty in any way. The sale agent's answer remained an unsympathetic 'No'.

Roger reluctantly decided to go ahead with the upgrade at the higher cost. However, when taking out two additional cell broadband contracts for himself and his wife, he chose to buy from alternative service providers. Roger is aware that he could migrate to another service provider but the administrative hassle and the fear of losing his cell number has so far prevented him from doing so.

MINI CASE STUDY QUESTIONS

1. Reading the case study, do you think that Roger is likely to be loyal to the company going forward (for example, is he likely to speak warmly of his service provider and recommend them to his friends and colleagues)?

2. Do you think that the company should in some way recognise Roger for his years of loyalty to the company?

3. How might the service provider have built a better relationship with Roger?

4. What benefits would such a relationship have for the service provider?

5. How could the service provider have used a technology solution to provide a better service to Roger thus building a better relationship with him?

6. If Roger does decide to end his relationship with the service provider, which of the metrics discussed in the chapter would capture this fact?

7. Do you think metrics are beneficial to companies in order to measure the effect of their CRM efforts? Explain why/why not.

References

Chapter 1

1. Winer, RS. 2001. A framework for customer relationship management. *California Management Review*, 43 (4), p. 89.

2. Pralahad, CK & Ramaswamy, V. 2004. Co-creation experiences: the next practice in value creation, *Journal of Interactive Marketing*, 18 (3), pp. 5–14.

3. Berndt, A. 2014. In Boshoff, C. *Services Marketing: A Contemporary Approach*. Cape Town: Juta, p. 348.

4. Ibid.

5. Kristensson, P, Matthing, J & Johansson, N. 2008. Key strategies for the successful involvement of customers in the co-creation of new technology-based services. *International Journal of Service Industry Management*, 19 (4), pp. 474–491.

6. Buttle, F. 2006. *Customer Relationship Management*. Oxford: Butterworth-Heinemann, pp. 3–5.

7. Bosch, J, Tait, M & Venter, E. 2011. *Business Management: An Entrepreneurial Perspective*. Port Elizabeth: Lectern, p. 383.

8. Gummesson, E. 2002. *Total Relationship Marketing*. Oxford: Butterworth-Heinemann, p. 14.

9. Borden, NH. 1962. Making better consumers. *The Journal of Marketing*, 26 (1), pp. 124–125.

10. Kotler, P. 1967. *Principles of Marketing*. Upper Saddle River: Prentice-Hall.

11. Egan, J. 2001. *Relationship Marketing*. Harlow: Pearson Education, pp. 11–13.

12. Sheth, JN & Parvatiyar, A. 1995. The evolution of relationship marketing. *International Business Review*, 4 (4), p. 397.

13. Hollensen, S. 2003. *Marketing Management: A Relationship Approach*. Harlow: Financial Times/Prentice-Hall, p. 12.

14. Hollensen, op. cit., p. 14.

15. Bosch, Tait & Venter, op. cit., p. 386.

16. Based on Cant, MC. 2004. *Essentials of Marketing*. Cape Town: Juta, pp. 154–158.

17. Bosch, Tait & Venter, op. cit., pp. 387–388.

18. Egan, op. cit., p. 17.

19. Gordon, op. cit., p. 5.

20. Grönroos, C. 1994. From marketing mix to relationship marketing: Towards a paradigm shift in marketing. *Management Decisions*, 32 (2), pp. 4–20.

21. Berry, L. 1983. *Relationship Marketing*. American Marketing Association, Chicago.

22. Du Plessis, F. 2014. In Boshoff, C. *Services Marketing: A Contemporary Approach*. Cape Town: Juta, p. 28.

23. Berndt, op. cit., p. 350.

24. Peppers, D & Rogers, M. 2004. *Managing Customer Relationships: A Strategic Framework*. Canada: John Wiley & Sons, Inc.

25. Bosch, Tait & Venter, op. cit., p. 27.

26. Morgan, RM & Hunt, SD. 1999. Relationship-based competitive advantage: the role of relationship marketing in marketing. *Journal of Business Research*, 46 (3), pp. 281–290.

27. Sheth, JN & Mittal, M. 2004. *Consumer Behaviour: A Managerial Perspective*. 2nd ed. United States of America: Thompson South-Western.

28. Peppers, D, Rogers, N & Dorf, B. 1999. *One to One Fieldbook*. New York: Currency Doubleday, p. 1.

29. Foss, B & Stone, M. 2002. CRM in *Financial Services: A Practical Guide to Making Customer Relationship Management Work*. London: Kogan Page Limited.

30. Available from: http://www.kidsrkids.com (accessed 1 August 2014).

31. Kotler, P. 2003. *Marketing Management*. Upper Saddle River: Prentice-Hall, p. 37.

32. Berndt, op. cit., p. 357.

33. Brink, A, Strydom, JW, Machado, R & Cant, MC. 2001. *Customer Relationship Management Principles*. Pretoria: Unisa, pp. 54–59.

34. Cant, M. 2013. *Essentials of Marketing*. Cape Town: Juta, p. 150.

35. Lemon, KN & Mark, T. 2006. Customer lifetime value as the basis of customer segmentation: Issues and challenges. *Journal of Relationship Marketing*, 5 (2/3), pp. 55–61.

36. Ryals, LJ. 2002. Are your customers worth more than money? *Journal of Retailing and Consumer Services*, 9, pp. 241–51.

37. Berndt, op. cit., p. 356.

38. Kolko, J & Gazala, ME. 2005. *Demystifying Segmentation*. Boston: Forrester Research.

39. Libai, B, Narayandas, D & Humby, C. 2002. Toward an individual customer profitability model. *Journal of Service Research*, 5 (1), pp. 69–76.

40. Ryals, LJ & Knox, S. 2005. Measuring risk-adjusted customer lifetime value and its impact on relationship marketing strategies and shareholder value. *European Journal of Marketing*, 39 (5/6), pp. 456–72.

41. Berndt, op. cit., pp. 354–355.

42. Liu, BS, Petruzzi, NC & Sudharshan, D. 2007. A service effort allocation model for assessing customer lifetime value in service marketing. *Journal of Services Marketing*, 21 (1), pp. 24–35.

43. Based on Brink, A. 2004. *Customer Relationship Management Principles*. Unisa: Centre for Business Management.

44. Bothma, C. 2013. *Product Management*. Cape Town: Juta. p. 59.

45. Available from: http://www.curvesafrica.com/about/history/ (accessed 1 August 2014).

46. Cant, M. 2013. *Essentials of Marketing*. 4th ed. Cape Town: Juta, p. 201.

47. Cant, op. cit., p. 193.

48. Cant, M. 2013. *Marketing: An Introduction*. Cape Town: Juta. p. 201.

49. Buttle, op. cit., pp. 249–253.

50. Gordon, op. cit., pp. 23–24.

51. Brunjes, B & Roderick, R. 2002. Customer relationship management: Why it does and does not work in South Africa. Paper presented at the IMM conference, Johannesburg, p. 10.

52. Kotler, 2003, op. cit., p. 679.

53. Berndt, op. cit., p. 353.

54. Accenture. 2002. *Computing SA*, 22 (26), 15 July, p. 13.

55. Du Plessis, op. cit. p. 11.

56. Buttle, op. cit., pp. 242, 247–251.

57. Du Plessis, op. cit. p. 11.

58. Buttle, op. cit., p. 252.

59. Buttle, op. cit., p. 253.

60. Accenture. n.d. The view from the top: What every CEO should know. Available from: http://www. accenture.com (accessed 23 May 2011).

61. Coetzer, J. 2000. Strategy important, but execution the key. *Business Day* survey, p. 15.

62. Buttle, op. cit., p. 237.

Chapter 2

1. Agnihotri, R. & Rapp, A A. (eds). 2010. *Effective Sales Force Automation and Customer Relationship Management: A Focus on Selection and Implementation*. New York: Business Expert Press, p. 56.

2. CRM Portals. 2014. *Pharmaceutical CRM*. Available from: http://www. crmportals.com/crmnews/Pharmaceutical%20CRM%20-%20Differentiate%20 the%20Product%20or%20Die%20or%20Do%20Customer%20Care.html (accessed 05 March 2014).

3. Kumar, V & Reinartz, W. 2012. *Customer Relationship Management: Concept, Strategy, and Tools*. 2nd ed. London: Springer-Verlag, p. 211.

4. Drotsky, A. & van Heerden, C H. (eds). 2013. *Applied Marketing Cases*. Cape Town: Juta and Co, p. 89.

5. Levy, M & Weitz, B A. 2009. *Retailing Management*. 7th ed. New York: McGraw-Hill, pp. 308–309.

6. Fjermesatd, J & Romano, N C. (eds). 2006. *Electronic Customer Relationship Management*. New York: M.E. Sharpe, p. 129.

7. Inc.com. 2012. *New Rules of Customer Engagement*. Available from: http://www.inc.com/wendy-lea/new-rules-of-customer-engagement.html (accessed 05 March 2014).

8. Drotsky, & van Heerden, op. cit., p. 89.

9. Pearce, R P & Mahieu, Y. 2002. *Customer Relationship Management: Five Lessons for a Better ROI*. Available from: http://iveybusinessjournal.com/topics/strategy/customer-relationship-management-five lessons-for-a-better-roi#.UyaovPmSzTo (accessed 12 March 2014).

10. Gilmore, J H & Pine, B J. 2000. *Markets of One*. Boston: Harvard Business School Publishing, p. 58.

11. Egan, J. 2008. *Relationship Marketing: Exploring Relational Strategies in Marketing*. 3rd ed. London: Pearson Education, p. 61.

12. Peppers, D & Rogers, M. 2010. *Managing Customer Relationships: A Strategic Framework*. New York: John Wiley & Sons.

13. Brettel, M, Koch, L T, Kollman, T & Witt, P. 2009. *Trust of Potential Buyers in New Entrepreneurial Ventures: An Analysis of Trust Drivers, the Relevance of Purchase Intentions. And the Moderating Effect of Product or Service Qualities*. Wiesbaden: Gabler, p. 54.

14. Gaol, F L, Kadry, S, Taylor, M & Li, P S. (eds). No date. *Recent Trends in Social and Behaviour Sciences*. London: Taylor & Francis Group, p. 146.

15. Buttle, F. 2009. *Customer Relationship Management: Concepts and Technologies*. 2nd ed. Burlington: Butterworth-Heinemann, p. 30.

16. Peppers & Rogers, op. cit.

17. Jackson, S, Sawyers, R & Jenkis, G. 2009. *Managerial Accounting: A Focus on Ethical Decision Making*. 5th ed. Mason, USA: Cengage Learning, p. 483.

18. Levy & Weitz, op. cit., p. 306.

19. Egan, op. cit., p. 55.

20. Data Base Marketing Institute. 2014. *How Customer Service Builds Loyalty and Profits*. Available from: http://www.dbmarketing.com/articles/Art183.htm (accessed 12 March 2014).

21. Solomon, M R, Marshall, G W. & Stuart, E W. 2012. *Marketing: Real People, Real Choices*. 7th ed. New Jersey: Pearson Education, p. 207.

22. Drotsky & van Heerden, op. cit., p. 2.

23. Data Base Marketing Institute. 2014. *Customer Migration*. Available from: http://www.dbmarketing.com/articles/Art121.htm (accessed 12 March 2014).

24. Allenby, G M. (ed.) 2010. *Perspectives on Promotion and Database Marketing: The Collected Works of* Robert C *Blattberg*. Singapore: World Scientific Publishing, p. 35.

25. Bidgoli, H. (ed). 2010. *The Handbook of Technology Management: Supply Chain Management, Marketing and Advertising and Global Management*. New York: John Wiley & Sons, p. 466.

26. Link Simulations. 2013. *Interpreting Retention Statistics and Customer Lifetime Value: A Tutorial*. Available from: http://www.links-simulations.com/SM/Retention StatisticsCLV.pdf (accessed 12 March 2014).

27. Kumar, V. 2008. *Managing Customers for Profit: Strategies to Increase Profits and Build Loyalty*. New Jersey: Wharton School Publishing, p. 25.

28. The University of Western Australia. 2010. *An investigation of customer lifetime value factors*. Available from: https://repository.uwa.edu.au/R/-?func=dbin-jump-full&object_id=26430&local_base=GEN01-INS01 (accessed 12 March 2014).

29. Bejou, D Keiningham, T L. & Aksoy, L. (eds). 2013. *Customer Lifetime Value: Reshaping the Way We Manage to Maximize Profit*s. Birmingham: Routledge, p. 49.

30. Harvard Business School Publishing. 2007. *Customer Lifetime Value Calculator*. Available from: http://hbsp.harvard.edu/multimedia/flashtools/cltv/ (accessed 15 March 2014).

31. Kiehls. 2011. *Objectives of IMC*. Available from: http://iheartkiehls.weebly.com/1/category/imc/1.html (accessed 15 March 2014).

32. Baines, P. & Fill, C. 2014. *Marketing*. 3rd ed. Oxford: Oxford University Press, p. 505.

33. Pheng, L S 1999. The extension of construction partnering for relationship marketing. *Marketing Intelligence & Planning*, 17(3), p. 157.

34. Drotsky & van Heerden, op. cit., p. 88.

Chapter 3

1. Sunday Times. 2005. *React Survey*. 2 October, p. 13.

2. Rajola, F. *Customer Relationship Management in the Financial Industry: Organizational Processes and Technology Innovation*. 2nd ed. London: Springer, p. 38.

3. Wellington, P. 2010. *Effective Customer Care*. London: Logan Page, pp. 120–121.

4. Van Heerden, C H. (ed). 2013. *Contemporary Retail and Marketing Case Studies.* Cape Town: Juta, pp. 110–112.

5. Ibid., pp. 176–178.

6. Christopher, M, Payne, A & Ballantyne, D. 2008. *Relationship Marketing.* Oxford: Butterworth-Heinemann.

7. Grönroos, C. 2007. *Service Management and Marketing: Customer Management in Service Competition.* 3rd ed. Chichester: Wiley, pp. 98–100.

8. Meier, H. (ed). no date. *Product-Service Integration for Sustainable Solutions.* Heidelberg: Springer, p. 77.

9. Kandampully, J, Mok, C & Sparks, B. DATE. *Service Quality Management in Hospitality Tourism and Leisure.* New York: Haworth Hospitality Press, p. 160.

10. Rootman, C, Tait, M & Bosch, J. 2007. The Influence of Bank Employees on Bank Customer Relationship Management. *Acta Commercii,* pp. 181–192.

11. Rao, KRM. 2011. *Services Marketing.* India: Pearson, p. 347.

12. The Guardian. 2007. *A fine line.* Available from: http://www.theguardian.com/ artanddesign/artblog/2007/jan/18/afineline (accessed 17 March 2014).

13. Allen, M. n.d. *Customer Relations Management.* University of Cambridge: Select Knowledge, p. 37.

14. Xu, J, Yasinzai, M & Lev, B. (eds). 2013. *Proceedings of the Sixth International Conference on Management Science and Engineering Management.* London: Springer, p. 434.

15. Conversation Agent. 2012. *Top Reasons Why Your Customer Service Fails.* Available from: http://www.conversationagent.com/2012/05/top-reasons-why-your-customer-service-fails.html (accessed 15 March 2014).

16. Survey Methods. 2011. *Benefits and Weaknesses of Customer Satisfaction Surveys.* Available from: http://blog.surveymethods.com/benefits-and-weaknesses-of-customer-satisfaction-surveys-2/ (accessed 17 March 2014).

17. Oliver, RL. 2010. Satisfaction: *A Behavioral Perspective on the Consumer.* 2nd ed. New York: M.E. Sharpe, p. 43.

18. Parasuraman, A, Zeithaml, VA & Berry, LL. 1994. Alternative Scales for Measuring Service Quality: A Comparative Assessment Based on Psychometric and Diagnostic Criteria. *Journal of Retailing,* 70(3), pp. 201–230.

19. Herbst, FJH. 2005. Unpublished course notes, University of Johannesburg.

20. Cronin, JJ & Taylor, SA. 1992. Measuring service quality: A re-examination and extension. *Journal of Marketing,* 56, p. 255.

21. Berndt, A. 2009. Investigating service quality dimensions in South African motor vehicle servicing. *African Journal of Marketing Management,* 1(1), pp. 1–9.

22. Haksever, C & Render, B. 2013. *Service Management: An Integrated Approach to Supply Chain Management and Operations.* New York: Pearson Education, p. 27.

23. Liyanage, UP. 1999. Five best management practices in the hotels sector in Sri Lanka. *Journal of Comparative International Management*, 2(1): p. 33.

24. Drotsky, A & van Heerden, CH. (eds). 2013. *Applied Marketing Cases.* Cape Town: Juta, pp. 3–4.

25. Machado, R & Diggines, C. (eds). 2012. *Customer Service*. Cape Town: Juta, p. 72.

26. Akhtar, A, Huda, SSMS & Dilshad, S. 2009. Critical Service Encounters: Employee's Viewpoint a Study on Transport Services in Dhaka City. *Journal of Social Sciences*, 1(2), p. 17.

27. Brink, A & Berndt, A. 2008. *Relationship Marketing and Customer Relationship Management*. Cape Town: Juta, p. 80.

28. Jones, P & Robinson, P. 2012. *Operations Management*. Oxford: Oxford University Press, p. 99.

29. Reimer, A & Kuehn, R. 2004. The impact of servicescape on quality perception. *European Journal of Marketing*, 39(7/), p. 797.

30. Sahaf, MA. 2013. *Strategic Marketing: Making Decisions for Strategic Advantage.* New Delhi: PHI Learning.

31. Data Apple. 2013. *Calculating Customer Lifetime Value with Recency, Frequency, and Monetary Value (RFM).* Available from: http://www.dataapple.net/?p=133 (accessed 20 March 2014).

32. Harvard Business School Publishing. 2007. *Customer Lifetime Value.* Available from: http://hbsp. harvard.edu/multimedia/flashtools/cltv/ (accessed 20 March 2014).

33. Startup Professionals Musings. 2014. *Startup 'Word-Of-Mouth' Is Not A Launch Strategy*. Available from: http://blog.startupprofessionals.com/2014/01/startup-word-of-mouth-is-not-launch.html (accessed 18 March 2014).

34. Spolsky, J. 2007. *Seven Steps to Remarkable Customer Service*. Available from: http://www.joelonsoftware.com/articles/customerservice.html (accessed 18 March 2014).

35. Jensen, CT, Cline, O & Owen, M. 2011. *Combining Business Process Management and Enterprise Architecture for Better Business Outcomes*. USA: IBM Red Books, p. 131.

36. Cant, MC, Van Heerden, CH & Ngambi, HC. 2013. *Marketing Management: A South African Perspective*. 2nd ed. Cape Town: Juta, p. 497.

37. Spolsky, op. cit.

38. Boshoff, C & Du Plessis, F. 2009. *Services Marketing: A Contemporary Approach*. Cape Town: Juta, p. 198.

39. Donaldson, B & O'Toole, T. *Strategic Market Relationships: From Strategy to Implementation*. West Sussex: John Wiley & Sons, p. 120.

40. Financial Services Commission of Ontario. 2013. *Customer Service Commitment.* Available from: https://www.fsco.gov.on.ca/en/about/Pages/service_commitment.aspx (accessed 18 March 2014).

41. Drotsky & Van Heerden, op. cit., pp. 75–79.

Chapter 4

1. Chu, PY & Yeh 2013. Municipal government business process reengineering: A case study of kaohsiung citizen electronic complaints System. Available from: http://wspg.nccu.edu.tw/download/topics/Panel_4.pdf. (accessed 12 May 2014).

2. Iliopoulos, E & Priporas, CV. 2011. The effect of internal marketing on job satisfaction in health services: a pilot study in public hospitals in Northern Greece. BMC Health Services Research, pp. 1–8

3. Gounaris, S. 200. Internal market orientation and job satisfaction. *Journal of Services Marketing*, 22(1), pp. 68–90.

4. Mieres, CG; Sanchez, JALA; Vijande, MLS. 2012. Internal marketing, innovation and performance in business service firms: The role of organisational unlearning. *International Journal of Management*, 29(4), pp. 403–429.

5. Done, I & Domazet, I. 2012. Improving the quality of human resources by implementation of internal marketing. Available from: http://mpra.ub.uni-muenchen.de/35363/1/Chapter_3_draft_Improving_the_Quality_of_Human_Resources_by_Implementation_of_Internal_Marketing.pdf. (accessed 8 May 2012).

6. Ballantyne, D, Christopher, M & Payne, A. 1995. Improving the quality of services marketing: (Re)design is the critical link. *Journal of Marketing Management*, 2 (1):15.

7. Ahmed, PK & Rafiq, M. 2002. *Internal Marketing: Tools and Concepts for Customer-focused Management*. Oxford: Butterworth-Heinemann, pp. 13–15.

8. Gummesson, E. 2002. *Total Relationship Marketing* (2nd ed). Oxford: Butterworth-Heinemann, p. 198.

9. Ahmed & Rafiq, op. cit., p. 11.

10. Payne, A, Christopher, M, Clark, M & Peck, H. 1995. *Relationship Marketing for Competitive Advantage*. Oxford: Butterworth-Heinemann, p. 12.

11. Lucas, RW. 2009. *Customer Service – Skills for Success*. New York: McGraw-Hill Erwin.

12. Roberts-Lombard, M. 2009. Employees as customers – An internal marketing study of the Avis car rental group in South Africa. *African Journal of Business Management*, 4(4), pp. 362–372.

13. De Bruin, LR. 2013. The influence of Internal Marketing on internal customer satisfaction within retail banking. Unpublished Masters dissertation. Johannesburg: University of Johannesburg.

14. Abzari, M & Ghujali, T. 2011. Examining the impact of internal marketing on organisational citizenship behaviour. *International Journal of Marketing Studies*, 3(4), pp. 95–104.

15. Saks, MA. 2006. Antecedents and consequences of employee engagement. *Journal of Managerial Psychology*, 21(7), pp. 600–619.

16. Luna-Arocas, R & Camps, J. 2008. A model of high performance work practices and turnover intentions. *Personnel Review*, 37, pp. 26–46.

17. Grayson, D & Sanchez-Hernandez, IM. (2010). Using internal marketing to engage employees in corporate responsibility. Cranefield University Working Paper Series, pp. 1–31.

18. Sincic, D & Vokic, NP. 2007. Integrating internal communications, human resource management and marketing concepts into the new internal marketing philosophy. Working paper. Faculty of Economics and Business, Zagreb University, pp. 1–13.

19. Mahmood, Z. 2013. Internal marketing provides a systematic framework to develop corporate culture and improve the internal organisational communication towards the implementation of quality management programs. Available from: http://faculty.kfupm.edu.sa/coe/sadiq/proceedings/SCAC2004/03.ASC018.EN.Mahmood.Internal%20Marketing%20Provides%20A%20Syste%20_1_.pdf (accessed 4 June 2014).

20. Sanchez-Hernandez, IM & Miranda, FJ. 2011. Linking internal market orientation and new service performance. *European Journal of Innovation and Management*, 14(2), pp. 207–226.

21. Hoffman, KD & Bateson, JEG. 2006. *Services Marketing: Concepts, Strategies and Cases* (3rd ed). Mason, Ohio: Thomson South-Western.

22. Green, S & Boshoff, C. 2002. An empirical assessment of the relationships between service quality, satisfaction and value: A tourism study. *Management Dynamics*, 11 (3), p. 4.

23. Klopper, HB, Berndt, A, Chipp, K, Ismail, Z, Roberts-Lombard, M, Subramani, D, Wakeham, M, Petzer, D, Hern, L, Saunders, S & Myers-Smith, P. 2006. *Marketing: Fresh Perspectives*. Cape Town: Pearson Education South Africa, p. 27.
Kaplan, RS & Norton, DP. 2004. The strategy map: guide to aligning intangible assets. *Strategy and Leadership*, 32(5), pp. 10–17.

24. Murby, L & Gould, S. 2005. *Effective Performance Management with the Balanced Scorecard*. CIMA, pp. 1–41.

25. Conradie, ES. 2012. The influence of internal marketing elements on the brand awareness of car rental customers in South Africa. Doctoral thesis, Department of Business Management, University of Johannesburg.

26. Yang, J, Alejandro, TGB & Boles, JS. 2011. The role of social capital and knowledge transfer in selling center performance. *Journal of Business & Industrial Marketing*, 26(3), pp. 152–161.

27. Peltier, J & Dahl, A. 2009. Relationship between employee satisfaction and hospital patient experience. Available from: http://www.info-now.com/typo3conf/ext/p2wlib/pi1/press2web/html/userimg/FORUM/Hospital%20Study%20Relationship%20Btwn%20Emp. %20Satisfaction%20and%20Pt.%20Experiences.pdf. (accessed 8 June 2014).

28. Paton, R & Karunaratne, N. 2009. Engagement and innovation: the Honda case. *VINE*, 39(4):280–297.

29. Yang & Alejandro, op. cit. p. 154.

30. Ndubisi, NO. 2007. Relationship marketing and customer loyalty. *Marketing Intelligence and Planning*, 25(1), pp. 98–106.

31. Eggers, JT. 2013. Psychological safety influences relationship behavior. Available from: https://www.aca.org/research/pdf/ResearchNotes_Feb2011.pdf. (accessed 23 May 2014).

    Williams, KC, 2013. Core qualities of successful marketing relationships. Available from: http://www.aabri.com/manuscripts/111023.pdf. (accessed 24 May 2014).

32. Slatten, T. 2011. Emotions in service encounters from the perspectives of employees and customers. Master's dissertation, Department of Business Studies, Karlstad University.

    Brown, J, Elliott, S, Christensen-Hughes, J, Lyons, S, Mann, S & Zdaniuk, A. 2009. Using HRM practice to improve productivity in the Canadian Tourism industry. Department of Business, University of Guelph.

33. Eggers, op. cit.

    Williams. op. cit.

    Ahmed , PK & Rafiq, M. 2003. Internal marketing issues and challenges. *European Journal of Marketing*, 37(9), pp. 1177–1186.

34. Panigyrakis, GG, & Theodoridis, PK. 2009. Internal marketing impact on business performance in a retail context. *International Journal of Retail and Distribution Management*, 37(7), pp. 600–628.

35. Matanda, MJ & Ndubisi, NO. 2013. Internal marketing, internal branding, and organisational outcomes: The moderating role of perceived goal congruence. *Journal of Marketing Management*, 29(9-10), pp. 1030–1055.

    Guenzi, P & Troilo, G. 2006. Developing marketing capabilities for customer value creation through Marketing – Sales integration. *Industrial Marketing Management*, 35, pp. 974–998.

36. Sambasivan, M, Siew-Phaik L, Mohamed, ZA & Leong YC. 2011. Impact of interdependence between supply chain partners on strategic alliance outcomes:

Role of relational capital as a mediating construct. *Management Decision*, 49(4), pp. 548–569.

37. Grönroos, C. 2007. *Service Management and Marketing: Customer Management in Service Competition.* (3rd ed). John Wiley and Sons Inc, UK.

38. Williams. op. cit.

Wang, S & Noe, R.A. 2010. Knowledge sharing: A review and directions for future research. *Human Resource Management Review* 20, pp. 115–131.

39. Ali, A & Haider, J. 2012. Impact of internal organisational communications on employee job satisfaction – Case of some Pakistani Banks. *Global Advanced Research Journal of Management and Business Studies*, 1, pp. 38–44.

40. Burin, C. 2011. The perceived influence of the elements of Internal Marketing on the brand image of staffing agencies in South Africa. Masters dissertation. hesis. Johannesburg: University of Johannesburg, pp. 59–145.

41. Roberts-Lombard, M. 2006. Verhoudingsbemarking by reisagentskappe in die Wes-Kaap provinsie. Doctoral thesis. Potchefstroom: North West University, pp. 199–218.

42. De Bruin, op. cit.

Chapter 5

1. Nguyen, B & Mutum, DS. 2012. A review of customer relationship management: successes, advances, pitfalls and futures. *Business Process Management Journal*, 18 (3), pp. 400–419.

2. Pitta, DA. 1998. Marketing one-to-one and its dependence on knowledge discovery in databases. *Journal of Consumer Marketing*, 15 (5), pp. 468–480.

3. Pine, BJ, Peppers, D & Rogers, M. 1995. Do you want to keep your customers forever. *Harvard Business Review*, March–April, pp. 103–114.

4. Peppers, D & Rogers, M. 1993. *The One-to-One Future*, London: Piatkus, p. 15.

5. Nguyen & Mutum, op. cit., p. 403.

6. Christopher, M, Payne, A & Ballantyne, D. 2002. *Relationship Marketing: Creating Stakeholder Value*. Oxford: Butterworth-Heinemann, p. 25.

7. Nguyen & Mutum, op. cit., p. 401.

8. Nguyen & Mutum, op. cit., p. 403.

9. Peppers & Rogers, op. cit., p. 23.

10. Nguyen & Mutum, op. cit., p. 403.

11. Gummesson, E. 2002. *Total Relationship Marketing*. Oxford: Butterworth-Heinemann, p. 45.

12. Pine et al., op. cit., p. 105.

13. Nguyen & Mutum, op. cit., p. 404.

14. Peppers & Rogers, op. cit., p. 27.

15. Peppers & Rogers, op. cit., p. 140.

16. Silver, D, Newnham, L, Barker, D, Weller, S & McFall, J. 2013. *Concurrent reinforcement learning from customer interactions.* Proceedings of the 30th International Conference on Machine Learning, Atlanta, Georgia, United States of America, JMLR: W&CP volume 28.

17. Peppers & Rogers, op. cit., p. 36.

18. Brink, A, Machado, R, Strydom, JW & Cant, MC. 2001. *Customer Relationship Management: Applied Strategy.* Study Guide 2. Pretoria: Unisa, p. 36.

19. Peppers & Rogers, op. cit., p. 213.

20. Nguyen & Mutum, op. cit., p. 404.

21. Clicks. n.d. Available from: https://clicks.co.za/clubcard (accessed 9 July 2014).

22. Pick n Pay. n.d. Available from: http://www.picknpay.co.za/smartshopper-about, http://www.picknpay.co.za/smartshopper-overview and http://www.picknpay.co.za/smartshopper-charities (accessed 9 July 2014).

23. Pine et al., op. cit., p. 110.

24. Peppers & Rogers, op. cit., p. 215.

25. Patino, A, Pitta, D & Quinones, R. 2012. Social media's emerging importance in market research. *Journal of Consumer Marketing*, 29 (3), pp. 233–237.

26. Gordon, IH. 1998. *Relationship Marketing.* Toronto: John Wiley, p. 216.

27. Gordon, op. cit., p. 218.

28. Brink et al., op. cit., p. 24.

29. Nguyen & Mutum, op. cit., pp. 404 and 410.

30. Hart, CWL. 1995. Mass customisation: Conceptual underpinnings, opportunities and limits. *International Journal of Service Industry Management*, 6 (2), pp. 36–45.

31. Ferguson, S, Olewnik, A, Malegaonkar, P, Cormier, P & Kansara, S. 2010. *Mass customization: A review of the paradigm across marketing, engineering and distribution domains.* Proceedings of the ASME International Design Engineering Technical Conferences & Computers and Information in Engineering Conference, Montreal, Quebec, Canada.

32. Sunikka, A & Bragge, J. 2012. Applying text-mining to personalization and customization research literature – Who, what and where? *Expert Systems with Applications*, 39, pp. 10049–10058.

33. Pollard, D, Chuo, S & Lee, B. 2008. Strategies for mass customization. *Journal of Business & Economics Research*, 6 (7), pp. 77–85.

34. Peppers, D & Rogers, M. 1997. *Enterprise One-to-One.* London: Piatkus, p. 142.

35. Pollard et al., op. cit., p. 78.

36. Gordon, op. cit., p. 176.

37. Peppers, D, Rogers, M & Dorf, B. 1999. Is your company ready for one-to-one marketing? *Harvard Business Review*, January–February, pp. 151–160.

38. Coelho, PS & Henseler, J. 2012. Creating customer loyalty through service customization. *European Journal of Marketing*, 46 (3/4), pp. 331–356.

39. Gordon, op. cit., p. 177.

40. Gordon, op. cit., p. 25.

41. Gordon, op. cit., p. 222.

42. Lin, R, Chen, R & Chiu, KK. 2010. Customer relationship management and innovation capability: An empirical study. *Industrial Management & Data Systems*, 110 (1), pp. 111–133.

43. Pollard et al., op. cit., p. 80.

44. Gordon, op. cit., p. 223.

45. Hart, op. cit., p. 40.

46. Pollard et al., op. cit., p. 84.

47. Coelho & Henseler, op. cit., p. 331.

48. Adapted from Gordon, op. cit., p. 224.

49. Brink et al., op. cit., pp. 31–34.

50. Woolworths. n.d. Available from: http://www.woolworthsholdings.co.za/corporate/profile_overview.asp (accessed 15 July 2014).

51. Gordon, op. cit., p. 236.

52. Pollard et al., op. cit., p. 77.

53. Peppers & Rogers, 1997, op. cit., p. 15.

54. Nguyen & Mutum, op. cit., p. 403.

55. Nguyen & Mutum, op. cit., p. 405.

56. Pine et al., op. cit., p. 103.

57. Peppers & Rogers,1997, op. cit., p. 170.

58. Pine et al., op. cit., pp. 110.

59. *Key findings – Motor trade sales, January 2011*. n.d. Available from: http://www.statssa.gov.za/publications/statskeyfindings.asp?PPN=p6343.2&SCH=4874 (accessed 15 July 2014).

60. *Used vehicle sales gain ground: TransUnion*. 2012. Available from: http://www.moneyweb.co.za/moneyweb-economic-trends/used-vehicle-sales-gain-ground-transunion (accessed 15 July 2014).

61. *Stats SA vehicle sales confirm positive news in Naamsa numbers*. 2013. Available from: http://www.bdlive.co.za/business/2013/04/18/stats-sa-vehicle-sales-confirm-positive-news-in-naamsa-numbers (accessed 15 July 2014).

62. Cape Jungle Kids. n.d. Available from: http://www.capejunglekids.co.za/ Available from: (accessed 9 July 2014).

Chapter 6

1. Van der Walt, A, Strydom, JW, Marx, S & Jooste, CJ. 1996. *Marketing Management*. 3rd ed. Cape Town: Juta.

2. Based on Gordon, IH. 1998. *Relationship Marketing*. Toronto: John Wiley, pp. 114–33.

3. Blois, KJ. 1996. Relationship marketing in organisational markets: When is it appropriate? *Journal of Marketing Management*, 12, pp. 161–73.

4. Gordon, op. cit., p. 128.

5. Hutt, MD & Speh, TW. 2001. *Business Marketing Management.* Fort Worth: Harcourt College Publishers, p. 89.

6. Day, op. cit., p. 25.

7. Hutt & Speh, op. cit., p. 90.

8. Nieman, G & Bennett, A (eds). 2002. *Business Management: A Value Chain Approach*.Pretoria: Van Schaik, p. 17.

9. Cronje, GJ de J, Du Toit, GS & Motlana, MDC. 2000. *Introduction to Business Management*. 5th ed. Cape Town: Oxford University Press, p. 422.

10. Du Plessis, PJ, Jooste, CJ & Strydom, JW. 2001. *Applied Strategic Marketing*. Sandown: Heinemann. p. 282.

11. Christopher, M, Payne, A & Ballantyne, D. 2002. *Relationship Marketing: Creating Stakeholder Value*. Oxford: Butterworth-Heinemann.

12. Available from: http://www.financialmail.co.za/features/2014/06/05/kalahari-surfers-only (accessed 4 June 2014).

13. Available from: http://www.fruits.co.za/services-fruits-unlimited.html (accessed 2 June 2014).

14. Available from: http://www.financialmail.co.za/fm/2010/01/29/farming (accessed 2 June 2014).

15. Peck, H, Payne, A, Christopher, M & Clark, M. 2004. *Relationship Marketing Strategy and Implementation*. Amsterdam: Elsevier Butterworth-Heinemann, p. 34.

16. Ibid.

17. Du Plessis et al., op. cit., p. 279–281.

18. Cronje et al., op. cit., p. 69.

19. Du Plessis, et al., op. cit.

20. Gummesson, E. 2002. *Total Relationship Marketing*. Oxford: Butterworth-Heinemann.

21. Available from: http://www.financialmail.co.za/features/2014/04/23/flysafair-preparing-for-takeoff (accessed 2 June 2014)

22. Du Plessis et al., op. cit., p. 289.

23. Ibid., p. 290.

24. Gummesson, op. cit., p. 157.

25. Hutt & Speh, op. cit., p. 102.

26. Gummesson, op. cit., p. 158.

27. Hutt & Speh, op. cit., p. 105.

28. Payne, A, Christopher, M, Clark, M & Peck, H. 2001. *Relationship Marketing for Competitive Advantage.* Oxford: Butterworth-Heinemann.

29. Available from: http://www.hybris.com/en/news-events/press-releases/131030-b2b-market#foot1 (accessed 2 June 2014).

30. Available from: http://www.brafton.com/glossary/business-to-business-b2b-marketing (accessed 2 June 2014).

31. Kenjale, K & Phatek, A. 2002. The benefit of B2B exchanges. Available from: http://www.destinationcrm.com/Articles/Web-Exclusives/Viewpoints/The-Benefits-of-B2B-Exchanges-48031.aspx (accessed 2 June 2014).

32. Available from: http://www.brafton.com/glossary/business-to-business-b2b-marketing (accessed 2 June 2014).

33. Available from: http://www.referenceforbusiness.com/small/Bo-Co/Business-to-Business-Marketing.html (accessed 2 June 2014).

34. Available from: http://www.wwre.org/c/document_library/get_file?uuid=630889bd-ed84-4762-9bb9-ae1fd4f4f08b&groupId=14 (accessed 2 June 2014).

35. Available from: http://www.unitrans.co.za/about (accessed 10 June 2014).

36. Available from: http://www.kap. co.za/wp-content/uploads/2014/02/KAP-Results_20140217.pdf (accessed 10 June 2014).

37. Available from: http://www.unitrans.co.za/about (accessed 10 June 2014).

Chapter 7

1. Polonsky, MJ & Scott, D. 2005. An empirical examination of the stakeholder strategy matrix. *European Journal of Marketing*, Vol 39 No. 9/10, p. 1200.

2. Lynch, R. 2000. *Corporate Strategy.* Harlow, England: Prentice-Hall. p. 520.

3. Christopher, M, Payne, A & Ballantyne, D. 2002. *Relationship Marketing Creating Stakeholder Value.* Butterworth-Heinemann: Oxford. p. 77.

4. Ibid., p. 80.

5. Morgan, RM & Hunt, SD. 1994. The Commitment-Trust Theory of Relationship Marketing. *Journal of Marketing*, 58 (3), pp. 20–38.

6. Morgan & Hunt, 1994 p. 21.

7. Peck, H, Payne, A, Christopher, M and Clark, M. 1999. *Relationship Marketing*. Elsevier: Amsterdam.

8. Christopher et al., op. cit., p. 80.

9. Anon, 2009. The Triple Bottom Line, The Economist, 17 November. Available from: http://www.economist.com/node/14301663 (accessed 13 June 2014).

10. Slaper, TF & Hall, TJ. n.d. The Triple Bottom Line: What Is It and How Does It Work? Available from: http://www.ibrc.indiana.edu/ibr/2011/spring/article2.html (accessed 13 June 2014).

11. Ibid.

12. Shridhar, K & Jones, G. 2011. The three fundamental criticisms of the Triple Bottom Line approach: An empirical study to link sustainability reports in companies based in the Asia-Pacific region and TBL shortcomings. *Asian Journal of Business Ethics 2*, pp. 91–111.

13. Available from: http://www.candorsolutions.co.za/king-iii/what-is-king-iii/ (accessed 13 June 2014).

14. Available from: http://www.pwc.co.za/en/king3/ (accessed 13 June 2014).

15. Available from: https://www.thedti.gov.za/economic_empowerment/bee.jsp (accessed 13 June 2014).

16. Available from: http://www.bbbeeact.co.za/ (accessed 13 June 2014).

17. Available from: http://www.theguardian.com/business/2014/may/09/margaret-hodge-urges-boycott-amazon-uk-tax-starbucks (accessed 27 June 2014).

18. Available from: http://getgrowingforbusiness.scotiabank.com/articles/what-investors-want-your-business (accessed 14 June 2014).

19. Payne, A, Holt, S & Frow, P. 2000. Integrating employee, customers and shareholder value through an enterprise performance opportunity for financial services. *International Journal of Bank Marketing*, 18 (6), p. 262.

20. Peck et al., op. cit., p. 240.

21. Available from: http://www.jimcollins.com/article_topics/articles/shareflipping.html (accessed 14 June 2014).

22. Lynch, op. cit., p. 521.

23. Linton, I. 2011. Objectives of Investor Relations. Available from: http://ehow.com/info_8292595_objectives-investor-relations.html (accessed 14 June 2014).

24. Cresswell, J & Kover, A. 2000. Annual Report Spin. *Fortune*, 141(9), p. 50.

25. Temkin, S. 2010. New Law 'will increase shareholder activism'. Available from: http://www.bdlive.co.za/articles/2010/05/20/new-law-will-increase-shareholder-activism;jsessionid=E4838388DEEF08AB681944816295F4CB.present2.bdfm (accessed 13 June 2014).

26. Ibid.

27. Steyn, L. 2011. Theo Botha – the shareholder activist. Available from: http://mg.co.za/article/2011-05-13-theo-botha-the-shareholder-activist (accessed 13 June 2014).

28. Kamhunga, S, 2011. Standard bosses admit investors disappointed. Available from: http://www.bdlive.co.za/articles/2011/05/27/standard-bosses-admit-investors-disappointed (accessed 13 June 2014).

29. Turney, M. n.d. Summarising the public relations process. Available from: http://www.nku.edu/~turney/prclass/readings/process_acronyms.html (accessed 13 June 2014).

30. Christopher et al., op. cit. p. 98.

31. Ibid.

32. Available from: http://vaalenvironmentalnews.blogspot.se/2012/04/stealing-our-tomorrow.html (accessed 13 June 2014).

33. Available from: http://ibasecretariat.org/lka_cape_comp_forgn_pla_0303.php (accessed 17 June 2014).

34. George, B. 2003. Managing stakeholder vs. responding to shareholders. *Strategy and Leadership*, 31 (6), pp. 36–40.

35. Watson, T, Osborne-Brown, S & Longhurst, M. 2002. Issues Negotiation™ – investing in Stakeholders. *Corporate Communications: An International Journal*, 7 (1), p. 55.

36. George, op. cit. p. 40.

37. Ibid.

38. Ibid.

39. Christopher et al., op. cit., p. 100.

40. Anon, n.d. Available from: https://www.icasa.org.za/AboutUs/tabid/55/Default.aspx (accessed 17 June 2014).

41. Anon, 2011. Marketing Practices now regulated by the Consumer Protection Act. Available from: http://www. moneyweb.co.za/moneyweb-soapbox/marketing-practices-now-regulated-by-the-consumer- (accessed 13 June 2014).

42. Anon, 2009. Consumer Protection Act crimps loyalty programmes. Available from: http://www.bizcommunity.com/Article/196/33/40401.html (accessed 14 June 2014).

43. Payne et al., op. cit., p. 259.

44. Ibid.

45. Payne, A, Ballantyne S & Christopher, M. 2004. A stakeholder approach to relationship marketing strategy: The development and use of the 'six markets' model. *European Journal of Marketing*, Vol 39, 7/8, p. 864.

46. Ibid., p. 866.

47. Lynch, op. cit, p. 219.

48. Ibid., p. 221.

49. Watson et al., op. cit., p. 55.

50. Ibid., p. 60.

51. Available from: http://earthoriented.wordpress.com/2013/04/21/south-africas-green-scorpions-eco-warriors-with-a-sting/http://earthoriented.wordpress.com/2013/04/21/south-africas-green-scorpions-eco-warriors-with-a-sting/ (accessed 6 June 2014).

52. Available from: http://www.sanews.gov.za/south-africa/green-scorpions-make-strides-compliance-enforcement (accessed 6 June 2014).

53. Available from: http://www.greenpeace.org/africa/en/Press-Centre-Hub/Press-releases/Greenpeace-congratulates-Green-Scorpions-on-exposing-Eskoms-environmental-crimes/ (accessed 12 June 2014).

54. Available from: http://www.inece.org/africa/prosecutors/d1_s2b.pdf (accessed 14 June 2014).

55. Available from: https://www.environment.gov.za/projectsprogrammes/emi/about

56. Ibid.

57. Available from: http://www.mediaclubsouthafrica.com/land-and-people/2092-green071210 (accessed 14 June 2014).

58. Available from: http://www.financialmail.co.za/fm/CoverStory/2012/08/01/is-water-sa-s-next-crisis (accessed 14 June 2014).

59. Available from: http://www.theatlantic.com/health/archive/2014/06/the-air-we-breathe/372411/ (accessed 14 June 2014).

60. Available from: http://mg.co.za/article/2014-06-26-rotten-egg-gas-suffocates-sa (accessed 28 June 2014).

61. Available from: http://www.financialmail.co.za/fm/2011/06/09/environment---amsa (accessed 14 June 2014).

62. Available from: http://www.greenworks.co.za/watchyourwastepage.html (accessed 14 June 2014).

63. Available from: http://www.bdlive.co.za/articles/2010/04/19/wildlife-reaction-unit-to-be-created (accessed 14 June 2014).

Chapter 8

1. Berndt, A. 2014. In Boshoff, C. Services marketing: a contemporary approach. Cape Town: Juta, p. 344.

2. Buttle, F. 2006. *Customer Relationship Management*. Burlington: Butterworth-Heinemann, p. 17.

3. Ibid., p. 4

4. Egan, J. 2001. *Relationship Marketing*. Harlow: Pearson Education, p. 206.

5. Du Plessis, F. 2014. In Boshoff, C. Services marketing: a contemporary approach. Cape Town: Juta, p. 15.

6. Grönroos, C. 2000. The relationship marketing process: Interaction, communication dialogue value. Paper presented at the second WWW Conference on Relationship Marketing.

7. Buttle, op. cit., p. 5.

8. Du Plessis, op. cit., p. 216.

9. Brunjes, B & Roderick, R. 2002. Customer relationship management: Why it does and does not work in South Africa. Presentation at the IIMM Marketing Educators' Conference, 26-27 September, p. 9.

10. Gordon, IH. 1998. *Relationship Marketing*. Toronto: John Wiley, p. 135.

11. Peppers & Rogers Group. 2001. Damn the technology hurdles – full speed ahead! *White Paper*, p. 2.

12. Du Plessis, op. cit., p. 222.

13. Buttle, op. cit., p. 6–9.

14. Cant, M. 2013. *Marketing: an introduction*. Cape Town: Juta, p. 59.

15. Ibid., p. 63.

16. Buttle, op. cit., p. 62.

17. Gummesson, E. 2002. *Total relationship marketing*. Oxford: Butterworth-Heinemann, p. 36.

18. Brunjes & Roderick, op. cit., p. 9.

19. Brink, A & Machado, R. 1999. *Relationship Marketing*. Pretoria: Unisa, p. 4.

20. Ryals, LJ & Knox, S. 2006. Measuring risk-adjusted customer lifetime value and its impact on relationship marketing strategies and shareholder value. *European Journal of Marketing* 39 (5/6), pp. 456–58.

21. Gordon, op. cit., p. 136.

22. Peppers & Rogers Group, op. cit., p. 4.

23. 1to1media. 2002. Available from: http://www.1to1.com (accessed 23 May 2011).

24. Buttle, op. cit., p. 45.

25. Ibid., p. 44.

26. Ibid., p. 21.

27. Payne, A & Frow, P. 2004. The role of mutichannel integration in customer relationship management. *Industrial Marketing Management*, pp. 527–38.

28. Kumar, V. 2006. CLV: The Databased Approach. Available from: http://jrm.haworthpress.com (accessed on 3 June 2006).

29. Reinartz, W & Kumar, V. 2002. The mismanagement of customer loyalty. *Harvard Business Review*, p. 93.

30. Berger, PD & Nasr, NI. 1998 Customer lifetime value: marketing models and applications. *Journal of Interactive Marketing* 12 (1), pp. 17–30.

31. Colgate, M & Stewart, K. 1998. The challenge of relationships in services: A New Zealand study. *International Journal of Service Industry Management*, 9 (5), pp. 454-468.

32. Based on Reinartz & Kumar, op. cit., p. 93; Gordon, op. cit., pp. 40–46.

33. Reinartz & Kumar, op. cit., p. 94.

34. Carr, NG. 1999. *Marketing: the economics of customer satisfaction.* Harvard Business Review, 77 (2), pp. 15–16.

35. Reinartz & Kumar, op. cit., p. 94.

36. Buttle, op. cit., pp. 205–209.

37. Ibid., p. 206.

38. Gordon, op. cit., p. 141.

39. Buttle, op cit., pp. 187–188.

40. Brink, A, Strydom, JW, Machado, R & Cant, MC. 2001. *Customer Relationship Management Principles.* Pretoria: Unisa, pp. 75–76.

41. Buttle, op cit., pp. 61–62.

42. Ibid., p. 51.

43. Sapa-AFP. 2014. Kenia voer 'selfoonbank' na Oos-Europa uit. Die Burger: Oos-Kaap, (14 August 2014), p. 13.

Chapter 9

1. Galbreath, J & Rogers, T. 1999. Customer relationship leadership: a leadership and motivational model for twenty-first century business. *The TQM Magazine.* 11(3), p. 168.

2. Du Plessis, PJ., Jooste, CJ. & Strydom, JW. 2001 *Applied Strategic Marketing.* Sandown : Heinemann, p. 396.

3. Gordon, IH. 1998. *Relationship Marketing.* Toronto: John Wiley & Sons. p. 160.

4. Oosthuizen, TFJ. (ed). 2002. *Managerial tasks for managerial success.* Johannesburg: Entropro. p. 79.

5. Warrick, D. 2009. Developing Organization Change Champions A High Payoff Investment! OD Practitioner, 41(1), pp. 14–19.

6. Galbreath & Rogers, op cit., p. 165.

7. Koen, JPL. 2001. *Customer Relationship Management...the tool that will win and keep customers.* Johannesburg: Wits Business School.

8. Gordon, op. cit., p. 66.

9. Galbreath & Rogers, op cit., p. 161.

10. Gordon, op. cit., p. 31.

11. Gordon, op. cit., p. 65.

12. Koen, op. cit., p. 3.

13. Gordon, op. cit., p. 162.

14. Wilson, AM. 2001. Understanding organisational culture and the implications for corporate marketing. *European Journal of Marketing*. 35(3/4), p. 354.

15. Du Plessis., op. cit., p. 395.

16. Smit, PJ & Cronjé, GJ de J. 1992. *Management Principles*. Cape Town: Juta & Co. p. 392.

17. Du Plessis et al., op. cit., p. 396.

18. Wilson, op. cit., p. 355.

19. Ibid., op. cit., p. 357.

20. Du Plessis, op. cit., p. 392.

21. Smit & Cronjé, op. cit., p. 252.

22. Koen. op. cit., p. 4.

23. Gordon, op. cit., p. 163–164.

24. Anon. 2010. A 12-point plan for Successful CRM. Available from: http://maximizercrm.co.za/articles_crm_planning/ (accessed 9 October 2014).

Chapter 10

1. Cravens, DW, Le Meunier-Fitzhugh, K & Piercy, NF. *The Oxford Handbook of Strategic Sales and Sales Management*. No page. Oxford, UK: Oxford University Press.

2. Goldenberg, BJ. 2008. *CRM in Real Time: Empowering Customer Relationships*. New Jersey: Information Today, p. 21.

3. Ibid.

4. The Chartered Institute of Marketing. *Cost of customer acquisition vs customer retention*. [Online] Available: http://www.camfoundation.com/PDF/Cost-of-customer-acquisition-vs-customer-retention.pdf (accessed: 05 March 2014).

5. Goldenberg, op. cit., p. 21.

6. Dahlen, M, Lange, F & Smith, T. *Marketing Communications: A Brand Narrative Approach*. Chichester, England: John Wiley & Sons, p. 258.

7. Rai, AK. 2013. *Customer Relationship Management: Concepts and Cases*. 2nd ed. New Delhi, India: PHI Learning, p. 269.

8. Bigstock. Call Centre. – Corporate office. Available from: http://www.bigstockphoto.com/image-731918/stock-photo-customer-support-centre (accessed 17 December 2014).

9. Bigstock. Call Centre. Available from: http://www.bigstockphoto.com/image-2648497/stock-photo-customer-call-centre (accessed 17 December 2014).

10. Van Heerden, CH. (ed). 2013. *Contemporary Retail and Marketing Case Studies.* Cape Town, South Africa: Juta and Co, pp. 39–40.

11. Wikipedia. 2011. Sales Force Management System. Available from: http://en.wikipedia.org/wiki/Sales_force_management_system (accessed: 05 March 2014).

12. Coronel, C, Morris, S & Rob, P. 2011. *Database Systems: Design, Implementation and Management.* 9th ed. Boston, USA: Cengage Learning, p. 555.

13. Peppers, D & Rogers, M. 2010. *Managing Customer Relationships: A Strategic Framework.* 2nd ed. New Jersey, USA: John Wiley, p. 212.

14. Brink, A & Berndt, A. 2010. *Relationship Marketing and Customer Relationship Management.* Cape Town: Juta, p. 35.

15. Lamb, CW, Hair, JF & McDaniel, C. 2011. *MKTG4.* Mason, USA: Cengage Learning, p. 331.

16. Brink & Berndt, op. cit., p. 36.

17. Rai, op. cit., p. 118.

Index